Algonquin Legends of New England

Charles Godfrey Leland

Alpha Editions

This edition published in 2024

ISBN : 9789366387765

Design and Setting By
Alpha Editions
www.alphaedis.com
Email - info@alphaedis.com

As per information held with us this book is in Public Domain.
This book is a reproduction of an important historical work. Alpha Editions uses the best technology to reproduce historical work in the same manner it was first published to preserve its original nature. Any marks or number seen are left intentionally to preserve its true form.

PREFACE.

When I began, in the summer of 1882, to collect among the Passamaquoddy Indians at Campobello, New Brunswick, their traditions and folk-lore, I expected to find very little indeed. These Indians, few in number, surrounded by white people, and thoroughly converted to Roman Catholicism, promised but scanty remains of heathenism. What was my amazement, however, at discovering, day by day, that there existed among them, entirely by oral tradition, a far grander mythology than that which has been made known to us by either the Chippewa or Iroquois Hiawatha Legends, and that this was illustrated by an incredible number of tales. I soon ascertained that these were very ancient. The old people declared that they had heard from their progenitors that all of these stories were once sung; that they themselves remembered when many of them were poems. This was fully proved by discovering manifest traces of poetry in many, and finally by receiving a long Micmac tale which had been sung by an Indian. I found that all the relaters of this lore were positive as to the antiquity of the narratives, and distinguished accurately between what was or was not pre-Columbian. In fact, I came in time to the opinion that the original stock of all the Algonquin myths, and perhaps of many more, still existed, not far away in the West, but at our very doors; that is to say, in Maine and New Brunswick. It is at least certain, as the reader may convince himself, that these Wabanaki, or Northeastern Algonquin, legends give, with few exceptions, in full and coherently, many tales which have only reached us in a broken, imperfect form, from other sources.

This work, then, contains a collection of the myths, legends, and folk-lore of the principal Wabanaki, or Northeastern Algonquin, Indians; that is to say, of the Passamaquoddies and Penobscots of Maine, and of the Micmacs of New Brunswick. All of this material was gathered directly from Indian narrators, the greater part by myself, the rest by a few friends; in fact, I can give the name of the aboriginal authority for every tale except one. As my chief object has been simply to collect and preserve valuable material, I have said little of the labors of such critical writers as Brinton, Hale, Trumbull, Powers, Morgan, Bancroft, and the many more who have so ably studied and set forth red Indian ethnology. If I have rarely ventured on their field, it is because I believe that when the Indian shall have passed away there will come far better ethnologists than I am, who will be much more obliged to me for collecting raw material than for cooking it.

Two or three subjects have, it is true, tempted me into occasional commenting. The manifest, I may say the undeniable, affinity between the myths and legends of the Northeastern Indians and those of the Eskimo could hardly be passed over, nor at the same time the identity of the latter and of the Shaman religion with those of the Finns, Laplanders, and Samoyedes. I believe that I have contributed material not devoid of value to those who are interested in the study of the relations of the aborigines of America with the Mongoloid races of the Old World. This is a subject which has been very little studied through the relations of these Wabanaki with the Eskimo.

A far more hazardous venture has been the indicating points of similarity between the myths or tales of the Algonquins and those of the Norsemen, as set forth in the Eddas, the Sagas, and popular tales of Scandinavia. When we, however, remember that the Eskimo once ranged as far south as Massachusetts, that they did not reach Greenland till the fourteenth century, that they had for three centuries intimate relations with Scandinavians, that they were very fond of legends, and that the Wabanaki even now mingle with them, the marvel would be that the Norsemen had not left among them traces of their tales or of their religion. But I do not say that this was positively the case; I simply set forth in this book a great number of curious coincidences, from which others may draw their own conclusions. I confess that I cannot account for these resemblances save by the so-called "historical theory" of direct transmission; but if any one can otherwise explain them I should welcome the solution of what still seems to be, in many respects, a problem.

I am, in fact, of the opinion that what is given in this work confirms what was conjectured by David Crantz, and which is thus expressed in his History of Greenland (London, 1767): "If we read the accounts which have been given of the most northerly American Indians and Asiatic Tartars, we find a pretty great resemblance between their manner of life, morals, usages, and notions and what has been said in this book of the Greenlanders, only with this difference: that the farther the savage nations wandered towards the North, the fewer they retained of their ancient conceptions and customs. As for the Greenlanders, if it be true, as is supposed, that a remnant of the old Norway Christians incorporated themselves and became one people with them, the Greenlanders may thence have heard and adopted some of their notions, which they may have new-modeled in the coarse mould of their own brain."

Among those who have greatly aided me in preparing this work I deem it to be a duty to mention MISS ABBY ALGER, of Boston, to whom it is cordially dedicated; the REV. SILAS T. RAND, of Hantsport, Nova Scotia, who lent me a manuscript collection of eighty-five Micmac tales, and communicated to me, with zealous kindness, much information by letter; and MRS. W. WALLACE BROWN, of Calais, Maine. It was through this lady that I derived a great proportion of the most curious folk-lore of the

Passamaquoddies, especially such parts as coincided with the Edda. With these I would include MR. E. JACK, of Fredericton, New Brunswick. When it is remembered that there are only forty-two of the Hiawatha Legends of Schoolcraft, out of which five books have been made by other authors, and that I have collected more than two hundred, it will be seen how these friends must have worked to aid me.

INTRODUCTION

Among the six chief divisions of the red Indians of North America the most widely extended is the Algonquin. This people ranged from Labrador to the far South, from Newfoundland to the Rocky Mountains, speaking forty dialects, as the Hon. J. H. Trumbull has shown in his valuable work on the subject. Belonging to this division are the Micmacs of New Brunswick and the Passamaquoddy and Penobscot tribes of Maine, who with the St. Francis Indians of Canada and some smaller clans call themselves the Wabanaki, a word derived from a root signifying white or light, intimating that they live nearest to the rising sun or the east. In fact, the French-speaking St. Francis family, who are known *par eminence* as "the Abenaki," translate the term by *point du jour*.

The Wabanaki have in common the traditions of a grand mythology, the central figure of which is a demigod or hero, who, while he is always great, consistent, and benevolent, and never devoid of dignity, presents traits which are very much more like those of Odin and Thor, with not a little of Pantagruel, than anything in the characters of the Chippewa Manobozho, or the Iroquois Hiawatha. The name of this divinity is Glooskap, meaning, strangely enough, the Liar, because it is said that when he left earth, like King Arthur, for Fairyland, he promised to return, and has never done so. It is characteristic of the Norse gods that while they are grand they are manly, and combine with this a peculiarly domestic humanity. Glooskap is the Norse god intensified. He is, however, more of a giant; he grows to a more appalling greatness than Thor or Odin in his battles; when a *Kiawaqu'*, or Jotun, rises to the clouds to oppose him, Glooskap's head touches the stars, and scorning to slay so mean a foe like an equal, he kills him contemptuously with a light tap of his bow. But in the family circle he is the most benevolent of gentle heroes, and has his oft-repeated little standard jokes. Yet he never, like the Manobozho-Hiawatha of the Chippewas, becomes silly, cruel, or fantastic. He has his roaring revel with a brother giant, even as Thor went fishing in fierce fun with the frost god, but he is never low or feeble.

Around Glooskap, who is by far the grandest and most Aryan-like character ever evolved from a savage mind, and who is more congenial to a reader of Shakespeare and Rabelais than any deity ever imagined out of Europe, there are found strange giants: some literal Jotuns of stone and ice, sorcerers who become giants like Glooskap, at will; the terrible Chenoo, a human being with an icy-stone heart, who has sunk to a cannibal and ghoul; all the weird monsters and horrors of the Eskimo mythology, witches and demons, inherited from the terribly black sorcery which preceded Shamanism, and compared to which the latter was like an advanced religion, and all the minor mythology of dwarfs and fairies. The Indian *m'teoulin*, or magician, distinctly taught that every created thing, animate or inanimate, had its indwelling spirit. Whatever had an *idea* had a soul. Therefore the Wabanaki mythology is strangely like that of the Rosicrucians. But it created spirits for the terrible Arctic winters of the north, for the icebergs and frozen wastes, for the Northern Lights and polar bears. It made, in short, a mythology such as would be perfectly congenial to any one who has read and understood the Edda, Beowulf, and the Kalevala, with the wildest and oldest Norse sagas. But it is, as regards spirit and meaning, utterly and entirely unlike anything else that is American. It is not like the Mexican pantheon; it has not the same sounds, colors, or feelings; and though many of its incidents or tales are the same as those of the Chippewas, or other tribes, we still feel that there is an incredible difference in the spirit. Its ways are not as their ways. This Wabanaki mythology, which was that which gave a fairy, an elf, a naiad, or a hero to every rock and river and ancient hill in New England, is just the one of all others which is least known to the New Englanders. When the last Indian shall be in his grave, those who come after us will ask in wonder why we had no curiosity as to the romance of our country, and so much as to that of every other land on earth.

Much is allowed to poets and painters, and no fault was found with Mr. Longfellow for attributing to the Iroquois Hiawatha the choice exploits of the Chippewa demi-devil Manobozho. It was "all Indian" to the multitude, and one name answered as well in poetry as another, at a time when there was very little attention paid to ethnology. So that a good poem resulted, it was of little consequence that the plot was a *melange* of very different characters, and characteristics. And when, in connection with this, Mr. Longfellow spoke of the Chippewa tales as forming an Indian Edda, the term was doubtless in a poetic and very general sense permissible. But its want of literal truth seems to have deeply impressed the not generally over particular or accurate Schoolcraft, since his first remarks in the Introduction to the Hiawatha Legends are as follows:—

"Where analogies are so general, there is a constant liability to mistakes. Of these foreign analogies of myth-lore, the least tangible, it is believed, is that which has been suggested with the Scandinavian mythology. That mythology is of so marked and peculiar a character that it has not been distinctly traced out of the great circle of tribes of the Indo-Germanic family. Odin and his terrific pantheon of war gods and social deities could only exist in the dreary latitudes of storms and fire which produce a Hecla and a Maelstrom. These latitudes have invariably produced nations whose influence has been felt in an elevating power over the world. From such a source the Indian could have derived none of him vague symbolisms and mental idiosyncrasies which have left him as he is found to-day, without a government and without a god."

This is all perfectly true of the myths of Hiawat'ha-Manobozho. Nothing on earth could be more unlike the Norse legends than the "Indian Edda" of the Chippewas and Ottawas. But it was not known to this writer that there already existed in Northeastern America a stupendous mythology, derived from a land of storms and fire more terrible and wonderful than Iceland; nay, so terrible that Icelanders themselves were appalled by it. "This country," says the Abbe Morillot, "is the one most suggestive of superstition. Everything there, sea, earth, or heaven, is strange." The wild cries which rise from the depths of the caverned ice-hills, and are reechoed by the rocks, icebergs, or waves, were dreadful to Egbert Olafson in the seventeenth century. The interior is a desert without parallel for desolation. A frozen Sahara seen by Northern lightning and midnight suns is but a suggestion of this land. The sober Moravian missionary Crantz once only in his life rose to poetry, when more than a century ago he spoke of its scenery. Here then was the latitude of storm and fire required by Schoolcraft to produce something wilder and grander than he had ever found among Indians. And here indeed there existed all the time a cycle of mythological legends or poems such as he declared Indians incapable of producing. But strangest of all, this American mythology of the North, which has been the very last to become known to American readers, is literally so nearly like the Edda itself that as this work fully proves, there is hardly a song in the Norse collection which does not contain an incident found in the Indian poem-legends, while in several there are many such coincidences. Thus, in the Edda we are told that the first birth on earth was that of a giant girl and boy, begotten by the feet of a giant and born from his armpit. In the Wabanaki legends, the first birth was of Glooskap, the Good principle, and Malsum the Wolf, or Evil principle. The Wolf was born from his mother's armpit. He is sometimes male and sometimes female. His feet are male and female, and converse. We pass on only twelve lines in the Edda (Vafthrudnismal, 36) to be told that the wind is caused by a giant in eagle's plumage, who sits on a rock far in the north "at the end of heaven." This is simply and literally the *Wochowsen* or Windblower of the Wabanaki word for word,—not the "Thunder-Bird" of the Western Indians. The second birth on earth, according to the Edda, was that of man. Odin found Ash and Elm "nearly powerless," and gave them sense. This was the first man and woman. According to the Indians of Maine, Glooskap made the first men from the *ash*-tree. They lived or were in it, "devoid of sense" till he gave it to them. It is to be observed that primevally among the Norse the *ash* alone stood for man. So it goes on through the whole Edda, of which all the main incidents are to be found among the sagas of the Wabanaki. The most striking of these are the coincidences between *Lox* (lynx, wolf, wolverine, badger, or raccoon, and sometimes man) and Loki. It is very remarkable indeed that the only two religions in the world which possess a devil in whom *mischief* predominates should also give to each the same adventures, if both did not come from the same source. In the Hymiskvida of the Edda, two giants go to fish for whales, and then have a contest which is actually one of heat against cold. This is so like a Micmac legend in every detail that about twenty lines are word for word the same in the Norse and Indian. The Micmac giants end their whale fishing by trying to freeze one another to death.

It is to the Rev. Silas T. Rand that the credit belongs of having discovered Glooskap, and of having first published in the Dominion Monthly several of these Northern legends. After I had collected nearly a hundred among the Passamaquoddy and Penobscot Indians, this gentleman, with unexampled kindness, lent me a manuscript of eighty-four Micmac tales, making in all nine hundred folio pages. Many were similar to others in my collection, but I have never yet received a duplicate which did not contain something essential to the whole. Though the old Indians all declare that most of their lore has perished, especially the more recondite mythic poems, I am confident that much more remains to be gathered than I have given in this work. As it is, I have omitted many tales simply because they were evidently Canadian French stories. Yet all of these, without exception, are half Indian, and it may be old Norse modified; for a French story is sometimes the same with one in the Eddas. Again, for want of room I have not given any Indian tales or chronicles of the wars with the Mohawks. Of these I have enough to make a very curious volume.

These legends belong to all New England. Many of them exist as yet among the scattered fragments of Indian tribes here and there. The Penobscots of Oldtown, Maine, still possess many. In fact, there is not an old Indian, male or female, in New England or Canada who does not retain stories and songs of the greatest interest. I sincerely trust that this work may have the effect of stimulating collection. Let every reader remember that everything thus taken down, and deposited in a local historical society, or sent to the Ethnological Bureau at Washington, will forever transmit the name of its recorder to posterity. Archaeology is as yet in its very beginning; when the Indians shall have departed it will grow to giant-like proportions, and every scrap of information relative to them will be eagerly investigated. And the man does not live who knows what may be made of it all. I need not say that I should be grateful for such Indian lore of any kind whatever which may be transmitted to me.

It may very naturally be asked by many how it came to pass that the Indians of Maine and of the farther north have so much of the Edda in their sagas; or, if it was derived through the Eskimo tribes, how these got it from Norsemen, who were professedly Christians. I do not think that the time has come for fully answering the first question. There is some great mystery of mythology, as yet unsolved, regarding the origin of the Edda and its relations with the faiths and folk-lore of the elder Shamanic beliefs, such as Lapp, Finn, Samoyed, Eskimo, and Tartar. This was the world's first religion; it is found in the so-called Accadian Turanian beginning of Babylon, whence it possibly came from the West. But what we have here to consider is whether the Norsemen did directly influence the Eskimo and Indians. Let us first consider that these latter were passionately fond of stories, and that they had attained to a very high standard of culture as regards both appreciation and invention. They were as fond of recitations as any white man is of reading. Their memories were in this respect very remarkable indeed. They have taken into their repertory during the past two hundred years many French fairy tales, through the Canadians. Is it not likely that they listened to the Northmen?

It is not generally noted among our learned men how long the Icelanders remained in Greenland, how many stories are still told of them by the Eskimo, or to what extent the Indians continue to mingle with the latter. During the eleventh, twelfth, and thirteenth centuries, says the Abbe Morillot, "there were in Greenland, after Archbishop Adalbert, more than twenty bishops, and in the colony were many churches and monasteries. In the Oestrbugd, one of the two inhabited portions of the vast island, were one hundred and ninety villages, with twelve churches. In Julianshaab, one may to-day see the ruins of eight churches and of many monasteries." In the fifteenth century all these buildings were in ruins, and the colony was exterminated by the pestilence or the natives. But among the latter there remained many traditions of the Scandinavians associated with the ruins. Such is the story of Oren'gortok, given by the Abbe Morillot, and several are to be found in Rink's Legends. When we learn that the Norsemen, during their three centuries of occupation of Greenland, brought away many of the marvelous tales of the Eskimo, it is not credible that they left none of their own. Thus we are told in the Floamanna Saga how a hero, abandoned on the icy coast of Greenland, met with two giant witches (Troldkoner), and cut the band from one of them. An old Icelandic work, called the Konungs Skuggsjo (Danish, Kongespeilet), has much to say of the marvels of Greenland and its monsters of the sea. On the other hand, Morillot declares that the belief in ghosts was brought to Greenland by the Icelanders and Scandinavians. The sagas have not been as yet much studied with a view to establishing how much social intercourse there was between the natives and the colonists, but common experience would teach that during three centuries it must have been something.

There has always been intercourse between Greenland and Labrador, and in this latter country we find the first Algonquin Indians. Even at the present day there are men among the Micmacs and Passamaquoddies who have gone on their hunting excursions even to the Eskimo. I myself know one of the latter who has done so, and the Rev. S. T. Rand, in answer to a question on the subject, writes to me as follows:—

"Nancy Jeddore, a Micmac woman, assures me that her father, now dead, used to go as far as the wild (heathen) Eskimo, and remained once for three years among the more civilized. She has so correctly described their habits that I am satisfied that her statements are correct." [Footnote: The word *Eskimo* is Algonquin, meaning to eat raw fish, *Eskumoga* in Micmac, and people who eat raw flesh, or *Eskimook*, that is, *eski*, raw, and *moo-uk*, people. This word recalls *in-noo-uk*, people, and spirits, in Eskimo, *Innue*, which has the same double meaning. This was all suggested to me by an Indian.]

These Eskimo brought from the Old World that primeval gloomy Shaman religion, or sorcery, such as is practiced yet by Laplanders and Tartars, such as formed the basis of the old Accadian Babylonian cultus, and such as is now in vogue among all our own red Indians. I believe that it was from the Eskimo that this American Shamanism all came. In Greenland this faith assumed its strangest form; it made for itself a new mythology. The Indians, their neighbors, borrowed from this, but also added new elements of an only *semi*-Arctic character. Thus there is a series of steps, but every one different, from the Eskimo to the Wabanaki, of Labrador, New Brunswick, and Maine, from the Wabanaki to the Iroquois, and from the Iroquois to the more western Indians. And while they all have incidents in common, the character of each is radically different.

It may be specially noted that while there is hardly an important point in the Edda which may not be found, as I have just shown, in Wabanaki legends, there is very little else in the latter which is in common with such Old World mythology as might have come to the Indians since the discovery by Columbus. Excluding French Canadian fairy tales, what we have left is chiefly Eskimo and Eddaic, and the proportion of the latter is simply surprising. There are actually more incidents taken from the Edda than there are from lower sources. I can only account for this by the fact that, as the Indians tell me, all these tales were once *poems*, handed down from generation to generation, and always sung. Once they were religious. Now they are in a condition analogous to that of the German Heldenbuch. They have been cast into a new form, but they are not as yet quite degraded to the nursery tale.

It may be objected that if the Norsemen in Greenland were Christians it is most unlikely that they would have taught the legends of the Edda to the heathen; to which I reply that some scholar a few centuries hence may declare it was a most improbable thing that Christian Roman Catholic Indians should have taught me the tales of Glooskap and Lox. But the truth is, we really know very little as to how soon wandering Vikings went to America, or how many were here.

I would say in conclusion that, while these legends of the Wabanaki are fragmentary and incomplete, they still read like the fragments of a book whose subject was once broadly and coherently treated by a man of genius. They are handled in the same bold and artistic manner as the Norse. There is nothing like them in any other North American Indian records. They are, especially those which are from the Passamaquoddy and Penobscot, inspired with a genial cosmopolite humor. While Glooskap is always a gentleman, Lox ranges from Punch to Satan; passing through the stages of an Indian Mephistopheles and the Norse Loki, who appears to have been his true progenitor. But neither is quite like anything to be found among really savage races. When it is borne in mind that the most ancient and mythic of these legends have been taken down from the trembling memories of old squaws who never understood their inner meaning, or from ordinary *senaps* who had not thought of them since boyhood, it will be seen that the preservation of a mass of prose poems, equal in bulk to the Kalevala or Heldenbuch, is indeed almost miraculous.

THE ALGONQUIN LEGENDS OF NEW ENGLAND.

GLOOSKAP THE DIVINITY.

Of Glooskap's Birth, and of his Brother Malsum the Wolf.

Now the great lord Glooskap, who was worshiped in after-days by all the Wabanaki, or children of light, was a twin with a brother. As he was good, this brother, whose name was Malsumsis, or Wolf the younger, was bad. Before they were born, the babes consulted to consider how they had best enter the world. And Glooskap said, "I will be born as others are." But the evil Malsumsis thought himself too great to be brought forth in such a manner, and declared that he would burst through his mother's side. [Footnote: The reader of Rabelais cannot fail to recall here the remarks of the author as to the extraordinary manner in which it pleased the giant Gargantua to come into the world. The Armenians believe that Christ was born through the right side of the Virgin. The Buddhists say the same of Buddha's birth. (Heth and Moab, London, 1883.) Another and as I believe the correct account declares that Malsum the Wolf was born from his mother's armpit.] And as they planned it so it came to pass. Glooskap as first came quietly to light, while Malsumsis kept his word, killing his mother.

The two grew up together, and one day the younger, who knew that both had charmed lives, asked the elder what would kill him, Glooskap. Now each had his own secret as to this, and Glooskap, remembering how wantonly Malsumsis had slain their mother, thought it would be misplaced confidence to trust his life to one so fond of death, while it might prove to be well to know the bane of the other. So they agreed to exchange secrets, and Glooskap, to test his brother, told him that the only way in which he himself could be slain was by the stroke of an owl's feather, [Footnote: There are different readings of this incident. In Mr. Band's manuscript the alleged means of Glooskap's death is described as being a cat-tail flag (*haw-kwee-usqu'*, Passamaquoddy), while a handful of bird's down is the bane of Malsum the Wolf. The termination *sis* is a diminutive, here meaning the younger.] though this was not true. And Malsumsis said, "I can only die by a blow from a fern-root."

It came to pass in after-days that Kwah-beet-a-sis, the son of the Great Beaver, or, as others say, Miko the Squirrel, or else the evil which was in himself, tempted Malsumsis to kill Glooskap; for in those days all men were wicked. So taking his bow he shot Ko-ko-khas the Owl, and with one of his feathers he struck Glooskap while sleeping. Then he awoke in anger, yet craftily said that it was not by an owl's feather, but by a blow from a pine-root, that his life would end.

[Illustration: Glooskap killing his brother the wolf]

Then the false man led his brother another day far into the forest to hunt, and, while he again slept, smote him on the head with a pine-root. But Glooskap arose unharmed, drove Malsumsis away into the woods, sat down by the brook-side, and thinking over all that had happened, said, "Nothing but a flowering rush can kill me." But the Beaver, who was hidden among the reeds, heard this, and hastening to Malsumsis told him the secret of his brother's life. For this Malsumsis promised to bestow on Beaver whatever he should ask; but when the latter wished for wings like a pigeon, the warrior laughed, and scornfully said, "Get thee hence; thou with a tail like a file, what need hast thou of wings?"

Then the Beaver was angry, and went forth to the camp of Glooskap, to whom he told what he had done. Therefore Glooskap arose in sorrow and in anger, took a fern-root, sought Malsumsis in the deep, dark forest, and smote him so that he fell down dead. And Glooskap sang a song over him and lamented.

The Beaver and the Owl and the Squirrel, for what they did and as they did it, all come again into these stories; but Malsumsis, being dead, was turned into the Shick-shoe mountains in the Gaspe peninsula.

For this chapter and parts of others I am indebted to the narrative of a Micmac Indian, taken down by Mr. Edward Jocly; also to another version in the Rand MS. The story is, in the main-points, similar to that given by David Cusick in his History of the Six Nations, of Enigorio the Good Mind, and Enigonhahetgea, Bad Mind, to which I shall refer anon.

It is very evident that in this tradition Glooskap represents the Good principle, and Malsumsis, the little wolf,—that is the Wolf who is the Younger, rather than little or small,—the Evil one. Malsum typifies destruction and sin in several of these tales. He will arise at the last day, when Glooskap is to do battle with all the giants and evil beasts of olden time, and will be the great destroyer. Malsum is the Wolf Fenris of this the true Indian Edda.

For a further comment on this birth of the twins and its resemblance to a passage in the Edda, the reader is referred to the notes on the next chapter.

How Glooskap made the Elves and Fairies, and then Man of an Ash Tree, and last of all, Beasts, and of his Coming at the Last Day.

(Passamaquoddy.)

Glooskap came first of all into this country, into Nova Scotia, Maine, Canada, into the land of the Wabanaki, next to sunrise. There were no Indians here then (only wild Indians very far to the west).

First born were the Mikumwess, the Oonabgemessuk, the small Elves, little men, dwellers in rocks.

And in this way he made Man: He took his bow and arrows and shot at trees, the basket-trees, the Ash. Then Indians came out of the bark of the Ash-trees. And then the Mikumwees said ... called tree-man.... [Footnote: The relater, an old woman, was quite unintelligible at this point.]

Glooskap made all the animals. He made them at first very large. Then he said to Moose, the great Moose who was as tall as Ketawkqu's, [Footnote: A giant, high as the tallest pines, or as the clouds.] "What would you do should you see an Indian coming?" Moose replied, "I would tear down the trees on him." Then Glooskap saw that the Moose was too strong, and made him smaller, so that Indians could kill him.

Then he said to the Squirrel, who was of the size of a Wolf, "What would you do if you should meet an Indian?" And the Squirrel answered, "I would scratch down trees on him." Then Glooskap said, "You also are too strong," and he made him little. [Footnote: Another account states that Glooskap took the Squirrel in his hands and smoothed him down.]

Then he asked the great White Bear what he would do if he met an Indian; and the Bear said, "Eat him." And the Master bade him go and live among rocks and ice, where he would see no Indians.

So he questioned all the beasts, changing their size or allotting their lives according to their answers.

He took the Loon for his dog; but the Loon absented himself so much that he chose for this service two wolves,—one black and one white, [Footnote: Dogs are used for beasts of burden, to draw sledges, in the North.] But the Loons are always his tale-bearers. Many years ago a man very far to the North wished to cross a bay, a great distance, from one point to another. As he was stepping into his canoe he saw a man with two dogs,—one black and one white,—who asked to be set across. The Indian said, "You may go, but what will become of your dogs?" Then the stranger replied, "Let them go round by land." "Nay," replied the Indian, "that is much too far." But the stranger saying nothing, he put him across. And as they reached the landing place there stood the dogs. But when he turned his head to address the man, he was gone. So he said to himself, "I have seen Glooskap."

Yet again,—but this was not so many years ago,—far in the North there were at a certain place many Indians assembled. And there was a frightful commotion, caused by the ground heaving and rumbling; the rocks shook and fell, they were greatly alarmed, and lo! Glooskap stood before them, and said, "I go away now, but I shall return again; when you feel the ground tremble, then know it is I." So they will know when the last great war is to be, for then Glooskap will make the ground shake with an awful noise.

Glooskap was no friend of the Beavers; he slew many of them. Up on the Tobaic are two salt-water rocks (that is, rocks by the ocean-side, near a freshwater stream). The Great Beaver, standing there one day, was seen by Glooskap miles away, who had forbidden him that place. Then picking up a large rock where he stood by the shore, he threw it all that distance at the Beaver, who indeed dodged it; but when another came, the beast ran into a mountain, and has never come forth to this day. But the rocks which the master threw are yet to be seen.

This very interesting tradition was taken down by Mrs. W. Wallace Brown from a very old Passamaquoddy Indian woman named Molly Sepsis, who could not speak a word of English, with the aid of another younger woman named Sarah.

It will be observed that it is said in the beginning that Glooskap produced the first human beings from, the ash-tree. Ash and Elm in the Edda were the Adam and Eve of the human race. There were no intelligent men on earth—

"Until there came three mighty and benevolent Aesir to the world from their assembly nearly powerless, Ash and Embla (Ash and Elm), void of destiny.

"Spirit they possessed not,
sense they had not,
blood nor motive powers,
nor goodly color.
Spirit gave Odin,
sense gave Hoenir,
blood gave Lodur,
and good color."

[Footnote: *The Edda of Saemund*, translated by Benjamin Thorpe. London: Trubner & Co. 1866. Voluspa, v. 17, 18.]

It is certain, however, that the *ash* was the typic tree of all life, since the next verse of the Voluspa is devoted to Yggdrasil, the tree of existence, or of the world itself. It may be observed that in the Finnish poem of Kalevala it is by the destruction of the great oak that Wainamoien, aided by the hero of the sea, causes all things to grow. The early clearing away of trees, as a first step towards culture, may be symbolized in the shooting of arrows at the ash.

The wolf, as a beast for the deity to ride, is strongly Eddaic.

"Magic songs they sung,
rode on wolves,

the god (Odin) and gods."
[Footnote: *Rognnir og regin*. Odin and the Powers. Note by B. Thorpe to the *Hrafnagalar Odins*, in Edda, p.30.]

We have here within a few lines, accordingly, the elm as the parent of mankind, and wolves as the beasts of transport for the supreme deity, both in the Indian legend and in the Edda.

As Glooskap is directly declared in one tradition to keep by him as an attendant a being who is the course of the sun and of the seasons, it may be assumed that the black and white wolf represent day and night.

Again, great stress is laid in the Glooskap legend upon the fact that the last great day of battle with Malsum the Wolf and the frost-giants, stone-giants, and other powers of evil, shall be announced by an earthquake.

"Trembles Yggdrasil's Ash yet standing, groans that aged tree.... and the Wolf runs.... The monster's kin goes all with the Wolf.... The stony hills are dashed together, The giantesses totter. Then arises Hlin's second grief When Odin goes with the wolf to fight."

Word for word, ash-tree, giantesses, the supreme god fighting with a wolf, and falling hills, are given in the Indian myth. This is not the Christian Day of Judgment, but the Norse.

In this myth Glooskap has two wolves, one black and the other white. This is an indication of day and night, since he is distinctly stated to have as an attendant Kulpejotei, who typifies the course of the seasons. In the Eddas (Ragnarok) we are told that one wolf now follows the sun, another the moon; one Fenris, the other Moongarm:—

"The moon's devourer
In a troll's disguise."

The magic arrows of Glooskap are of course worldwide, and date from the shafts of Abaris and those used among the ancient Jews for divination. But it may be observed that those of the Indian hero are like the "Guse arrows," described in Oervarodd's Saga, which always hit their mark and return to the one who shoots them. [Footnote: *The Primitive Inhabitants of Scandinavia*. By Svent Nilsson. Edited by Sir John Lubbock, 1868.]

It is important here to compare this *old* Algonquin account of the Creation with that of the Iroquois, or Six Nations, as given by David Cusick, himself an Indian:—

"There was a woman who was with child, with twins. She descended from the higher world, and was received on the turtle. While she was in the distress of travail, one of the infants in her womb was moved by an evil desire, and determined to pass out under the side of the parent's arm, and the other infant endeavored in vain to prevent his design. They entered the dark world by compulsion, and their mother expired in a few minutes. One of them possessed a gentle disposition, and was named Enigorio, the Good Mind. The other possessed an insolence of character, and was called Enigonhahetgea; that is, the Bad Mind. The Good Mind was not content to remain in a dark situation, and was desirous to create a great light in the dark world; but the Bad Mind was desirous that the world should remain in its original state. The Good Mind, determined to prosecute his design, began the work of creation. Of his mother's head he made the sun, of her body the moon. After he had made creeks and rivers, animals and fishes, he formed two images of the dust of the ground in his own likeness, male and female, and by his breathing into their nostrils he gave them living souls, and named them *ea gwe howe*, that is a real people; and he gave the Great Island all the animals—of game for the inheritance of the people.... The Bad Mind, while his brother was making the universe, went through the island, and made numerous high mountains and falls of water and great steeps, and also created reptiles which would be injurious to mankind; but the Good Mind restored the island to its former condition. The Bad Mind made two images of clay in the form of mankind, but while he was giving them existence they became *apes*. The Good Mind discovered his brother's contrivances, and aided in giving them living souls.

Finding that his brother continually thwarted him, the Good Mind admonished him to behave better. The Bad Mind then offered a challenge to his brother, on condition that the victor should rule the universe. The Good Mind was willing. He falsely mentioned that whipping with flags [bulrushes] would destroy his *temporal* life, and earnestly solicited his brother to observe the instrument of death, saying that by using deer-horns he would expire. [This is very obscure in Cusick's Indian-English.] On the day appointed the battle began; it lasted for two days; they tore up the trees and mountains; at last the Good Mind gained the victory by using the horns. The last words uttered by the Bad Mind were that he would have equal power over the souls of mankind after their death, and so sank down to eternal doom and became the Evil Spirit."

Contrasted with this hardly heathen cosmogony, which shows recent Bible influence throughout, the Algonquin narrative reads like a song from the Edda. That the latter is the original and the older there can be no doubt. Between the "Good Mind," making man "from the dust of the earth," and Glooskap, rousing him by magic arrows from the ash-tree, there is a great difference. It may be observed that the fight with horns is explained in another legend in this book, called the Chenoo, and that these horns are the magic horns of the Chepitch calm, or Great Serpent, who is somewhat like the dragon.

In the Algonquin story, two Loons are Glooskap's "tale-bearers," which occasion him great anxiety by their prolonged absences. This is distinctly stated in the Indian legend, as it is of Odin's birds in the Edda. Odin has, as news-bringers, two ravens.

"Hugin and Munin Fly each day over the spacious earth. I fear for Hugin that he comes not back, yet more anxious am I for Munin."

The Loons, indeed, occasioned Glooskap so much trouble by absences that he took wolves in their place. The ravens of the Edda are probably of biblical origin. But it is a most extraordinary coincidence that the Indians have a corresponding perversion of Scripture, for they say that Glooskap, when he was in the ark, that is as Noah, sent out a white dove, which returned to him colored black, and became a raven. This is not, however, related as part of the myth.

The Ancient History of the Six Nations, by David Cusick, gives us in one particular a strange coincidence with the Edda. It tells us that the Bad Mind, the principle of Evil, forced himself out into life, as Cusick expresses it in his broken Indian-English, "under the side of the parent's arm;" that is, through the armpit. In the Edda (Vafthrudnismal, 33) we are told of the first beings born on earth that they were twins, begotten by the two feet of a giant, and born out of his armpit.

"Under the armpit grew, 't is said of the Hrimthurs, a girl and boy together; foot with foot begat, of that wise Jotun, a six-headed son."

There are in these six lines six coincidences with red Indian mythology: (1.) The Evil principle as a Jotun's first-born in the one and the Bad Mind in the other are born of the mother's armpit. (2.) In one of the tales of Lox, the Indian devil, also a giant, we are told that his feet are male and female. (3.) In both faiths this is the first birth on earth. (4.) The six-headed demon appears in a Micmac tale. (5.) There is in both the Eddaic and the Wabanaki account a very remarkable coincidence in this: that there is a Titanic or giant birth of twins on earth, followed by the creation of man from the ash-tree. (6.) The Evil principle, whether it be the Wolf-Lox, in the Wabanaki myths, or Loki in the Norse, often turns himself into a woman. Thus the male and female sex of the first-born twins is identified.

According to the Edda, the order of births on earth was as follows:—

First, two giants were born from the mother's armpit.

Secondly, the dwarfs were created.

Thirdly, man was made from the ash-tree.

According to the Wabanaki, this was the order:—

First, two giants were born, *one* from his mother's armpit.

Secondly, the dwarfs (Mikumwessuk) were created from the bark of the ash-tree.

Thirdly, man was made from the *trunk* of the ash.

The account of the creation of the dwarfs is wanting in the present manuscript.

Of the Great Deeds which Glooskap did for Men; how he named the Animals, and who they were that formed his Family.

(Passamaquoddy.)

Woodenit atbk-hagen Gloosekap: [Footnote: Passamaquoddy.] this is a story of Glooskap. It is told in traditions of the old time that Glooskap was born in the land of the Wabanaki, which is nearest to the sunrise; but another story says that he came over the sea in a great stone canoe, and that this canoe was an island of granite covered with trees. When the great man, of all men and beasts chief ruler, had come down from this ark, he went among the Wabanaki. [Footnote: This part of the legend is from a very singular and I may add almost unintelligible manuscript, *Storey about Glooscap*, written in English by a Passamaquoddy Indian. The word *ark* which occurs in it reminds me that the Indian from whom I obtained it once asked me if I did not think that Glooskap was the same as Noah. This sentence is as follows in the Indian-English of the original: "Gloosecap hat left from ark come crosse even wiht wabnocelel."] And calling all the animals he gave them each a name: unto the Bear, *mooin*; and asked him what he would do if he should meet with a man. The Bear said, "I fear him, and I should run." Now in those days the Squirrel (*mi-ko*) was greater than the Bear. Then Glooskap took him in his hands, and smoothing him down he grew smaller and smaller, till he became as we see him now. In after-days the Squirrel was Glooskap's dog, and when he so willed, grew large again and slew his enemies, however fierce they might be. But this time, when asked what he would do should he meet with a man, Mi-ko replied, "I should run up a tree."

Then the Moose, being questioned, answered, standing still and looking down, "I should run through the woods." And so it was with Kwah-beet the Beaver, [Footnote: This is very obscure in the original manuscript. It reads "Herask beaber did do anything just look behager."] and Glooskap saw that of all created beings the first and greatest was Man.

Before men were instructed by him, they lived in darkness; it was so dark that they could not even see to slay their enemies. [Footnote: This was read to me by an Indian from a wampum record, now kept at Sebayk. I do not think I am mistaken in the phrase. It probably refers to ignorance of warlike weapons.] Glooskap taught them how to hunt, and to build huts and canoes and weirs for fish. Before he came they knew not how to make weapons or nets. He the Great Master showed them the hidden virtues of plants, roots, and barks, and pointed out to them such vegetables as might be used for food, as well as what kinds of animals, birds, and fish were to be eaten. And when this was done he taught them the names of all the stars. He loved mankind, and wherever he might be in the wilderness he was never very far from any of the Indians. He dwelt in a lonely land, but whenever they sought him they found him. [Footnote: This is from the Rand manuscript. The writer remarks that these expressions were the very words of a Micmac Indian named Stephen Flood, "who had no idea that he was using almost the identical expressions of Holy Writ with reference to God."] He traveled far and wide: there is no place in all the land of the Wabanaki where he left not his name; hills, rocks and rivers, lakes and islands, bear witness to him.

Glooskap was never married, yet as he lived like other men he lived not alone. There dwelt with him an old woman, who kept his lodge; he called her Noogumee, "my grandmother." (Micmac.) With her was a youth named Abistariaooch, or the Martin. (M.) And Martin could change himself to a baby or a little boy, a youth or a young man, as befitted the time in which he was to act; for all things about Glooskap were very wonderful. This Martin ate always from a small birch-bark dish, called *witch-kwed-lakun-cheech* (M.), and when he left this anywhere Glooskap was sure to find it, and could tell from its appearance all that had befallen his family. And Martin was called by Glooskap Uch-keen (M.), "my younger brother." The Lord of men and beasts had a belt which gave him magical power and endless strength. And when he lent this to Martin, the younger brother could also do great deeds, such as were only done in old times.

Martin lived much with the Mikumwess or Elves, or Fairies, and is said to have been one of them.

How Win-pe the Sorcerer, having stolen Glooskap's Family, was by him pursued, and how, Glooskap for a Merry Jest cheated the Whale. Of the Song of the Clams, and how the Whale smoked a Pipe.

(Micmac.)

N'*kah-ne-oo*. In old times (P.), in the beginning of things, men were as animals and animals as men; how this was, no one knows. But it is told that all were at first men, and as they gave themselves up to this and that desire, and to naught else, they became beasts. But before this came to pass, they could change to one or the other form; yet even as men there was always something which showed what they were.

Now Glooskap lived on an island named Aja-lig-un-mechk, and with him were many Indians with the names and natures of animals and birds.

These men, but most of all Pulowech, the Partridge, having acquired power themselves, became jealous of Glooskap, and made up their minds to depart when he was away, taking with them Martin and the grandmother. For they had great hope that Glooskap, being left alone on the island, would perish, because they knew not his power. There is another story which says that he was living at the mouth of the Oolostook, at a place called Menogwes (St. John, N. B.), and went away into the forest as far as Goolwahgik (Juan), and had been gone six weeks, when he returned home and found the old woman, whose name was Mooinarkw, [Footnote: Mr. Rand translates this Micmac word as Mrs. Bear.] and Martin had been taken away. Following their tracks to the shore he saw one of his greatest enemies, a terrible sorcerer named Win-pe, just pushing off in his canoe. And with him were his wife and child and Dame Bear and Martin. They were still within call, and Glooskap cried from the shore to the grandmother to send back his dogs, which were not larger than mice, and, as some stories tell us, were squirrels. So she took a *woltes-takun*, which is a small wooden platter, and on such Indian dice are tossed. This she put in the water, and placed the dogs on it, and it floated to the shore, and Glooskap took it up. Win-pe with his family and prisoners pushed on to Passamoogwaddy (M.), and thence to Grand Manan; and after remaining there a while he crossed over to Kes-poog-itk (Yarmouth), and so went slowly along the southern coast through Oona-mahgik (Cape Breton), and over to Uktukkamkw (Newfoundland), where he was slain.

Now whether it was to gain magical power, or to weaken that of Win-pe, or to chasten the others by suffering, who knows? But Glooskap rested seven years alone before he pursued the enemy, though some say it was seven months. And when the time had come, he took his dogs and went to the shore, and looked far out to sea over the waves, and sang the magic song which the whales obey. [Footnote: In the *Tales and Traditions of the Eskimo*, by Dr. Henry Rink, we are told in the story of Akigsiak that an old man taught the hero a magic lay for luring a whale to him. In another, Katersparsuk sings such a song to the walrus.] Soon there rose in the distance a small whale, who had heard the call, and came to Glooskap; but he was then very great, and he put one foot on the whale to test his weight, and the fish sank under him. So he sent it away.

Then the lord of men and beasts sang the song again, and there came the largest, a mighty female, and she bore him well and easily over to Kes-poog-itk. But she was greatly afraid of getting into shoal water, or of running ashore, and this was what Glooskap wished her to do that he might not wet his feet. So as she approached she asked him if land were in sight. But he lied, and said "No." So she went on rapidly.

However, she saw shells below, and soon the water grew so shoal that she said in fear, "*Moon-as-taba-kan-kari-jean-nook*? (M.) Does not the land show itself like a bow-string?" And he said, "We are still far from land."

Then the water grew so shoal that she heard the song of the Clams as they lay under the sand, singing to her that she should throw him off and drown him. For these Clams were his deadly enemies. But Bootup the Whale did not understand their language, so she asked her rider—for he knew Clam—what they were chanting to her. And he replied in a song:—

"They tell you to hurry (*cussal*) (M),
To hurry, to hurry him along,
Over the water,
Away as fast as you can!"

Then the Whale went like lightning, and suddenly found herself high on the shore. Then she lamented and sang:—

"Alas, my grandchild (*noojeech*),
Ah, you have been my death;
I can never leave the land,
I shall swim in the sea no more."

But Glooskap sang:—

"Have no fear, *noogumee*,
You shall not suffer,
You shall swim in the sea once more."

[Illustration: GLOOSKAP LOOKING AT THE WHALE SMOKING HIS PIPE]

Then with a push of his bow against her head he sent her off into deep water. And the Whale rejoiced greatly. But ere she went she said, "Oh, my grandson, *K'teen pehabskwass n'aga tomawe*?" (P.). "Hast thou not such a thing as an old pipe and some tobacco?" He replied,—

"Ah yes.
You want tobacco,
I behold you."

So he gave her a short pipe and some tobacco, and thereunto a light. And the Whale, being of good cheer, sailed away, smoking as she went, while Glooskap, standing silent on the shore, and ever leaning on his maple bow, beheld the long low cloud which followed her until she vanished in the far away.

In a Passamaquoddy tale of Pook-jin-skwess the Witch, the Clams sing a song deriding the hero. The words are:—

"Mow chow nut-pess sell
Peri marm-hole wett."

These words are not Indian, but they are said to mean,—

You look very funny with your long hair streaming in the wind,
And sailing on a snail's horn.

The large Clams sing this in a bass voice, the small ones in falsetto. The gypsies say that a Snail, when put on a pie, utters four cries, or squeaks; hence in Germany the Romany call it *Stargoli*: that is, *shtor-godli*, four cries.

Of the Dreadful Deeds of the Evil Pitcher, who was both Man and Woman, and how she fell in love with Glooskap, and, being scorned, became his Enemy. Of the Toads and Porcupines, and the Awful Battle of the Giants.

(Passamaquoddy.)

When Glooskap came into the world it abounded in giants, monsters, sorcerers and witches, fiends and devils. Among the witches there was, one whom the Passamaquoddy call Pook-jin-skwess, or the Pitcher [Footnote: It is not impossible that this well-known Indian witch gave her name to Moll Pitcher, the famous fortune-teller of Lynn.] And they have a legend that she once fell in love with Glooskap when he was young and had not gained the power of his riper age. He fled before her, and she pursued him. It was a dreadful flight, since to make rapid steps both took the form of giants by their *m'-te-oulin* (P.), or magic power. It was like an awful storm in winter, the wind chasing the cloud; it was like a frightful tempest in summer, the lightning chasing the thunder. As the snow lay deep, both had snow-shoes on. When they came to the shore Glooskap leaped from the main-land to the island of Grand Manan, [Footnote: A leap of about nine miles.] and so escaped her. Now the snow-shoes of Glooskap were *sams'ook* (P.), or round, while those of Pook-jin-skwess were long and pointed, [Footnote: The Penobscots give the long shoes to Glooskap.] and the marks of them as they jumped are to be seen deep in the rocks to this day.

When Glooskap came to the camp, which was at Ogumkegeak (M.), now called Liverpool, he found no one. But there lay the *witch-kwed-lakun-cheech* (M.), or birch-bark dish of Martin, and from it, or, as another legend states, from an old man and woman who dwelt hard by, he learned that Win-pe and the families had been gone for seven years, along a road guarded by wicked and horrible beings, placed by Win-pe to prevent the Great Master from finding him. For it was a great triumph for him to keep Glooskap's friends as slaves, and all the land spoke thereof.

And these monsters were Pook-jin-skwess, or the Evil Pitcher herself, in many forms; for she could be man or woman, [Footnote: In the *Tales and Traditions* of the Eskimo, we are told that a woman named Arnakuak, being apparently gifted by magic with the ability to change her sex, had her daughter-in-law; Ukuamak, for a wife, and, having eloped with her, was followed and killed by her own son. As this is almost immediately followed by a story of a man who gave birth to a child, it would appear that the idea was common to both Eskimo and Indians. Only the wicked magicians in Indian tales change their sex, like Loki in the Edda.] or many of them, and also several girls, when she willed it. Now it is a great part of Indian *m'teoulin* (P.) to know what one's enemies are planning and plotting, and all their tricks and darkened paths; and in this Glooskap went beyond them all, for before his time every one went his own way, even in wickedness. But Glooskap first of all threw out his soul unto others.

And when he came to Ogumkeok he found a hut, and in it, seated over a fire, the ugliest old hag he had ever seen, trembling in every limb, as if near death, dirty, ragged, and loathsome in all ways. Looking up at him with bleared eyes, she begged him to gather her a little firewood, which he did. And then she prayed him to free her from the *wah gook*(M.), or vermin, with which she was covered, and which were maddening her with their bites. These were all devils in disguise, the spirits of foul poison, such as she deemed must kill even the Master. Now Glooskap, foreseeing all this, had taken with him, as he came, from a bog many cranberries. And bidding Pook-jin-skwess bend over, he began to take from her hair the hideous vermin, and each, as he took it, became a horrid porcupine or toad. [Footnote: In the Eskimo mythology, *Arnarkuagsak*, the old woman of the sea, is tormented by vermin about her head. These are really the souls of still-born or murdered infants, who have become imps. The first thing which the *angakok* or sorcerer, who visits her must do is to free her from these pests. The descent of the sorcerer to this mother of all the monsters of the sea, who are at the same time *giants*, when they choose to assume the human form, recalls that of Odin to Hela. Both make this journey to hell, not for themselves, but in the interests of mankind.] Then the hag asked, "Have you found one?" "I have," replied the Master. "*Basp!*" (M.) "Crush it!" was her answer, and Glooskap crushed a cranberry; and she, hearing the noise, thought that he had done as she bid, and that the poison on his fingers would penetrate to his life. But he put the imps, one by one, under the wooden platter, which lay before him. As this went on he put the witch to sleep. When she awoke he was gone. The foul porcupines and toads were swarming all over the ground, having upset their hive. And filled with fury at being made a jest of, since it was a great despite that he had not even found it worth while to kill her when asleep, she burst out into her own form, which was beautiful as sin, wild as the devil, and gathering up all her imps, and making herself far more magical by fiercer will, went onward to encounter him again.

Then Glooskap came to a narrow pass in the hills. Here were two terrible beasts, as one story has it, or two monstrous dogs, [Footnote: The Indians had dogs before the coming of the whites. They were wolf-like.] as it is told in another. And they attacked him; but he set his own at them, and they, growing to tremendous size, killed the others. His dogs were so trained that when called to come off they went on, and the more they were bid to be quiet the more they bit.

Soon he came to the top of a high hill, and looking thence over all the land saw afar off a large wigwam, and knew in his heart that an enemy dwelt therein. And coming to it he found an old man and his two daughters. [Footnote: In another account, an old sorceress and her daughters; also an old man and his wife and daughters. According to two versions, these are all separate wizards, but the whole spirit of the Passamaquoddy legends make them Pook-jin-skwess alone.] Now the girls came out greeting [Footnote: In the story of the Rabbit and Lusifee the sorcerer singly twice assumes the form of an old man and his two daughters. There is yet another story, in which a magician thus triples himself with two daughters. It is, I believe, Eskimo, but I cannot distinctly remember as to this.] him with very pleasant glances, wooing softly and sweetly; they offered him a string of sausages, such as the Indians make from the entrails of the bear by only turning them inside out. For the fat, which clings to the outside, fills the skin. When these are washed and dried and smoked, many deem them delicious. But these which the girls offered, as girls do, to show their love, by casting the string round the neck of the favored youth, were enchanted, and had they once put the necklace upon him he would have been overpowered. However, they knew not of this new magic which the Master had brought into the land, by which one can read the heart; so, as they sidled up unto him with smiles and blandishments, waving in the wind as they danced their garlands of enchanted sausages, he looked as if he wanted to be won. And when his dogs growled at them he cried, "*Cuss*!" (M.), which means *Stop*! but which the dogs only knew as "Hie, at them!" So they flew at the witches, and these flashed up like fire into their own dreadful forms of female fiends. Then there was a terrible tumult, for never before in the land of the Wabanaki had there been such a battle. All the earth and rocks around were torn up. All the while the Master cried to the dogs, "Stop! These are my sisters. Come off, ye evil beasts! Let them alone! Cease, oh cease!" Yet the more he exhorted them to peace the more they inclined to war, and the more fiercely they fought, until the witches fled.

[Illustration: GLOOSKAP SETTING HIS DOGS ON THE WITCHES]

Then he entered the wigwam where the old sorcerer sat, waiting for him as food. And the Master said, "Are you hungry? Or do you love sausages? Here they are!" Instantly casting the links around his neck, he was taken, and Glooskap slew him with one blow.

Then, going on, he reached the Strait of Camsoke [Footnote: Camsoke means, "There is a high bluff on the opposite side of the river."—S. T. Rand.] (M.), or Canso, and to cross over again sang the song which wins the whales, and one of these rising, carried him to the opposite shore. Thence he made the circle of Oona-mah-gik, keeping round by the southern coast, and coming to the old camps where his enemy had been. From the *witch-kwed-lakun-cheech*, or birch-bark dish, left by Martin, he learned how long they had been gone. [Footnote: As the gypsy leaves his *patteran*, or sign, so the Indian makes marks which set forth clearly enough how long he has camped at any place, and how many were in the party, etc. It may be supposed that Martin, not daring to attract Win-pe's attention, effected this by a few secret scratches. Thus three lines and a crescent or moon would mean three nights.] When he came to Uk-tu-tun (M., Cape North) he found they had rowed to Uk-tuk-amqw (M., Newfoundland), and had left three days before.

Then again he sang, and once more a whale carried him over. And now he knew that he was indeed coming to what he sought, for in the deserted camp he found the embers of a fire, still smoking. Advancing rapidly, he saw near the next camp Martin, seeking wood to burn. The youth and the old Dame Bear had been most cruelly treated by Win-pe, and they were nearly starved, but Martin's clothes were good. [Footnote: There is a reason for this singular detail. Nancy Jeddore, the Indian from whom Mr. Rand learned one version of this legend, informed him that the Martin, thin at all times, always has a fine fur, however starved he may be. Dying with hunger, he is always well dressed.] And Martin was so sunk in sorrow that he did not hear Glooskap call him, and not till the Master threw a small stick at him did he look up, and even then he thought it had fallen from a tree. Then, seeing him, he cried out with joy; but Glooskap, who was hiding in the woods, bade him be silent. "Wait till it is dark," he said, "and I will go to your wigwam. Now you may go home and tell your grandmother."

In the other story (M.) it is narrated that as Martin with the grandmother were on the road, and Dame Bear bore him as almost a babe on her back, he turned his head and saw Glooskap following them, and cried out,—

"Where, oh where,
Where is my brother?
He who fed me often
On the marrow of the moose!"

And she replied,—

"Alas for thee, boy!
He is far, far away;
You will see him no more."

But the little fellow, seeing him again, sang as before, and Dame Bear, turning her head and beholding her Master, was so moved that she fainted and fell to the ground. Then Glooskap raised her in his arms, and when she had recovered she related how cruelly they had been treated by Win-pe. And Glooskap said, "Bear with him yet a little while, for I will soon pay him in full for what he has done."

Then the Master bade the old woman go back to the camp with Martin, and say nothing. It was the youth's duty to go for water and tend the baby in its swinging cot. And Glooskap told him all that he should do. When he should bring water he must mix with it the worst filth, and so offer it to Win-pe, the sorcerer.

And even as he ordered it was done, and Martin meekly offered the foul drink to the evil man, who at the smell of it cried aloud, "*Uk say!*" (M., Oh, horror!) and bade him bring a cleaner cup. But Martin, bearing the babe, threw it into the fire, and, running to the spot where Glooskap hid, cried out, "*Nse-sako! nse-sako!*" (M., My brother! my brother!) Win-pe, pursuing him, said, "Cry out to him; your brother cannot help you now. He is far away from here, on the island where I left him. Cry out well, for now you must die!" All this had been done that Win-pe's power might be put to sleep by anger, and his mind drawn to other things. And the Master rose before him in all his might, and stepped forward, while Win-pe drew backward a pace to recover his strength. And with great will the Master roused all the magic within him, and, as it came, he rose till his head was above the tallest pine; and truly in those days trees were giants beyond those of this time. But the lord of men and beasts laughed as he grew till his head was far above the clouds and reached the stars, and ever higher, till Win-pe was as a child at his feet. And holding the man in scorn, and disdaining to use a nobler weapon, he tapped the sorcerer lightly with the end of his bow, like a small dog, and he fell dead.

How the Story of Glooskap and Pook-jin-skwess, the Evil Pitcher, is told by the Passamaquoddy Indians. [Footnote: In this story Glooskap is called Pogumk, the Black Cat or Fisher, that is, a species of wild cat, while Martin is a N'mockswess, sable. There seems to be no settled idea as to what was the *totem* or innate animal nature of the lord of men and beasts. I have a series of pictures scraped on birch-bark illustrating these myths, executed by a Passamaquoddy, in which Glooskap and the adopted grandmother in the stone canoe are represented as wood-chucks, or ground-hogs. (Mon-in-kwess, P.)]

(Passamaquoddy.)

There was a village of Indians who were all Black Cats, or Po'gum'k. One of them, the cleverest and bravest, went forth every day with bow and arrow, tomahawk and knife, and killed moose and bear, and sent meat to the poor, and so he fed them all. When he returned they came to him to know where his game lay, and when he had told them they went forth with toboggins [Footnote: Toboggin, a sled made very simply by turning up the ends of one or more pieces of wood to prevent them from catching in the snow.] and returned with them loaded with meat. And the chief of the Black Cats was by his mother the son of a bear. [Footnote: A confused but important point in all these myths.]

Pook-jin-skwess, the Witch, was a Black Cat. She was a woman or a man as she willed to be; but in these days she was a man. And she, being evil, hated the chief, and thought long how she could kill or remove him, and take his place. Now, one day when all the camp had packed what they had, being about to travel, Pitcher asked the chief to go with him, or with her, as you may will, down to the water-side to gather gulls' eggs. And then they went far out in a canoe, and very far, and still farther, till they came to an island, and there they landed, and while Pogumk (who was Glooskap) sought for eggs, the false-hearted Pitcher stole away in the *akweden* (P., canoe), and as she paddled she sang a song—

"Nikhed-ha Pogumk min nekuk,
Netswil sagamawin!" (P)

"I have left the Black Cat on an island,
I shall be the chief of the Fishers now!"

So she came to the village, and the next day they all departed through the woods; there was not one of them left save the one who was worth them all. And at night they camped, expecting every day that the chief would come to them, and till then Pitcher was in his place.

Now on the thirtieth day the chief remembered his friend the Fox, who had *m'teoulin* (P.), or magic power. And he sang a song, and the Fox heard it, although he was miles away, beyond forests and mountains. And thus knowing all, he went to the shore and swam to the island, where he found the chief. At this time the Black Cat could not swim such a distance, [Footnote: The most powerful *manitous*, or magicians, in the Chippeway tales, as well as in all others of the Indians, may exhaust their power and be forced to depend on that of inferiors in the great art. In this tale Glooskap is decidedly under a cloud.] but the Fox offered to take him to the mainland. Then they waded into the water, and the Fox said, "Close thine eyes and hold fast to my tail as tightly as thou canst, and be of good faith, oh, my elder brother, and we shall soon gain the shore." Saying this, he swam away and his friend followed. And it went well with them, but the chief grew weary, and he opened one eye a little, and saw that they were not ten feet from the shore. And being of little faith he thought, for he spoke not aloud, "We shall never get to land." But the Fox replied, "Do not believe it." But the journey lasted long, for what seemed to Pogumk to be ten feet was ten miles, and the wind was high and the waters were wild, for Pitcher had called forth a storm. So they swam all day and all the evening before they landed. "And now, my elder brother," said the Fox, "you may go your way." And he went to the camp of the Black Cats.

When he came to the camp it was cold, and there were only ashes, for the people had gone on. So he followed them, and in one day came near them. And the first whom he overtook was his mother, bearing his younger brother Sable ('Nmmok-swess, P.) on her back, so that while she looked forward he looked behind. And as Pogumk peeped out from among the leaves, Sable saw him, and said, "Here comes my brother!" And she turned, but saw nothing, for the chief suddenly hid himself behind a tree. Then they went on, and Sable cried again, "Indeed, mother, I behold my elder brother!" And this time the mother, glancing quickly, caught him, and they all laughed for joy, and she threw Sable down in the leaves, like a stick. Then the chief bade Sable run to the camp. "And when you are there," he said, "build up a great fire of hemlock bark, and take Pitcher's babe, even the babe which she loves, and which you tend, and throw it into the fire, and run to me as fast as you can, for verily thou wilt be in dire need to do so."

And as he commanded it was done; and when the fire was hot, Sable threw the babe into it, and it was burned to death. And Pitcher, being, as one may well believe, maddened at such a sight, pursued him as a starving wolf pursues a rabbit. Then Sable, in great fear, cried aloud, "Oh, my elder brother, my brother!" And Pitcher screamed, "Call aloud to him, for you must run as far as the island where Pogumk is, to save yourself!" And at that word Pogumk stepped forward and confronted her, and said, "Truly, she need not run so far."

And seeing him and hearing this, fear came upon her; but she laughed aloud to hide it, and said, "I did but chase him in sport, for I love Sable." But Pogumk replied grimly, "I know thee and thy tricks, thou the evil one." Then, as his magic had come to him, he used his power, and put Pitcher with her back against a tree; and there she stayed, stuck to it, unable to get away. But the chief and Sable went to the camp. Now Pitcher had a hatchet and wedge, and with much ado she cut herself away, and the Black Cats heard her pounding and chopping all night long. And in the morning she came to them, and there was a great piece of wood sticking to her back, and they laughed her to scorn, and sang at her,—

"He who made the chief
Stay on a distant island,
He is stuck by the chief
Fast with his back to a tree."

Now Pitcher the Witch, being mad with shame and spite, fled from the face of man, and ran through the woods like a wild wolf. And so she came to Bar Harbor (Pes'sonkqu', P.), and sat down on a log, and said, with her heart full of bitterness and malice, "I would that I could become something which should torment all men." And as she said this she became a mosquito (T'sis-o, P.), and so it came to pass that mosquitoes were made. And to this day men see that wherever the Black Cat is, there too is the Sable not far away. [Footnote: The Passamaquoddy version relates that Pitcher in her flight pursued a moose to Bar Harbor, where, having killed him and drawn out the entrails, she petrified him. A Penobscot woman told me she had often seen the moose rock there, and the "inments." But she attributed the deed to Glooskap, to whom it properly belongs, his petrified moose and dogs and the print of his bow, etc., being still shown in Nova Scotia; and it is also said that it was at Freshwater, after returning from Bar Harbor (Maine), that Pitcher was changed into a mosquito. Another story states that Pook-jin-skwess, having pursued young men all her life, changed into a mosquito that she might continue to prey on them.]

Of this Pook-jin-skwess it was said that she had children of her own, begotten by sorcerers and giants and monsters; but as they were all ugly she stole from the Indian women their fairest babes, and brought them up as if they were her own, that she might not be entirely put to shame because of her children. And once she had thus stolen a boy, and when he grew up some one said to him that he should not believe that she was his mother, but should question her as to it. Now the youth, reflecting on this, observed that his brothers and sisters were all as ugly as evil beasts and no better behaved, while he himself was comely and good. Then he asked her what this might mean. And she replied, laughing, "Because they were all begotten (or born) in the night-time, but you are a child of the day and of light." [Footnote: There is probably an allusion in this to the Wabanaki, or Children of Light; that is, the Algonquin. This story was told me by Noel Josephs, a Passamaquoddy. I have been told by an old Passamaquoddy woman that the descendants of Pook-jin-skwess were the 'Nmmok-skwess. This stealing the white boy is related in another tale more folly. It may refer to the early dark Eskimo.]

How Glooskap became friendly to the Loons, and made them his Messengers.

(Micmac.)

When Glooskap was pursuing Win-pe, he one day on Uktukamkw saw from afar flying over water the Kwe-moo (M.), or Loons. And thrice did their chief make the circle of the lake, coming near to the land of men and beasts every time, as if he would fain seek somewhat. Then Glooskap asking him what he wanted, Kwe-moo replied that he would be his servant and friend. So Glooskap taught him a strange long cry like the howl of a dog, and when the loons were in need of him or would pray to him they were to utter this cry.

And it came to pass that when he was in Newfoundland he came to an Indian town, and they who dwelt therein were all Kwee-moo-uk, or Loons. And they, as men, were exceeding glad to see their lord, who had blessed them as birds, and did their best to please him. So he made them his huntsmen and messengers, and in all the tales of Glooskap the Kweemoo ever appears as faithful to him. Whence to this day, when the Indians hear the cry of the Loon, they say, "*Kwemoo el-komik-too-ajul Gloocapal*" (He is calling upon Glooskap).

How Glooskap made his Uncle Mikchich the Turtle into a Great Man, and got him a Wife. [Footnote: This legend of the tortoise is carefully compiled from six different versions: the narration of Tomah Josephs, a Passamaquoddy; the Anglo-Indian manuscript, already cited; two accounts in the Rand manuscript; the author quoted without credit in *The Maritime Provinces*; and one by Mrs. W. Wallace Brown. As the totem of the Tortoise was of the highest rank among the Algonquins, this account of its origin is of corresponding interest. Having employed an old Indian to carve the handle of a war or scalping knife for me, such as was used by his Passamaquoddy ancestors, he carved on it a tortoise. It was especially the totem of the Lenni-Lenape, called by the Passamaquoddies *Lel-le-mabe*, "the people."] Of Turtles' Eggs, and how Glooskap vanquished a Sorcerer by smoking Tobacco.

(Micmac and Passamaquoddy.)

Now when Glooskap left Uktukamkw, or Newfoundland, it was in a canoe, and he came to Piktook (M. for Pictou), which means the bubbling up of air, because there is much bubbling in the water near that place. And here there was an Indian village, and in that place the Master met with a man whom he loved all his life.

And this was not because this man, whose name in Micmac is Mikchich and in Passamaquoddy Chick-we-notchk, meaning the Turtle, was great, or well favored, or rich. For truly he was none of these, being very poor and lazy, no longer young, and not very clever or wise in any way. It is said that he was indeed Glooskap's uncle, but others think that this was by adoption. However, this old fellow bore all his wants with such good nature that the

Master, taking him in great affection, resolved to make of him a mighty man. Which came to pass, and that in a strange manner, as we shall see.

For coming to Piktook, where there were above a hundred wigwams, Glooskap, being a very handsome, stately man, with the manner of a great chief, was much admired, and that not a little by all the women, so that every one wished to have him in the house. Yet he gave them all the go-by, and dwelt with his old uncle, in whose quaint ways and old-time stories he took great delight. And there was to be a great feast with games, but Glooskap did not care to go, either as a guest or a performer in the play.

Still he inquired of Mikchich if he would not take part in it, telling him that all the maidens would be there, and asking him why he had never married, and saying that he should not live alone. Then the uncle said: "Poor and old and plain am I; I have not even garments fit for a feast; better were it for me to smoke my pipe at home." "Truly, if that be all, uncle," replied Glooskap, "I trow I can turn tailor and fit you to a turn; and have no care as to your outside or your face, for to him who knows how, 't is as easy to make a man over as a suit of clothes." "Yes; but, nephew," said Mikchich, "how say you as to making over the inside of a mortal?" "By the great Beaver!" answered the Master, "that is something harder to do, else I were not so long at work in this world. But before I leave this town I shall do that also for you; and as for this present sport, do but put on my belt." And when he had done that, Mikchich became so young and handsome that no man or woman ever saw the like. And then Glooskap dressed him in his own best clothes, and promised him that to the end of his days, whenever he should be a man, he would be the comeliest of men; and because he was patient and tough, he should, as an animal, become the hardest to kill of all creatures on the face of the earth, as it came to pass.

So Mikchich went to the feast. Now the chief of Piktook had three beautiful daughters, and the youngest was the loveliest in the land. And on her he cast his eyes, and returning said, "I have seen one whom I want." Now all the young men in Piktook desired this girl, and would kill any one who would win her.

So the next day Glooskap, taking a bunch of *wawbap* (P., wampum), went, to the chief and proposed for Mikchich, [Footnote: All invitations to festivals, or formal ceremonies, proposals of marriage, etc., were preceded among these tribes by a gift of wampum.] and the mother at once said "Yes." So the girl made up a bed of fresh twigs and covered it with a great white bear-skin, and went to Mikchich, and they returned and had dried meat for supper. So they were married.

Now Turtle seemed to be very lazy; and when others hunted he lounged at home. One day his young wife said to him that if this went on thus they must soon starve. So he put on his snow-shoes and went forth, and she followed him to see what he would do. And he had not gone far ere he tripped and fell down, and the girl, returning, told her mother that he was worthless. But the mother said, "He will do something yet. Be patient."

One day it came to pass that Glooskap said to Mikchich, "To-morrow there will be a great game at ball, and you must play. But because you have made yourself enemies of all the young men here, they will seek to slay you, by crowding all together and trampling upon you. And when they do this it will be by your father-in-law's lodge, and to escape them I give you the power to jump high over it. This you may do twice, but the third time will be terrible for you, and yet it must be."

All this happened as he foretold; for the young men indeed tried to take his life, and to escape them Mikchich jumped over the lodge, so that he seemed like a bird flying. But the third time he did this he was caught on the top of the tent-poles, and hung there dangling in the smoke which rose from below.

[Illustration: THE MUD TURTLE JUMPING OVER THE WIGWAM OF HIS
FATHER-IN-LAW.]

Then Glooskap, who was seated in the tent, said, "Uncle, I will now make you the *sogmo*, or great chief of the Tortoises, and you shall bear up a great nation." Then he smoked Mikchich [Footnote: In a verbal Passamaquoddy narrative (John Gabriel), and in one given in *The Maritime Provinces*, this was effected by Glooskap with tobacco-smoke from his pipe. In Mr. Rand's manuscript it is the smoke of the tent-fire. The Passamaquoddy narrations are invariably more spirited and *humorous* than the Micmac.] so long that his skin became a hard shell, and the marks of the smoke may be seen thereon to this day. And removing his entrails he destroyed them, so that but one short one was left. And he cried aloud, "*Milooks*! (M.) My nephew, you will kill me!" But the nephew replied, "Not so. I am giving you great life. From this time you may roll through a flame and never feel it, and live on land or in the water. And though your head be cut off, it will live for nine days, and your heart, even, shall beat as long when taken from your body." So Mikchich rejoiced greatly.

And this came betimes, for he soon had need of it all. For the next day all the men went on a hunt, and the Master warned him that they would seek to slay him. Now the young men went on before, and Turtle lingered behind; but all at once he made a magic flight far over their heads, unseen, and deep in the forest he slew a moose. Then he drew this to the snow-shoe track or road, and when his foes came up there he sat upon the moose, smoking, and waiting for them. Now Glooskap had told them that they would see some one come out ahead of them all that day, and when this came to pass they were more angered in their hearts than ever.

So they plotted to kill Turtle, and his nephew, who was about to leave, told him how it would be. "First of all, they will build a mighty fire and throw you in it. But do thou, O uncle, go cheerfully, for by my power thou wilt in nowise suffer. Then they will speak of drowning, but thou must beg and pray that this may not be; and then they will the more seek to do so, and thou shalt fight them to the bitter end, and yet it shall be."

And as he said, so it came to pass; and Mikchich, being of good cheer, bade farewell to his nephew. [Footnote: This is amusingly, though not very clearly, set forth in the Indian manuscript as follows: "Make believe but you dond want be trown. So he shaken hands witt is nuncel kick hororch good by do him. Tell is uncle you—I shall not be kill and I am going Lever (to live)—we may meet again."] And they seized him and threw him into a great fire, but he turned over and went to sleep in it, being very lazy; and when the fire had burnt out he awoke, and called for more wood, because it was a cold night.

Then they seized him yet again, and spoke of drowning. But, hearing this, he, as if he were in mortal dread, begged them not to do this thing. And he said they might cut him to pieces, or burn him, as they would, but not to throw him into the water. [Footnote: This in the original is extremely like Brer Rabbit's prayer not to be thrown into the brier-bush. As this legend is one of the oldest of the Algonquin, and certainly antedating the coming of the whites, I give it the priority over the negro.] Therefore they resolved to do so, and dragged him on. Then he screamed horribly and fought lustily, and tore up trees and roots and rocks like a madman; but they took him into a canoe and paddled out into the middle of the lake (or to the sea), and, throwing him in, watched him sink as he vanished far down below. So they thought him dead, and returned rejoicing.

Now the next day at noon there was a hot sunshine, and something was seen basking on a great rock, about a mile out in the lake. So two young men took a canoe and went forth to see what this might be. And when they came to the edge of the rock, which was about a foot high, there lay Mikchich sunning himself; but seeing them coming to take him, he only said, "Good-by," and rolled over plump into the water, where he is living to this day. In memory whereof all turtles, when they see any one coming, tip-tilt themselves over into the water at once.

And Turtle lived happily with his wife, and she had a babe. New it happened in after-days that Glooskap came to see his uncle, and the child cried. "Dost thou know what he says?" exclaimed the Master. "Truly, not I," answered Mikchich, "unless it be the language of the Mu-se-gisk (P., Spirits of the Air), which no man knoweth." "Well," replied Glooskap, "he is talking of eggs, for he says '*Hoo-wah! hoo-wah!*' which methinks is much the same as '*Waw-wun, waw-wun.*' And this in Passamaquoddy means egg." "But where are there any?" asked Mikchich. Then Glooskap bade him seek in the sand, and he found many, and admired and marveled over them greatly; and in memory of this, and to glorify this jest of Glooskap, the Turtle layeth eggs even to this day.

* * * * *

The great Glooskap was a right valiant smoker; in all the world was no man who loved a pipe of good tobacco so much as he. In those days the summers were longer in the land of the Wabanaki, the sun was warmer, and the Indians raised *tomawe* (tobacco, P.), and solaced themselves mightily therewith. [Footnote: I have met with an old Indian woman in New Brunswick who told me that her grandmother remembered to have seen tobacco raised there by the Passamaquoddy.] And there came to Glooskap a certain evil-minded magician, who sought to take his life, as the Master very well knew, for he read the hearts of men as if they had been strings of wampum. And this *m'teoulin* (P., magician), believing himself to be greatest in all things, thought to appall Glooskap by outdoing him at first in something at which he excelled; for a fish is frightened when another swims faster, but not till then.

And the man sat down to smoke with an exceeding long pipe with a great bowl, but that of Glooskap grew to be much greater. Then, having filled his pipe, the sorcerer exhausted and burnt it out at one pull, and then blew all the smoke out of his nose at one puff. So he sat and looked at the Master. But Glooskap, whose pipe held ten times as much tobacco, did the same, and blowing it out split the rocky ground, so that a great chasm opened before them. Then they were silent awhile, till the Master said, "If you can do that you may kill me." But he could not, and so went back with shame to those who had sent him. [Footnote: In this "tale of tobacco," told me by John Gabriel, the evil-minded magician is described as a Black Cat. This is probably an error, as Glooskap himself appears as chief of the Black Cats in another tale. It may be, however, that this was Pook-jin-skwess in disguise.]

How Glooskap sailed through the great Cavern of Darkness.

(Micmac.)

Now it is told in another tradition—and men tell even this differently—that *pitche*, in these old times (P.) Glooskap's seven neighbors, who were all so many different animals, took away his family, and that he followed them, even as it has been written, unto Newfoundland. And when he came there it was night, and, finding Marten alone, he took him forth into the forest to seek food, putting his belt on the boy, which gave him such power that he hunted well and got much meat.

So it came to pass that the next morning Dame Kah-kah-gooch, the Crow, [Footnote: *Kah-kah-gooch*, Micmac, *Kah-kah-goos*, Passamaquoddy. The Crow is represented in several stories as always peeping, spying, begging, pilfering, and tale-bearing about a town. The Passamaquoddy Indians hare peculiar superstitions as regards killing the crow.] observed that Marten was drying meat on his wigwam. And this she spread abroad. But when the people learned that the child had done this, a great fear came upon them all, and they sat every man in his lodge and awaited death, for they knew that the Master had come.

And he indeed came; but when he saw them all as frightened as rabbits before the wild-cat, he laughed aloud and forgave them, for he was noble and generous. And as they were hungry—for he had come in hard times—he gave them much venison, and sorrow departed from their wigwams. But as they had left him of old, he now left them. When they knew him not they left him to die; now that they knew him they feared lest they should perish without him. But he turned his steps towards other paths.

Now having made a canoe, the Master, with Marten and Dame Bear, went upon a mighty river. As the story says, it was broad and beautiful at first, and so they sailed away down towards its mouth. Then they came to great cliffs, which gathered round and closed over them. But the river ran on beneath these, and ever on far underground, deeper and deeper in the earth, till it dashed headlong into rapids, among rocks and ravines, and under cataracts which were so horrible that death seemed to come and go with every plunge of the canoe. And the water grew narrower and the current more dreadful, and fear came upon Marten and the woman, so that they died. But the Master sat with silent soul, though he sang the songs of magic, and so passed into the night, but came forth again into sunlight. And there was a lonely wigwam on the bank, into which he bore Marten and the grandmother, and saying, "*Numchahse*! arise!" lo, they arose, and deemed they had only slept. And now Glooskap had gained the greatest power. [Footnote: This incident of the passage underground is deeply suggestive of Wabeno mystery and initiation. It will strike every student of classic lore as almost identical with much that he has read. If it has not the same symbolical meaning here, it has apparently none whatever.]

This incident of passing through darkness, on a roaring stream in a frail bark, before emerging to sunlight or illumination, was not only in the ancient heathen myths. We are reminded of it by the storm through which Jesus passed with the disciples. That it made a great impression upon the Indians is shown by its being told of Pulewech, the Partridge, who is a type of Glooskap, and who, like him, makes war on the powers of evil, set forth in the Porcupines. The Indians, who imagined and selected so many wild and terrible tests to form the Shaman, or sorcerer, as well as the warrior, would hardly neglect that of *de profundis clamari*, the storm, the waves, darkness, and the roaring flood.

If there is really any Norse influence in this tale, this river must be the one mentioned in the Vafthrudnismal,—

"Ifing the stream is called which earth divides between the Jotuns and the gods. Open it shall run throughout all time. On that stream no ice shall he."

It will be observed that, having gone down or across this stream, Pulewech finds himself in the country of the Evil sorcerers; that is, Jotunheim. To conquer a river among the Norse, in a dream, was a sign of victory; to be carried away by one was a terrible omen.

"Methought a river ran Through the whole house, that it roared violently, rushed over the benches, brake the feet of yon brothers twain; Nothing the water spared; Something that will portend."

(Atlamal, in Groenlewzku, 25.)

Of the Great Works which Glooskap made in the Land.

(Micmac, Passamaquoddy, Penobscot.)

Over all the Land of the Wabanaki there is no place which was not marked by the hand of the Master. And it is to be seen on hills and rivers and great roads, as well as mighty rocks, which were in their day living monsters.

For there is a very wonderful highway from Cwesowra legek [Footnote: Hardwood Point, Fort Cumberland.] to Parrsborough, running parallel with the river now called Hebert, and this road is called by Indians Ou-wokun, the Causeway, but by white men, or the Iglesmani, the Boar's Back. For it is said that he meant to visit Partridge Island and Cape Blomidon, but they who were with him had got tired of the sea, and wished to cross over by land. And while they were resting and getting ready for their trip across, the Master, raising his magic power to a great deed to be spoken of forever, went away a little time, and cast up a great and beautiful level ridge, throwing it over bogs and streams; and on this they traveled, rejoicing, and, having reached the island, awaited him.

And yet again the Master did a mighty deed. It came to pass in those days that the Beavers had built a dam across from Utkoguncheek, or Cape Blomidon, to the opposite shore, and thereby made a pond that filled all the valley of Annapolis. Now in those times the Beavers were monstrous beasts, and the Master, though kind of heart, seems to have had but little love for them ever since the day when Qwah-beetsis, the son of the Great Beaver, tempted Malsum to slay his brother. Now the bones of these Beavers may be found to this day, and many there are on Oonamahgik, and their teeth are six inches across, and there are no such *qwah-beet* to-day. [Footnote: Both Mr. Rand and myself have been solemnly assured by Indians who had seen these antediluvian remains that they are the petrified relics of Glooskap's victims.] And these are the remains of the Beavers who built the dam at Cape Blomidon and forded the Annapolis Valley. Now Glooskap would have a hunt and do a deed which should equal the great whale-fishing of Kit-pooseeog-unow. So he cut the great dam near the shore, and bade Marten watch; for he said, "I mistrust that there is a little Beaver hiding hereabouts." And when the dam was cut from where it joined the shore there was a mighty rush of many waters, so that it swung round to the westward, yet it did not break away from the other shore. Therefore the end of it lodged with a great split therein when the flood had found a free course, and the whole may be seen there still, even to this day, and may be seen by all of those who pass up the bay; and this point, or Cape Split, is called by the Micmacs Pleegun, which, being interpreted, means the opening of a beaver dam.

Then, to frighten the Beaver, Glooskap threw at it a few handfuls of earth, and these, falling somewhat to the eastward of Partridge Island, became the Five Islands. And the pond which was left was the Basin of Minas.

And yet another tradition tells that, after cutting the dam, Glooskap sat and watched, but no beaver came out; [Footnote: This is the Anglo-Indian manuscript, already referred to.] for *Qwah-beet* had gone out of a back door. So he took a rock and threw it afar, [Footnote: "He took Rock tructed 150 miles ip River to sker beaber bock down, but beaber has gone ober granfalls."]—one hundred and fifty miles,—to scare the Beaver back again; but the Beaver had gone over the Grand Falls, and the stone remaineth there even to this day.

The Story of Glooskap as told in a few Words by a Woman of the Penobscots.

"Glus-gahbe gave names to everything. He made men and gave them life, and made the winds to make the waters move. The Turtle was his uncle; the Mink, *Uk-see-meezel*, his adopted son; and *Monin-kwessos*, the Woodchuck, his grandmother. The Beaver built a great dam, and Glus-gahbe turned it away and killed the Beaver. At Moose-tchick he killed a moose; the bones may be seen at Bar Harbor turned to stone. He threw the entrails of the Moose across the bay to his dogs, and they, too, may be seen there to this day, as I myself have seen them; and there, too, in the rock are the prints of his bow and arrow." [Footnote: Many a place is pointed out as the locality of the same legend. In addition to those in New Brunswick and Bar Harbor, Thoreau found another in Maine, which he thus describes:—

"While we were crossing this bay" (that is, the mouth of Moose River), "where Mount Kineo rose dark before us, within two or three miles, the

Indian repeated the tradition respecting this mountain's having been anciently a cow-moose,—how a mighty Indian hunter, whose name I forget, succeeded in killing this queen of the moose tribe with great difficulty, while her calf was killed somewhere among the islands in Penobscot Bay; and to his eyes this mountain had still the form of the moose in a reclining posture, its precipitous side presenting the outline of her head. He told this at some length, though it did not amount to much, and with apparent good faith, and asked us how we supposed the hunter could have killed such a mighty moose as that; how we could do it. Whereupon a man-of-war to fire broadsides into her was suggested, etc. An Indian tells such a story as if he thought it deserved to have a good deal said about it, only he has not got it to say; and so he makes up for the deficiency by a drawling tone, long-windedness, and a dumb wonder which he hopes will be contagious."

This concluding criticism is indeed singularly characteristic of Mr. Thoreau's own nasal stories about Nature, but it is as utterly untrue as ridiculous when applied to any Indian storytelling to which I have ever listened, and I have known the near relatives of the Indians of whom he speaks, and heard many of them tell their tales. This writer passed months in Maine, choosing Penobscot guides expressly to study them, to read Indian feelings and get at Indian secrets, and this account of Glooskap, whose name he forgets, is a fair specimen of what he learned. Yet he could in the same book write as follows: "The Anglo-American can indeed cut down and grub up all this waving forest, And make a stump and vote for Buchanan on its ruins; but he cannot Converse with the spirit of the tree he fells, he cannot read the poetry and mythology which retires as he advances."

If Mr. Thoreau had known the Indian legend of the spirit of the fallen tree—and his guide knew it well—he might have been credited with speaking wisely of the poetry and *mythology* which he ridicules the poor rural Yankees for not possessing.

Such a writer can, indeed, peep and botanize on the grave of Mother Nature, but never evoke *her* spirit.

The moving the island is evidently of Eskimo origin, since Crantz (*History of Greenland*) heard nearly the same story of some magician-giant. It was probably suggested by the very common floating away of ice-islands.]

How Glooskap, leaving the World, all the Animals mourned for him, and how, ere he departed, he gave Gifts to Men.

(Micmac.)

Now Glooskap had freed the world from all the mighty monsters of an early time: the giants wandered no longer in the wilderness; the *cullo* terrified man no more, as it spread its wings like the cloud between him and the sun; the dreadful Chenoo of the North devoured him not; no evil beasts, devils, and serpents were to be found near his home. And the Master had, moreover, taught men the arts which made them happier; but they were not grateful to him, and though they worshiped him they were not the less wicked.

"Now when the ways of men and beasts waxed evil they greatly vexed Glooskap, and at length he could no longer endure them, and he made a rich feast by the shore of the great Lake Minas. All the beasts came to it, and when the feast was over he got into a great canoe, and the beasts looked after him till they saw him no more. And after they ceased to see him, they still heard his voice as he sang; but the sounds grew fainter and fainter in the distance, and at last they wholly died away; and then deep silence fell on them all, and a great marvel came to pass, and the beasts, who had till now spoken but one language, were no longer able to understand each other, and they fled away, each his own way, and never again have they met together in council. Until the day when Glooskap shall return to restore the Golden Age, and make men and animals dwell once more together in amity and peace, all Nature mourns. And tradition says that on his departure from Acadia the Great Snowy Owl retired to the deep forests, to return no more until he could come to welcome Glooskap; and in those sylvan depths the owls even yet repeat to the night *Koo-koo-skoos*! which is to say in the Indian tongue, 'Oh, I am sorry! Oh, I am sorry!' And the Loons, who had been the huntsmen of Glooskap, go restlessly up and down through the world, seeking vainly for their master, whom they cannot find, and wailing sadly because they find him not." [Footnote: This passage is one of seven on the subject of Glooskap, cited in Osgood's *Maritime Provinces*, without giving either the name of the author or the book from which they were taken.]

But ere the Master went away from life, or ceased to wander in the ways of men, he bade it be made known by the Loons, his faithful messengers, that before his departure years would pass, and that whoever would seek him might have one wish granted, whatever that wish might be. Now, though the journey was long and the trials were terrible which those must endure who would find Glooskap, there were still many men who adventured them. [Footnote: There is a great embarrassment of riches, or rather a great wealth of embarrassment, as regards this chapter. In the Rand manuscript there are three histories of the adventures of the pilgrims who sought Glooskap. Another and very different was given to me by John Gabriel. In one account there are three travelers, in another four; others speak of seven and twelve. Finally, there are many incidents which apparently belong to this part of the Glooskap cycle, scattered here and there in different disconnected legends.

Mrs. W. Wallace Brown was told by the Passamaquoddy Indians that when Glooskap departed he took with him the king of each of the different kinds of animals; so that the wolves, loons, etc., mourn not only for the lord, but for their masters.]

Now ye shall hear who some of these were and what happened to them. And this is the first tale as it was told me in the tent of John Gabriel, the Passamaquoddy.

When all men had heard that Glooskap would grant a wish to any one who would come to him, three Indians resolved to try this thing; and one was a Maliseet from St. John, and the other two were Penobscots from Old Town. And the path was long and the way was hard, and they suffered much, and they were seven years on it ere they came to him. But while they were yet three months' journey from his dwelling, they heard the barking of his dogs, and as they drew nearer, day by day, it was louder. And so, after great trials, they found the lord of men and beasts, and he made them welcome and entertained them.

But, ere they went, he asked them what they wanted. And the eldest, who was an honest, simple man, and of but little account among his people, because he was a bad hunter, asked that he might excel in the killing and catching of game. Then the Master gave him a flute, or the magic pipe, which pleases every ear, and has the power of persuading every animal to follow him who plays it. And he thanked the lord, and left.

Now the second Indian, being asked what he would have, replied, 'The love of many women.' And when Glooskap asked how many, he said, "I care not how many; so that there are but enough of them, and more than enough." At hearing this the Master seemed displeased, but, smiling anon, he gave him a bag which was tightly tied, and told him not to open it until he had reached his home. So he thanked the lord, and left.

Now the third Indian was a gay and handsome but foolish young fellow, whose whole heart was set on making people laugh, and on winning a welcome at every merry-making. And he, being asked what he would have or what he chiefly wanted, said that it would please him most to be able to make a certain quaint and marvelous sound or noise, [Footnote: Pedere, crepitare.] which was frequent in those primitive times among all the Wabanaki, and which it is said may even yet be heard in a few sequestered wigwams far in the wilderness, away from men; there being still here and there a deep magician, or man of mystery, who knows the art of producing it. And the property of this wondrous sound is such that they who hear it must needs burst into a laugh; whence it is the cause that the men of these our modern times are so sorrowful, since that sound is no more heard in the land. And to him Glooskap was also affable, sending Marten into the woods to seek a certain mystical and magic root, which when eaten would make the miracle the young man sought. But he warned him not to touch the root ere he got to his home, or it would be the worse for him. And so he kindly thanked the lord, and left.

It had taken seven years to come, but seven days were all that was required to tread the path returning to their home, that is, for him who got there. Only one of all the three beheld his lodge again. This was the hunter, who, with his pipe in his pocket, and not a care in his heart, trudged through the woods, satisfied that so long as he should live, there would always be venison in the larder.

But he who loved women, and had never won even a wife, was filled with anxious wishfulness. And he had, not gone very far into the woods before he opened the bag. And there flew out by hundreds, like white doves, swarming all about him, beautiful girls, with black burning eyes and flowing hair. And wild with passion the winsome witches threw their arms about him, and kissed him as he responded to their embraces; but they came ever more and more, wilder and more passionate. And he bade them give way, but they would not, and he sought to escape, but he could not; and so panting, crying for breath, smothered, he perished. And those who came that way found him dead, but what became of the girls no man knows.

Now the third went merrily onward alone, when all at once it flashed upon his mind that Glooskap had given him a present, and without the least heed to the injunction that he was to wait till he had reached his home drew out the root and ate it; and scarce had he done this ere he realized that he possessed the power of uttering the weird and mystic sound to absolute perfection. And as it rang o'er many a hill and dale, and woke the echoes of the distant hills, until it was answered by the solemn owl, he felt that it was indeed wonderful. So he walked on gayly, trumpeting as he went, over hill and vale, happy as a bird.

But by and by he began to weary of himself. Seeing a deer he drew an arrow and stealing silently to the game was just about to shoot, when despite himself the wild, unearthly sound broke forth like a demon's warble. The deer bounded away, and the young man cursed! And when he reached Old Town, half dead with hanger, he was worth little to make laughter, though the honest Indians at first did not fail to do so, and thereby somewhat cheered his heart. But as the days went on they wearied of him, and, life becoming a burden, he went into the woods and slew himself. And the evil spirit of the night-air even Bumole, [Footnote: For an account of Bumole, or Pamola, see the chapter on Supernatural Beings. Bumole seems to have been the personification of the night-hawk.] or Pamola, from whom came the gift, swooped down from the clouds and bore him away to 'Lahmkekqu', the dwelling place of darkness, and he was no more heard of among men.

As regards the destruction of the giants by Glooskap, it may be observed that the same tradition exists among the Six Nations. Cusick tells us that about 1250 years before Columbus discovered America a powerful tribe called Otne-yar-heh, that is, Stone Giants, who were ravenous cannibals, overran the country, and nearly exterminated the inhabitants. These Stone Giants practiced, themselves in rolling on the sand; by this means their bodies became hard. Then Tas-enyawa-gen, the Holder of the Heavens, came to earth as a giant, and being made their chief, led them into a hollow, where he overwhelmed them with rocks. Only one escaped to the far North. The reader will recognize in these the Chenoos, or Kewahqu', who cover themselves with pitch and roll on the ground. But no one can deny that, while that which Cusick narrates has much in common with the mythology of the Wabanaki, it is much less like that of the Edda; that Indian grotesqueness has in it greatly perverted an original: and finally, that it certainly occupies a position midway between the mythology of the Northeastern Algonquins and that of the Chippewas, Ottawas, and other Western tribes. Examination shows this in every story. Thus the Wabanaki warrior makes his bow infallible in aim by stringing it with a cord made of his sister's hair. This is Norse, as it was of old Latin. But in the Iroquois the young man "adorns his arms with the hairs of his sister." Here the tradition has begun to weaken.

It may be interesting to visitors to Niagara to know that the army of Stone Giants crossed the river during their journey just below the Falls.

How Glooskap had a great Frolic with Kitpooseagunow, a Mighty Giant who caught a Whale.

(Micmac.)

N'kah-nee-oo. In the old time (P.) Glooskap came to Pulewech Munegoo (M., Partridge Island), and here he met with Kitpooseagunow, [Footnote: *Kitpooseagunow*, "one born after his mother's death," is a magician-giant, who plays in the Algonquin mythology a part only inferior to that of Glooskap, whom he in every way resembles. Both are benevolent, both make war on wicked sorcerers and evil wild beasts, and both, finally, are much like Gargantua and Pantagruel in their sense of humor. They are sometimes made the heroes of the same adventure in different stories. The true origin of the name, according to Mr. Rand, is as follows: "After a cow moose or caribou has been killed, her calf is sometimes taken out alive, and reared by hand. As may be supposed, the calf is very easily tamed. The animal thus born is called *Kitpooseagunow*, and from this a verb is formed which denotes the act."— *Legends of the Mic Macs, Old Dominion Monthly*, 1871.

This giant was also called the Protector of the Oppressed. He probably represents the Glooskap myth in another form.] whose mother had been slain by a fearful cannibal giant. And it was against these that he made war all his life long, as did Glooskap. Whence it came to pass that they loved one another, which did not at all hinder them from having a hearty and merry encounter, in which they missed but little of killing one or the other, and all in the best natured way in the world.

[Illustration: Glooskap and Keanke spearing the whale]

Now, having come to Pulewech Munegoo, the lord of men and beasts was entertained by Kitpooseagunow. And when the night came, he who was born after his mother's death said to his guest, "Let us go on the sea in a canoe and catch whales by torchlight;" to which Glooskap, nothing loath, consented, for he was a mighty fisherman, as are all the Wabanaki of the seacoast. [Footnote: Glooskap would seem to have been the prototype of the giant fisher so well known in song:—

"His rod was made of a sturdy oak,
His line, a cable, in storms ne'er broke;
He baited his hook with a dragon's tail,
And sat on a rock and bobbed for whale."

A fabulous monster, apparently identical with the dragon, is common in Micmac stories.]

Now when they came to the beach there were only great rocks, lying here and there; but Kitpooseagunow, lifting the largest of these, put it on his head, and it became a canoe. And picking up another, it turned to a paddle, while a long splinter which he split from a ledge seemed to be a spear. Then Glooskap asked, "Who shall sit in the stern and paddle, and who will take the spear?" Kitpooseagunow said "That will I." So Glooskap paddled, and soon the canoe passed over a mighty whale; in all the great sea there was not his like; but he who held the spear sent it like a thunderbolt down into the waters, and as the handle rose again to sight he snatched it up, and the great fish was caught. And as Kitpooseagunow whirled it on high, the whale, roaring, touched the clouds. Then taking him from the point, the fisher tossed him into the bark as if he had been a trout. And the giants laughed; the sound of their laughter was heard all over the land of the Wabanaki. And being at home, the host took a stone knife and split the whale, and threw one half to the guest Glooskap, and they roasted each his piece over the fire and ate it.

Now the Master, having marked the light, which was long in the heaven after the sun went down, said, "The sky is red; we shall have a cold night." And his host understood him well, and saw that he would make it cold by magic. So he bade Marten bring in all the fuel he could find, and all there was of the oil of a porpoise; and this oil he so multiplied by magic that there was ten times more of it. And they sat them down and smoked, and told tales of old times; but it grew ever colder and colder. And at midnight, when all was burnt out, Marten froze to death, and then the grandmother, but the two giants smoked on, and laughed and talked. Then the rocks out-of-doors split with the cold, the great trees in the forest split; the sound thereof was as thunder, but the Master and he who was born after his mother's death laughed even louder. And so they sat until the sun rose. Then Glooskap said to the dead woman, "*Noogume, numchahse!*" (M.) "Grandmother, arise!" and to his boy, "*Abistanooch numchahse!*" "Marten, arise!" and they arose, and went about their work.

And the morning being bright, they went forth far into the forest to find game. But they got very little, for they caught only one small beaver, and Glooskap gave up his share of this to Kitpooseagunow. And he, taking the skin, fastened it to his garter, whence it dangled like the skin of a mouse at the knee of a tall man. But as he went on through the woods the skin grew larger and larger and larger, till it broke away by its own weight. Then the giant twisted a mighty sapling into a withe, and fastened it around his waist. But it still grew apace as he went on, till, trailing after, it tore down all the forest, pulling away the trees, so that Kitpooseagunow left a clean, fair road behind him. [Footnote: Many of these stories have received later additions, which can be detected by their occurring only in single versions of them. In the story of Kitpooseagunow (Rand's manuscript) the giants arrive at a "large town," and go to a "store," where they sell the skin for all the money, goods, houses, and lands which, the merchant possesses. "And the skin was so heavy that it took the greater part of the day to weigh it."]

And when the night came on they fished again, as they had done before; and again it was said, but this time by the host, "The sky is red; we shall have a cold night." So they heaped up wood more than the first time, but now it was far colder. And soon the boy was dead, and the grandmother also lay frozen. But when the sun rose the Master brought them back to life, and, bidding good-by to Kitpooseagunow, went his way. [Footnote: It is possible that there is a version of this story in which Glooskap kills his friend with frost, and then revives him. In one story it is a *frozen stream*, incarnate as a man, which attempts in vain to freeze Glooskap. The extraordinary manner in which host and guest, or even intimate friends, endeavor to *kill* one another in the most good-natured rivalry, is of constant occurrence in the Eskimo legends. It is not infrequent among our own backwoods or frontier-men.

The stone-canoe occurs in Eskimo legends (*vide* Rink), as it does in those of all American Indians.]

The most striking feature, however, of this legend is its Norse-like breadth or grandeur and its genial humor, which are very remarkable characteristics for the fictions of savages. Its resemblance to the Scandinavian tales is, if accidental, very remarkable. The two heroes are, like Thor and Odin, giant heroes who make war on Jotuns and Trolls; that is, giant-like sorcerers. It is their profession; they live in it. No one can read Beowulf or the Eddas without being struck by the great resemblance between Grendel, the hideous, semi-human night prowler, and the Kewahqu', a precisely similar monster, who rises from the depths of waters to wantonly murder man. I do not recall any two beings in any other two disconnected mythologies so strangely similar. The fishing for the whale recalls that which is told in the Older Edda (Hymiskrida, 21), where Hymir succeeds in hooking two of these fish:—

"Then he and Hymir rowed out to sea. Thor rowed oft with two oars, and so powerfully that the giant was obliged to acknowledge they were speeding very fast. *He himself rowed at the prow.*"

If the reader will compare this account of the Edda with the Micmac story, he cannot fail to be struck with the great resemblance between them. It is even specified in both that the hero, though a guest, paddles. And in both instances the host catches a whale. Now compare with this the legend of Manobozho-Hiawatha, who merely catches the great sunfish, and is swallowed by it. Does it not seem as if the Western Indians had here borrowed from the Micmacs, and the Micmacs from the Norse? Whether this was done directly or through the Eskimo is as yet a problem. It may also be noted that both in the Edda and in the Micmac story, it is declared that one of the giants picked up the boat and carried it.

It may be observed that most of these Indian traditions were originally poems. It is probable that all were sung, while they still retained the character of serious mythical or sacred narrative. Now they are in the transition state of heroic tales. But they unquestionably still retain many passages of very great antiquity, and it is not impossible that Eskimo and even Norse songs are still preserved in them. In this tale the following coincidences with passages in the Elder Edda (Hymiskrida) are remarkable. In both the host asks his guest to go with him to catch whales, to which the latter assents.

"'We three to-morrow night
Shall be compelled
On what we catch to live.'
Thor said he would
On the sea row."

Kitpooseagunow picks up the heavy canoe, with its oars and a spear, and carries them.

"Thor went, grasped the prow quickly with its hold-water, lifted the boat together with its oars and scoop; bore to the dwelling the curved vessel."

Glooskap asks which of the two shall take the paddle, and which sit in the stern. Hymir inquires,—

"Wilt thou do half the work with me? either the whales home to the dwelling bear, Or the boat fast bind?"

Kitpooseagunow drew up a whale.

"The mighty Hymir, He alone two whales drew up with his hook."

After this whale-fishing, the Scandinavian giants at home have a trial of strength and endurance. Thor throws a cup at Hymir. This cup can only be broken on Hymir's head, which is of ice, and intensely hard.

"That is harder
than any cup."

This is therefore an effort on the part of Thor to overcome Cold. Hymir is the incarnation of Cold itself.

"The icebergs resounded as the churl approached; the thicket on his cheeks was frozen. In shivers flew the pillars At the Jotun's glance."

That is, the frost cracks the stones and rocks. In the Indian tale the two giants try to see which can freeze the other. In both there is distinctly a contest. In the Norse tale Strength or Heat fights Frost; in the American, Frost is battled with by Frost as a rival.

It may be observed that the Indian tale is far from being perfect, and that in all probability the whole of it includes a fishing for the sea-serpent.

It is plainly set forth in the Edda that Cold may be overcome by a magic spell. Thus Groa (Grougaldr, 12) promises her son a rune to effect this:—

"A seventh (charm) I will sing thee: If on a mountain high frost should assail thee, deadly cold shall not thy body injure, nor draw it to thy limbs."

How Glooskap made a Magician of a Young Man, who aided another to win a Wife and do Wonderful Deeds.

(Micmac.)

It is well known unto all Indians who still keep the true faith of the olden time that there are wondrous dwellers in the lonely woods, such as elves and fairies, called by the Micmacs *Mikumwessos*, and by the Passamaquoddies *Oonahgawessos*. And these can work great wonders, and also sing so as to charm the wildest beasts. From them alone come the magic pipes or flutes, which sometimes pass into possession of noted sorcerers and great warriors; and when these are played upon, the woman who hears the melody is bewitched with love, and the moose and caribou follow the sound even to their death. And when the *Megumawessos* are pleased with a mortal they make him a fairy, even like themselves.

N'Karnayoo. In old times there was an Indian village, and in it were two young men, [Footnote: According to another Micmac version of this legend, the elder of these pilgrims was Keekwahjoo, the Badger, and the younger Caktoogwasees, or Little Thunder.] who had heard that Glooskap, ere he left the world, would bestow on those who came to him whatever they wanted. So they went their way, an exceeding long pilgrimage, until they came to a great island, where he dwelt. And there they first met with Dame Bear and Marten, and next with the Master himself. Then they all, sitting down to supper, had placed before them only one extremely small dish, and on this there was a tiny bit of meat, and nothing more. But being a bold and jolly fellow, the first of the pilgrims, thinking himself mocked for sport, cut off a great part of the meat, and ate it, when that which was in the dish grew in a twinkling to its former size; and so this went on all through the supper, every one eating his fill, the dish at the end being as full as ever.

Of these two, one wished to become a Mikum-wess, and the other to win a very beautiful girl, the daughter of a great chief, who imposed such cruel tasks on all who came for her, that they died in attempting them.

And the first was taken by Glooskap; and after he had by a merry trick covered him with filth and put him to great shame, he took him to the river, and after washing him clean and combing his hair gave him a change of raiment and a hair string of exceeding great magic virtue, since when he had bound it on he became a Mikumwess, having all the power of the elfin-world. And also because he desired to excel in singing and music, the Master gave him a small pipe, and it was that which charmed all living beings; [Footnote: The identity of these incidents with those of "classic" times is worth noting. There is a lustration and the clothing the neophyte in a new garment, and he receives the magic fillet, as in the Mysteries of the old world. Nor is the resemblance of the pipe to that of Orpheus less striking. In many respects this is the most remarkable old Indian myth I have ever met with.] and then singing a song bade him join in with him. And doing this he found that he could sing, and ever after had a wondrous voice.

Now to seek the beautiful girl it was necessary to sail afar over the sea; and during this adventure the Mikumwess was charged to take care of the younger pilgrim. So he begged the Master to lend him his canoe. And Glooskap answered, "Yes, I will do this for thee, if thou wilt honestly return it when thou needest it no more. Yet in very truth I did never yet lend it to mortal man but that I had to go after it myself." [Footnote: One of the traits of *bonhomie* and common humanity which continually occur in the Glooskap tales, even in the most serious situations and solemn myths. In this respect the resemblance of the Northwest Algonquin tales to the Norse is truly striking. The canoe is among all Indians, even in Central America, exactly what the umbrella is in civilized society. With all his immense originality Glooskap had a number of "old Joes," of which he never seems to have tired. One was the inexhaustible dish, and another the giant skunk set upon end to salute his visitors, and this of the canoe was probably the commonest of all. He is a true Indian divinity, shining like the lightning and striking only when there is a storm, but appearing like the Aurora Borealis, or even the Robin Goodfellow-Will-o'-the-Wisp at others.]

Thereupon the young man promised most faithfully that he would indeed return the canoe, and with this they got them ready for the journey. But when they came to the bay there was no canoe, and they knew not what was to be done. But Glooskap pointed to a small island of granite which rose amid the waves, and it was covered with tall pine-trees. "There is my canoe!" said he; [Footnote: Another standard "piece of witt" with the incorrigible joker. Glooskap's "floating island" was served up as a dessert to all guests, and I doubt not that if the double meaning of the word had been known to him, they would have had that too.] and when he had taken them unto it, it became a real canoe, with masts, and they set sail on it, rejoicing.

So they came in time to a very large island, where they drew up the canoe and hid it in the bushes. Then they went forward to seek for people, and found a village in which dwelt the chief who had the beautiful daughter, in seeking whom so many had lost their lives.

And having found him, they went into his wigwam, and were placed on the seat of honor. Now when an Indian seeks a wife, he or his mutual friend makes no great ado about it, but utters two words, which tell the whole story. And these are *Sewin-coadoo-gwah-loogwet'*, which mean—in Micmac, "I am tired of living alone." And the chief, hearing this, consented that the young man should marry her whom he sought; but on one condition: and this was that he should slay and bring unto him the head of a certain horned dragon, called in Micmac *Chepichealm*. [Footnote: Vide "Supernatural Beings." The *Chepichealm* (M.) is an immense horned serpent or wingless dragon. It is probably identical with the Wiwillmekq' (P. and Pen.), which is a singular horned worm found on trees or by water. It is believed to be capable of assuming a vast size and to be gifted with supernatural powers.] So this was agreed upon, and the two strangers went to the wigwam which was assigned them.

Now in the night he that was Mikumwess arose and went alone and afar until he came to the den of the dragon, and this was a great hole in the ground. And over this he laid a mighty log, and then began the magic dance around the den. So the serpent, or the great Chepichcalm, hearing the call, came forth, putting out his head after the manner of snakes, waving it all about in every way and looking round him. While doing this he rested his neck upon the log, when the Indian with a blow of his hatchet severed it. Then taking the head by one of the shining yellow horns he bore it to his friend, who in the morning gave it to the chief. And the old man said to himself, "This time I fear me I shall lose my child."

Yet the young man had more to do; for the chief said, "I would fain see my son coast down yonder hill on hand-sled." Now this lull was an exceeding high mountain; the sides thereof were ragged with rocks and terrible with trees and ice. Then two toboggins [Footnote: Toboggin: a sled or sledge.] were brought out, one of them for the two strangers, and this he that was Mikumwess was to direct. And on the other were two powerful men, and these were both *boo-oinak*, [Footnote: Magicians, the original of *pow-wow-in*. It is apparently the same in meaning as the *angakok* of the neighboring Eskimo.] who hoped to see the former soon fall out, and then to run over them. And at the word they went flying fearfully down the mountain, and yet ever faster, as if to death. And soon he that sought the girl went whirling headlong from the sled, and the two *boo-oinak* gave a loud hurrah; for they knew not that this had been done with intent by the Mikumwess, that he might get them before him. So he put forth his hand, and, seizing the younger man, turned a little aside, but in an instant went on after; and erelong the sled of the *boo-oinak* stopped, but the other, bounding upwards from a mighty wall of ice, flew far over their heads onwards; nor did it stop in the valley, but, running with tremendous speed up the opposite hill and into the village, struck the side of the chief's wigwam, ripping it up from end to end ere it stopped. And the old man, seeing this, said, "This time I have lost my daughter!"

Yet the young man had more to do; for the chief said, "There is here a man who has never been beaten in running, and thou must strive with him in that and overcome him, to win thy wife." And the race was appointed; but ere it came off he that was Mikumwess lent to his friend the magic pipe to give him power. [Footnote: It may be observed that Indian magic depends on fetich, or objects having innate power. Glooskap himself relies on his belt, and when he lends it to Marten, the boy becomes "manitoo," as the more Western Indians term it. There is in the early red Indian mythology really no God; only more or less powerful magicians.] And when he that was the racer of the village met the young man, the youth said, "Who art thou?" and he replied, "I am Wey-ad-esk" (the Northern Lights, M.); "but who art thou?" And he answered, "I am Wosogwodesk" (the Chain Lightning). And they ran. In an instant they were no longer in sight; they were far away over the most distant hills. Then all sat and waited, and ere it was noon he that was the Chain Lightning returned, and he was not out of breath, nor weary, and he had gone round the world. And at evening they saw the Northern Lights return, and he trembled and quivered with fatigue; yet for all that he had not been round the world, but had turned back. And the old chief, seeing him beaten, exclaimed, "This time I shall lose my child!"

And yet there was another trial of the young man ere he could win her whom he wanted. For the chief had a man whom no one could overcome in swimming and diving, and it was chiefly in this last thing that he excelled. And the young man must strive with him. And when they met he asked the man of the village his name, and he replied, "I am an *Ukchigumooech*" (a Sea Duck, M.); "but who are you?" And he answered, "I am a *Kweemoo*" (a Loon, M.). So they dived, and after a time the Sea Duck rose again for breath, but those who waited waited long indeed ere they saw the Loon. And an hour passed, and he came not, and yet another ere they beheld him; but when he at last rose the old chief said, "This is the end of all our weary work, for this time truly I have lost my child."

Yet it was not the end of the wonderful deeds which were done in that village by the power of the great Glooskap. For the Mikumwess, at the great dance which was held that evening at the wedding, astonished all who beheld him. As he danced around the circle, upon the very hard beaten floor, they saw his feet sink deeper at every step, and ever deeper as the dance went on; ploughing the ground up into high, uneven ridges, forming a trench as he went, until at length only his head was to be seen. [Footnote: This is very characteristic of the true magician, both in the Algonquin and Eskimo folk-lore. "The *angakok*," or sorcerer of Greenland, "after meeting with *tomarsuk*, or guardian spirits, sometimes manifested it by his feet sinking into the rocky ground *just as if in snow*." (Rink.) This phrase indicates the Northern origin of the idea, which occurs in many Indian stories. I have been assured in all faith that there is a Passamaquoddy *m'teoulin*, or sorcerer, now living, who can walk up to his knees in a floor or in the paved street, and an honest and trustworthy Indian assured me that he had seen him do it.]

And this ended the dancing for that night, since the ground was no longer to be danced upon by anybody except wizards and witches.

Then the young man and his wife and the Mikumwess entered their canoe and sailed *boosijk* (homewards, M.). And yet their trials were not over. [Footnote: These subsequent trials were not inflicted by the old chief, but were, as appears by comparison with other legends, simply jokes played by the incorrigible Glooskap. It is most probable that in its original form this remarkable myth was all *maya*, or illusion, and the whole a series of illusions, caused by the arch-conjurer, typifying natural phenomena.] For they had not gone far ere they saw an awful storm coming to meet them; and he that had the Elfin spells knew that it was raised by *boo-oin*, or sorcery, since these storms are the worst of all. Then, without fear, he rose, and, filling his lungs and puffing his cheeks, he blew against the tempest, wind against wind, until he blew the wind away, and the great water was '*aoobuneak*', as calm and smooth as before.

So they sailed on over the sunlit sea, but it was not long before the Elf-gifted saw rising among the waves far before them a dark mass, which soon proved to be a tremendous Beast coming to attack them. And as he drew near they saw it was Quahbeet, the giant beaver, and his eyes were angry. [Footnote: From the beginning, when *Quahbeetsis*, the son of the Beaver, inspired Malsumsis with hatred of Glooskap, this quadruped appears as an enemy.] But the Mikumwess, seeing this, steered straight to meet the monster, and, coming to him, said, "I am the great hunter of beavers; lo, I am their butcher; many a one has fallen by my hand." [Footnote: This is oddly like the speech of the beaver-killer in *The Hunting of the Snark*.] Now the Beaver had placed himself under water, with his tail out of it and rising upwards, that he might sink the canoe with a blow thereof; for the Beaver strikes mightily in such wise, as is his wont. But he of the magic power, with one blow of his tomahawk, cut the tail from the body, and sailed onward.

Yet they had not gone far ere, on rounding a point, they saw before them another animal of giant size, who likewise had his tail in the air, waiting to overcome them, and this was A-bekk-thee-lo (M.), the Skunk. Yet ere he made his hideous attack the Mikumwess, ever on the watch, caught up his spear, and, hurling it, pierced A-bekk-thee-lo, who did but kick two or three times ere he died. And, stepping ashore, he who had slain him took a pole, a long dead pine, which lay upon the sand, and, transfixing the Skunk, lifted him high in air, and, planting the tree on the ground, left him, saying scornfully, as he left, "*Lik cho je nain!*" which, being interpreted, meaneth, "And now show your tail there!" [Footnote: The Skunk is here a parody on the Beaver.]

So they returned safely. And Glooskap met them at the landing, and his first words were, "Well, my friends, I see that you have brought back my canoe." And they answered, "We have, indeed." Then he inquired," Has all gone well with ye?" And they replied that it had. Then Glooskap, laughing, let them know that in all they had experienced he had been busy, and that in all their triumphs he had had a hand. And to the Mikumwess he said, "Go now thy ways, thou and these, and ever lead happy lives: thou amid the Elfin, they among mankind. And be sure of this, that if danger or trouble should come to you, you have but to think of me, and verily aid will come." So they rose and went to their wigwams. [Footnote: In its earlier form this must have been a very remarkable narrative, or poem. That the two combatants in the race were originally the personified Northern Lights and Lightning, and that these were *not* merely names assumed for boasting, is shown by the incident that the Lightning actually *passed round the world*, while the Aurora Borealis only covered a portion of it. The diving is either a later addition, or it represents the same stupendous spirits taking on the appearance of mastering the element of water as well as that of fire. Without carrying the Solar myth theory to extremes, it cannot be denied that Glooskap appears in several of these stories as Spring, or as the melter of ice, the conqueror of the frozen stream and of the iceberg. In this narrative he is active and creative Nature itself, directing and sporting with the warring elements. His vast practical joking cannot fail to remind the reader yet again of the Norse deities and their jovial household godhood.

This tradition is Micmac, and taken almost entirely from Mr. Rand's manuscript. It should be borne in mind that it is not from a single story of this collection, but from a careful analysis and comparison of them all, that their entire value is to be ascertained.

Certain incidents in this tale deserve special attention. The young men go to a land of evil sorcerers, of *boo-oin*. When one is required to run a race he conquers because he is really the Lightning. When Thor visits Utgard Loki, there is also a race, in which Hugi wins, because he is *Thought* disguised as a man. Glooskap has a canoe, which is sometimes immensely large, but which at other times shrinks to a very small size. In the Edda, Odin is said to have had made for him by the dwarfs a boat, Skidbladnir, which, like Glooskap's bark, expanded or diminished. Sigurd, in the New Edda, is obliged to kill a dragon, and it is very remarkable that he does it by a special previous preparation. That is to say, he digs a little ditch, and when the dragon crawls over it the hero pierces him with his sword. In this story the Indian lays a log over the dragon's hole, to enable him to chop his head off. The dragon, or horned snake, is an old-time tradition in America, or pre-Columbian.]

How a Certain Wicked Witch sought to cajole the Great and Good Glooskap, and of her Punishment.

(Micmac.)

N'karnayoo, of old time. Once it came to pass that Glooskap met with an evil witch, and she had made herself like unto a fair young girl, and believed that he could not know who she was. And she asked him to take her with him in his canoe. So they sailed out over a summer sea: and as they went the witch sought to beguile him with sweet words; but he answered naught, for he wist well what kind of passenger he had on board. And as they went on she played her cajoleries, but he remained grim as a bear. Then she, being angry, showed it, and there arose a great storm. The wind howled over the waves as they rose and fell, like white wolves jumping while they run, the first lightnings flashed, and the sky grew dark as night. The Master was angered that so mean a creature dared to play him such tricks, and, paddling the canoe to the beach, he leaped ashore. Then giving the bark, with the witch in it, a push out to sea, he cried to her, "Sail thou with the devil! But never be in human form again, O she-beast!"

Then she, being frightened, said, "Master, what wilt thou that I become?" And he replied, "Whatever thou wilt; that grace alone I give thee." And in despair she plunged into the waters, and became a *keegunibe*, a ferocious fish, which has upon its back a great fin, which it shows like a sail when swimming through the water. So the canoe and the witch became one in the evil fish, and the Indians to this day when they see it, cry, "See the witch, who was punished by the great Master!"

Now of sinful men, evil beasts, foul sorcerers, witches, and giants, there were in those days many who sought to do great harm to Glooskap; but of them all there did not escape any; verily, no, not one. [Footnote: A Micmac story, from the Rand manuscript. I believe that the fish here spoken of is a shark.]

Of other Men who went to Glooskap for Gifts.

(Micmac.)

N'karnayoo: wood-enit-atokhagen Glooskap. Of the old times: this is a story of Glooskap. Now there went forth many men unto Glooskap, hearing that they could win the desires of their hearts; and all got what they asked for, in any case; but as for having what they wanted, that depended on the wisdom with which they wished or acted.

The good Glooskap liked it not that when he had told any one evenly and plainly what to do, that man should then act otherwise, or double with him. And it came to pass that a certain fool, of the kind who can do nothing unless it be in his own way, made a long journey to the Master. And his trials were indeed many. For he came to an exceeding high mountain in a dark and lonely land, where he heard no sound. And the ascent thereof was like a smooth pole, and the descent on the other side far worse, for it hung over the bottom. Yet it was worse beyond, for there the road lay between the heads of two huge serpents, almost touching each other, who darted their terrible tongues at those who went between. And yet again the path passed under the Wall of Death. Now this wall hung like an awful cloud over a plain, rising and falling at times, yet no man knew when. And when it fell it struck the ground, and that so as to crush all that was beneath it.

But the young man escaped all these trials, and came to the island of the Great Master. And when he had dwelt there a certain time, and was asked what he would have, he replied, "If my lord will, let him give me a medicine which will cure all disease." More than this he asked not. So the Master gave him a certain small package, and said, "Herein is that which thou seekest; but I charge thee that thou lettest not thine eyes behold it until thou shalt reach thy home." So he thanked the Master, and left.

But he was not far away ere he desired to open the package and test the medicine, and, yet more, the truth of the Master. And he said to himself, "Truly, if this be but a deceit it was shrewdly devised to bid me not open it till I returned. For he knew well that once so far I would make no second journey to him. Tush! if the medicine avail aught it cannot change in aught." So he opened it, when that which was therein fell to the ground, and spread itself like water everywhere, and then dried away like a mist. And when he returned and told his tale, men mocked him.

Then again there were three brothers, who, having adventured, made known their wishes. Now the first was very tall, far above all his fellows, and vain of his comeliness. For he was of those who put bark or fur into their moccasins, that they may be looked up to by the little folk and be loved by the squaws; and his hair was plastered to stand up on high, and on the summit of it was a very long turkey-tail feather. And this man asked to become taller than any Indian in all the land. [Footnote: This story has been told to me in three different forms. I have here given it with great care in what I conceive to be the original. In one version it is the pine, in another the cedar-tree.]

And the second wished that he might ever remain where he was to behold the land and the beauty of it, and to do naught else.

And the third wished to live to an exceeding old age, and ever to be in good health.

Now the three, when they came to the island, had found there three wigwams, and in two of these were dwellers, not spoken of in other traditions. In one lived *Cool-puj-ot*, a very strange man. For he has no bones, and cannot move himself, but every spring and autumn he is *rolled over with handspikes* by the order of Glooskap, and this is what his name means in the Micmac tongue. And in the autumn he is turned towards the west, but in the spring towards the east, and this is a figure of speech denoting the revolving seasons of the year. With his breath he can sweep down whole armies, and with his looks alone he can work great wonders, and all this means this weather,— frost, snow, ice, and sunshine. [Footnote: Mr. Rand (manuscript, p. 471) says that all of this explanation was given *verbatim* by a Micmac named Stephen Flood, who was a "very intelligent and reliable Indian." Cool-puj-ot is almost identical with Shawandasee, the guardian of the South. "He is represented as an affluent, plethoric old man, who has grown unwieldy from repletion, and seldom moves. He keeps his eyes steadfastly fixed on the north. When he sighs in autumn, we have those balmy southern airs, which communicate warmth and delight over the northern hemisphere, and make the Indian summer." The "affluence" and "grown unwieldy from repletion," in this account, are probably due to Schoolcraft's florid style. (*Hiawatha*

Legends.) Shawandasee is identical with Svasud of the Edda. (Vafthrudnisnal, 27.)]

And in the other wigwam dwelt *Cuhkw* (M.), which means Earthquake. And this mighty man can pass along under the ground, and make all things shake and tremble by his power.

Now when Glooskap had heard what these visitors wished for, he called Earthquake, and bid him take them all three and put them with their feet in the ground. And he did so, when they at once became three trees: as one tradition declares, pines; and another, cedars.

So that he that would be tall became exceeding tall, for his head rose above the forest; and even the turkey-feather at the top thereof is not forgotten, since to this day it is seen waving in the wind. And he who will listen in a pine-wood may hear the tree murmuring all day long in the Indian tongue of the olden time,—

"Ee nil Etuchi nek m'kilaskitopp
Ee nil Etuche wiski nek n'kil ooskedjin."
[Footnote: Passamaquoddy.]

Oh, I am such a great man!
Oh, I am such a great Indian!

And the second, who would remain in the land, remains there; for while his roots are in the ground he cannot depart from it.

And the third, who would live long in health, unless men have cut him down, is standing as of yore. [Footnote: In another version of this tale, Glooskap transformed him into an old gnarled and twisted cedar, with limbs growing out rough and ugly all the way from the bottom. "There," he said to the cedar-tree, "I cannot say how long you will live; only the Great Spirit above can tell that; but you will not be disturbed for a good while, as no one can have any object in cutting you down. You are yourself unfit for any earthly purpose, and the land around you is useless for cultivation. I think you will stand there for a long while." (Rand manuscript.)

It should be added that in one version we are told that the seeds from these cedars or pines were blown by the wind, and so spread forth all over the earth. The planting of the cedar by Earthquake possibly indicates the storms by which seeds are blown afar.]

Of Glooskap and the Three Other Seekers.

(Micmac.)

Of old time. Now when it was noised abroad that whoever besought Glooskap could obtain the desire of his heart, there were three men who said among themselves, "Let us seek the Master." So they left their home in the early spring when the bluebird first sang, and walked till the fall frosts, and then into winter, and ever on till the next midsummer. And having come to a small path in a great forest, they followed it, till they came out by a very beautiful river; so fair a sight they had never seen, and so went onward till it grew to be a great lake. And so they kept to the path which, when untrodden, was marked by blazed trees, the bark having been removed, in Indian fashion, on the side of the trunk which is *opposite* the place where the wigwam or village lies towards which it turns. So the mark can be seen as the traveler goes towards the goal, but not while leaving it.

[Illustration: GLOOSKAP TURNING A MAN INTO A CEDAR-TREE]

Then after a time they came to a long point of land running out into the lake, and, having ascended a high hill, they saw in the distance a smoke, which guided them to a large, well-built wigwam. And, entering, they found seated on the right side a handsome, healthy man of middle age, and by the other a woman so decrepit that she seemed to be a hundred years old. Opposite the door, and on the left side, was a mat, which seemed to show that a third person had there a seat.

And the man made them welcome, and spoke as if he were *weleda'asit kesegvou* (M.)—well pleased to see them, but did not ask them whence they came or whither they were going, as is wont among Indians when strangers come to their homes or are met in travel. Erelong they heard the sound of a paddle, and then the noise of a canoe being drawn ashore. And there came in a youth of fine form and features and well clad, bearing weapons as if from hunting who addressed the old woman as *Kejoo*, or mother, and told her that he had brought game. And with sore ado—for she was feeble—the old dame tottered out and brought in four beavers; but she was so much troubled to cut them up that the elder, saying to the younger man *Uoh-keen*! (M.), "My brother," bade him do the work. And they supped on beaver. So they remained for a week, resting themselves, for they were sadly worn with their wearisome journey, and also utterly ragged. And then a wondrous thing came to pass, which first taught them that they were in an enchanted land. For one morning the elder man bade the younger wash their mother's face. And as he did this all her wrinkles vanished, and she became young and very beautiful; in all their lives the travelers had never seen so lovely a woman. Her hair, which had been white and scanty, now hung to her feet, dark and glossy as a blackbird's breast. Then, having been clad in fine array, she showed a tall, lithe, and graceful form at its best.

And the travelers said to themselves, "Truly this man is a great magician!" They all walked forth to see the place. Never was sunshine so pleasantly tempered by a soft breeze; for all in that land was fair, and it grew fairer day by day to all who dwelt there. Tall trees with rich foliage and fragrant flowers, but without lower limbs or underbrush, grew as in a grove, wide as a forest, yet so far apart that the eye could pierce the distance in every direction.

Now when they felt for the first time that they were in a new life and a magic land, he that was host asked them whence they came and what they sought. So they said that they sought Glooskap. And the host replied, "Lo, I am he!" And they were awed by his presence, for a great glory and majesty now sat upon him. As the woman had changed, so had he, for all in that place was wonderful.

Then the first, telling what he wanted, said, "I am a wicked man, and I have a bad temper. I am prone to wrath and reviling, yet I would fain be pious, meek, and holy."

And the next said, "I am very poor, and my life is hard. I toil, but can barely make my living. I would fain be rich."

Now the third replied, "I am of low estate, being despised and hated by all my people, and I wish to be loved and respected." And to all these the Master made answer, "So shall it be!"

And taking his medicine-bag (*Upsakumoode*, M.) he gave unto each a small box, and bade them keep it closed until they should be once more at home. [Footnote: In this version (Rand manuscript) there is a fourth Indian introduced,—he who would fain be tall and long-lived, and is changed to a tree. As it is precisely the same tale as that of the three who became cypresses or pines, I have not repeated it.] And on returning to the wigwam he also, gave to each of them new garments; in all their lives they had never seen or heard of such rich apparel or such ornaments as they now had. Then when it was time to depart, as they knew not the way to their home, he arose and went with them. Now they had been more than a year in coming. But he, having put on his belt, went forth, and they followed, till in the forenoon he led them to the top of a high mountain, from which in the distance they beheld yet another, the blue outline of which could just be seen above the horizon. And having been told that their way was unto it, they thought it would be a week's journey to reach it. But they went on, and in the middle of the afternoon of the same day they were there, on the summit of the second mountain. And looking from this afar, all was familiar to them—hill and river, and wood and lakes; all was in their memory. "And there," said the Master, pointing unto it,—"there is your own village!" So he left them alone, and they went on their way, and before the sun had set were safe at home.

Yet when they came no one knew them, because of the great change in their appearance and their fine attire, the like of which had never been seen by man in those days. But having made themselves known to their friends, all that were there of old and young gathered together to gaze upon and hear what they had to say. And they were amazed.

Then each of them, having opened his box, found therein an unguent, rich and fragrant, and with this they rubbed their bodies completely. And they were ever after so fragrant from the divine anointing that all sought to be near them. Happy were they who could but sniff at the blessed smell which came from them.

Now he who had been despised for his deformity and weakness and meanness became beautiful and strong and stately as a pine-tree. There was no man in all the land so graceful or of such good behavior.

And he who had desired abundance had it, in all fullness, his wish. For the moose and caribou came to him in the forest, the fish leaped into his nets, all men gave unto him, and he gave unto all freely, to the end.

And he that had been wicked and of evil mind, hasty and cruel, became meek and patient, good and gentle, and he made others like himself. And he had his reward, for there was a blessing upon him as upon all those who had wished wisely even unto the end of their days. [Footnote: This beautiful story, in its original simplicity, reminds one of the tenderest biblical narratives. There is in it nothing reflected or second-hand; it is a very ancient or truly aboriginal tale. I can but sincerely regret my utter inability to do justice to it. The pen of a great master would be required to describe the fairyland freshness and light of Glooskap's home as it is *felt* in the original by men far more familiar with the forest in all its loveliness at all seasons than any white writer can be. The *naivete* or simplicity of the pilgrims is as striking as that of the narrator or poet, to whom fine clothes—a Homeric trait—are as wonderful as all the deeds of magic which he describes.

In this and other tales a man is represented as being punished by being turned into a tree, so that he can never leave a certain spot. This is a kind of imprisonment. In the Edda the Ash Yggdrasil is the prison of Iduna.

"She ill brooked her descent under the hoar tree's trunk confined."

(*Hrofnagaldr Odins*, 7.)

It is to keep a man or a woman in a certain place, as prisoner, that the characters described in the Indian and Norse myths are put into trees.

This was related to Mr. Rand by Benjamin Brooks, a Micmac.]

Of Glooskap and the Sinful Serpent.

(Passamaquoddy.)

Of old time it befell that Glooskap had an enemy, an evil man, a sinful beast, a great sorcerer. And this man, after trying many things, made himself a great serpent, hoping so to slay the Master.

Of old time Glooskap met a boy whose name was '*Nmmokswess*, the Sable. [Footnote: Evidently no other than Marten, or the Abistanooch of the Micmac mythology.] And the boy had a flute: whoever played on it could entice unto him all the animals. And once, when the Master was afar, the boy broke the flute, and in his great sorrow he would not return home, but wandered away into the wilderness. Now Glooskap knew in his heart that the flute was broken: he who is a magician knows at once of a great evil. And coming home, he asked of the grandmother where the boy was, and she could only weep. Then the Master said, "Though I roam forever, yet will I find the boy." So he went forth, and he tracked him in the snow for three days; and on the third night he heard some one singing in a hollow; and it was a magic song, that which the *m'teoulin* sings when he is in dire need and death is near. And making a circle round about the place, Glooskap looked down and saw a wigwam, and heard the voice more distinctly as he drew nearer; and it was the voice of the boy, and he was singing a song against all of the snake kind. And he was wandering about the wigwam, seeking a straight stick.

Then Glooskap understood all the thing, and how the boy had been enticed into the wilderness by the evil arts of At-o-sis, the Snake, and that the Great Serpent was in the wigwam, and had sent him out to seek a straight stick. Then Glooskap, singing again softly, bade him get a very crooked one, and told what more to do. So the boy got an exceedingly crooked one; and when he entered, the Snake, seeing it, said, "Why hast thou got such a bad stick?" And the boy, answering, said, "Truly, it is very crooked, but that which is crookedest may be made straightest, and I know a charm whereby this can be done; for I will but heat this stick in the fire, and, then I will make it quite straight, as you shall see." Now At-o-sis was very anxious to behold this wonderful thing, and he looked closely; but the boy, as soon as the end of the stick was red-hot, thrust it into his eyes and blinded him, and ran forth. Yet the Snake followed him; but when he was without the wigwam he met the Master, who slew him out of hand. [Footnote: This curious legend is suggestive of Ulysses and the Cyclops. The enemies of Glooskap are all cannibals; the boy is sent out for a straight stick to serve as a spit to roast him on. It is not impossible that the Snake, in some perfect version of the tale, has but a single eye since many of the evil creatures of red Indian mythology are half stone lengthwise. But the whole story is full of strange hints. It was told me by Tomah Josephs, at Campobello, N. B.]

Of old times. This is an end of the story.

The Tale of Glooskap as told by another Indian. Showing how the Toad and Porcupine lost their Noses.

(Micmac.)

In the old time. Far before men knew themselves, in the light before the sun, Glooskap and his brother were as yet unborn; they waited for the day to appear. Then they talked together, and the youngest said, "Why should I wait? I will go into the world and begin my life at once." Then the elder said, "Not so, for this were a great evil." But the younger gave no heed to any wisdom: in his wickedness he broke through his mother's side, he rent the wall; his beginning of life was his mother's death.

Now, in after years, the younger brother would learn in what lay the secret of the elder's death. And Glooskap, being crafty, told the truth and yet lied; for his name was the Liar, yet did he never lie for evil or aught to harm. So he told his brother that the blow of a ball, or handful of the down of feathers, would take away his life; and this was true, for it would stun him, but it would not prevent his returning to life. Then Glooskap asked the younger for his own secret. And he, being determined to give the elder no time, answered truly and fearlessly, "I can only be slain by the stroke of a cat-tail or bulrush."

And then the younger, having gathered the down of bird's feathers, struck the elder, so that he fell dead, and therein he told the truth. But he soon recovered, and in that was his deceit. Howbeit it was well for the world and well for him that he then gathered bulrushes and smote his younger brother, so that he died. But the plant never grew that could harm the Master, wherefore he is alive to this day.

Who was his mother? The female Turtle was his mother.

The Master was the Lord of Men and Beasts. Beasts and Men, one as the other, he ruled them all Great was his army, his tribe was All. In it the Great Golden Eagle was a chief; he married a female Caribou. The Turtle was Glooskap's uncle; he married a daughter of the Golden Eagle and Caribou. Of all these things there are many and long traditions. Our people tell them in the winter by the fire: the old people know them; the young forget them and the wisdom which is in them.

When the Turtle married, the Master bade him make a feast, and wished that the banquet should be a mighty one. To do this he gave him great power. He bade him go down to a point of rocks by the sea, where many whales were always to be found. He bade him bring one; he gave him power to do so, but he set a mark, or an appointed space, and bade him not go an inch beyond it. So the Turtle went down to the sea; he caught a great whale, he bore it to camp; it seemed to him easy to do this. But like all men there was in him vain curiosity; the falsehood of disobedience was in him, and to try the Master he went beyond the mark; and as he did this he lost his magic strength; he became as a man; even as a common mortal his nerves weakened, and he fell, crushed flat beneath the weight of the great fish.

Then men ran to Glooskap, saying that Turtle was dead. But the Master answered, "Cut up the Whale; he who is now dead will revive." So they cut it up; (and when the feast was ready) Turtle came in yawning, and stretching out his leg he cried, "How tired I am! Truly, I must have overslept myself." Now from this time all men greatly feared Glooskap, for they saw that he was a spirit.

It came to pass that the Turtle waxed mighty in his own conceit, and thought that he could take Glooskap's place and reign in his stead. So he held a council of all the animals to find out how he could be slain. The Lord of Men and Beasts laughed at this. Little did he care for them!

And knowing all that was in their hearts, he put on the shape of an old squaw and went into the council-house. And he sat down by two witches: one was the Porcupine, the other the Toad; as women they sat there. Of them the Master asked humbly how they expected to kill him. And the Toad answered savagely, "What is that to thee, and what hast thou to do with this thing?" "Truly," he replied, "I meant no harm," and saying this he softly touched the tips of their noses, and rising went his way. But the two, witches, looking one at the other, saw presently that their noses were both gone, and they screamed aloud in terror, but their faces were none the less flat. And so it came that the Toad and the Porcupine both lost their noses and have none to this day.

Glooskap had two dogs. One was the Loon (Kwemoo), the other the Wolf (Malsum). Of old all animals were as men; the Master gave them the shapes which they now bear. But the Wolf and the Loon loved Glooskap so greatly that since he left them they howl and wail. He who hears their cries over the still sound and lonely lake, by the streams where no dwellers are, or afar at night in the forests and hollows, hears them sorrowing for the Master.

I am indebted for this legend to Mr. Edward Jack, of Fredericton, N. B. "I give it to you," he writes, "just as it came from an Indian's lips, as he sat before the fire in my room this evening, smoking his tobacco mixed with willow bark. He has an endless store of Indian lore." It may be observed that this story gives a far more ingenious reason for Glooskap's telling his brother what would be his bane than appears in the other version. For he tells him what would indeed deprive him of life, but not forever.

No one can compare the story of Glooskap with that of Manobozho-Hiawatha and the like, as given by Schoolcraft or Cusick, and not decide that the latter seems to be a second-hand version of the former. In one we have the *root* of the bulrush,—not the light, feathery rush itself. In this story, as in that of Balder and Loki, it is the very apparent harmlessness of the bane which points the incident. Manobozho's father *says* that a black rock will kill him; but it does not, although he flies before it. Glooskap declares that a handful of down will cause his death. The *double entendre* of the swoon is entirely wanting in the Western tale, as is the apparent harmlessness of the medium of death. In the Edda the mistletoe, the softest, and apparently the least injurious, of plants, kills Balder; in the Wabanaki tale it is a ball of down or a rush. The Chippewas change it, like savages, to a substantial root and a black rock, thereby manifesting an insensibility to the point of the original, which is that the most trifling thing may be the cause of the most terrible events.

How Glooskap changed Certain Saucy Indians into Rattlesnakes

(Passamaquoddy.)

You know At-o-sis, the Snake? Well, the worst of all is Rattlesnake. Long time ago the Rattlesnakes were saucy Indians. They were very saucy. They had too much face. They could not be put down by much, and they got up for very little.

When the great Flood was coming Glooskap told them about it. They said they did not care. He told them the water would come over their heads. They said that would be very wet. He told them to be good and quiet, and pray. Then those Indians hurrahed. He said, "A great Flood is coming." Then they gave three cheers for the great Flood. He said, "The Flood will come and drown you all." Then these Indians hurrahed again, and got their rattles, made of turtle-shells, in the old fashion, fastened together, filled with pebbles, and rattled them and had a grand dance. Afterwards, when the white men brought cows and oxen into the country, they made rattles of horns.

Yes, they had a great dance. The rain began to fall, but they danced. The thunder roared, and they shook their rattles and yelled at it. Then Glooskap was angry. He did not drown them in the Flood, however, but he changed them into rattlesnakes. Nowadays, when they see a man coming, they lift up their heads and move them about. That's the way snakes dance. And they shake the rattles in their tails just as Indians shake their rattles when they dance. How do you like such music?

A Passamaquoddy tale related by an old woman to Mrs. W. Wallace Brown. These Indians still keep up a very curious snake-dance.

How Glooskap bound Wuchowsen, the Great Wind-Bird, and made all the Waters in all the World Stagnant.

(Passamaquoddy.)

The Indians believe in a great bird called by them *Wochowsen* or *Wuchowsen*, meaning Wind-Blow or the Wind-Blower, who lives far to the North, and sits upon a great rock at the end of the sky. And it is because whenever he moves his wings the wind blows they of old times called him that.

When Glooskap was among men he often went out in his canoe with bow and arrows to kill sea-fowl. At one time it was every day very windy; it grew worse; at last it blew a tempest, and he could not go out at all. Then he said, "Wuchowsen, the Great Bird, has done this!"

He went to find him; it was long ere he reached his abode. He found sitting on a high rock a large white Bird.

"Grandfather," said Glooskap, "you take no compassion on your *Koosesek*, your grandchildren. You have caused this wind and storm; it is too much. Be easier with your wings!"

The Giant Bird replied, "I have been here since ancient times; in the earliest days, ere aught else spoke, I first moved my wings; mine was the first voice,— and I will ever move my wings as I will."

Then Glooskap rose in his might; he rose to the clouds; he took the Great Bird-giant Wuchowsen as though he were a duck, and tied both his wings, and threw him down into a chasm between deep rocks, and left him lying there.

The Indians could now go out in their canoes all day long, for there was a dead calm for many weeks and months. And with that all the waters became stagnant. They were so thick that Glooskap could not paddle his canoe. Then he thought of the Great Bird, and went to see him.

As he had left him he found him, for Wuchowsen is immortal. So, raising him, he put him on his rock again, and untied one of his wings. Since then the winds have never been so terrible as in the old time. The reader will find the main incident of this story repeated in "Tumilkoontaoo, the Broken Wing," from the Micmac, in which there is no mention of Glooskap. This of *Wuchowsen* is from the Passamaquoddy manuscript collection by Louis Mitchell. It is unquestionably the original. Glooskap, as the greatest magician, most appropriately subdues the giant eagle of the North, the terrible god of the storm.

No one who knows the Edda will deny that Wuchowsen, or the Wind-blower, as he appears in the Passamaquoddy tale, is far more like the same bird of the Norsemen than the grotesque Thunder Bird of the Western tribes. He is distinctly spoken of by the Indians of Maine as a giant and a bird in one, sitting on a high cliff at the end of the sky, the wind—not thunder—coming from his pinions:—

"Tell me ninthly,
Since thou art called wise,
Whence the wind comes,
That over ocean passes,
Itself invisible to man.

"Hraesvelg he is called
Who at the end of heaven sits,
A Jotun (giant) in eagle's plumage:
From his wings comes,
It is said, the wind.
That over all men passes."

(The Lay of Vafthrudnir. The Edda, trans. by B. Thorpe.)

How Glooskcap conquered the Great Bull-Frog, and in what Manner all the Pollywogs, Crabs, Leeches, and other Water Creatures were created.

(Passamaquoddy and Micmac.)

N'karnayoo, of old times, there was an Indian village far away among the mountains, little known to other men. And the dwellers therein were very comfortable: the men hunted every day, the women did the work at home, and all went well in all things save in this. The town was by a brook, and except in it there was not a drop of water in all the country round, unless in a few rain-puddles. No one there had ever found even a spring.

Now these Indians were very fond of good water. The brook was of a superior quality, and they became dainty over it.

But after a time they began to observe that the brook was beginning to run low, and that not in the summer time, but in autumn, even after the rains. And day by day it diminished, until its bed was as dry as a dead bone in the ashes of a warm fire.

Now it was said that far away up in the land where none had ever been there was on this very stream another Indian village; but what manner of men dwelt therein no one knew. And thinking that these people of the upper country might be in some way concerned in the drought, they sent one of their number to go and see into the matter.

And after he had traveled three days he came to the place; and there he found that a dam had been raised across the rivulet, so that no water could pass, for it was all kept in a pond. Then asking them why they had made this mischief, since the dam was of no use to them, they bade him go and see their chief, by whose order this had been built.

And when he came to him, lo, there lay lazily in the mud a creature who was more of a monster than a man, though he had a human form. For he was immense to measure, like a giant, fat, bloated, and brutal to behold. His great yellow eyes stuck from his head like pine-knots, his mouth went almost from ear to ear, and he had broad, skinny feet with long toes, exceeding marvelous.

The messenger complained to this monster, who at first said nothing, and then croaked, and finally replied in a loud bellow,—

"Do as you choose,
Do as you choose,
Do as you choose.

"What do I care?
What do I care?
What do I care?

"If you want water,
If you want water,
If you want water,
Go somewhere else."

Then the messenger remonstrated, and described the suffering of the people, who were dying of thirst. And this seemed to please the monster, who grinned. At last he got up, and, making a single spring to the dam, took an arrow and bored a hole in it, so that a little water trickled out, and then he bellowed,—

"Up and begone!
Up and begone!
Up and begone!"

So the man departed, little comforted. He came to his home, and for a few days there was a little water in the stream; but this soon stopped, and there was great suffering again.

Now these Indians, who were the honestest fellows in all the world, and never did harm to any one save their enemies, were in a sorry pickle. For it is a bad thing to have nothing but water to drink, but to want that is to be mightily dry. And the great Glooskap, who knew all that was passing in the hearts of men and beasts, took note of this, and when he willed it he was among them; for he ever came as the wind comes, and no man wist how.

And just before he came all of these good fellows had resolved in council that they would send the boldest man among them to certain death, even to the village which built the dam that kept the water which filled the brook that quenched their thirst, whenever it was not empty. And when there he was either to obtain that they should cut the dam, or do something desperate, and to this intent he should go armed, and sing his death-song as he went. And they were all agog.

Then Glooskap, who was much pleased with all this, for he loved a brave man, came among them looking terribly ferocious; in all the land there was not one who seemed half so horrible. For he appeared ten feet high, with a hundred red and black feathers in his scalp-lock, his face painted like fresh blood with green rings round his eyes, a large clam-shell hanging from each ear, a spread eagle, very awful to behold, flapping its wings from the back of his neck, so that as he strode into the village all hearts quaked. Being but simple Indians, they accounted that this must be, if not Lox the Great Wolverine, at least Mitche-hant, the devil himself in person, turned Wabanaki; and they admired him greatly, and the squaws said they had never seen aught so lovely.

Then Glooskap, having heard the whole story, bade them be of good cheer, declaring that he would soon set all to rights. And he without delay departed up the bed of the brook; and coming to the town, sat down and bade a boy bring him water to drink. To which the boy replied that no water could be had in that town unless it were given out by the chief. "Go then to your chief," said the Master, "and bid him hurry, or, verily, I will know the reason why." And this being told, Glooskap received no reply for more than an hour, during which time he sat on a log and smoked his pipe. Then the boy returned with a small cup, and this not half full, of very dirty water.

So he arose, and said to the boy, "I will go and see your chief, and I think he will soon give me better water than this." And having come to the monster, he said, "Give me to drink, and that of the best, at once, thou Thing of Mud!" But the chief reviled him, and said, "Get thee hence, to find water where thou canst." Then Glooskap thrust a spear into his belly, and lo! there gushed forth a mighty river; even all the water which should have run on while in the rivulet, for he had made it into himself. And Glooskap, rising high as a giant pine, caught the chief in his hand and crumpled in his back with a mighty grip. And lo! it was the Bull-Frog. So he hurled him with contempt into the stream, to follow the current.

And ever since that time the Bull-Frog's back has crumpled wrinkles in the lower part, showing the prints of Glooskap's awful squeeze.

Then he returned to the village; but there he found no people,—no, not one. For a marvelous thing had come to pass during his absence, which shall be heard in every Indian's speech through all the ages. For the men, being, as I said, simple, honest folk, did as boys do when they are hungry, and say unto one another, "What would you like to have, and what you?" "Truly, I would be pleased with a slice of hot venison dipped in maple-sugar and bear's oil." "Nay, give me for my share succotash and honey." Even so these villagers had said, "Suppose *you* had all the nice cold, fresh, sparkling, delicious water there is in the world, what would *you* do?"

And one said that he would live in the soft mud, and always be wet and cool.

And another, that he would plunge from the rocks, and take headers, diving into the deep, cold water, drinking as he dived.

And the third, that he would be washed up and down with the rippling waves, living on the land, yet ever in the water.

Then the fourth said, "Verily, you know not how to wish, and I will teach you. I would live in the water all the time, and swim about in it forever."

Now it chanced that these things were said in the hour which, when it passes over the world, all the wishes uttered by men are granted. And so it was with these Indians. For the first became a Leech, the second a Spotted Frog, the third a Crab, which is washed up and down with the tide, and the fourth a Fish. Ere this there had been in all the world none of the creatures which dwell in the water, and now they were there, and of all kinds. And the river came rushing and roaring on, and they all went headlong down to the sea, to be washed into many lands over all the world. [Footnote: This was told by Tomah Josephs. It is given much more imperfectly in the tale of Kitpooseagunow in the Rand manuscript, and in the Anglo-Indian "Storey of Glooscap." I have taken very great pains in this, as in all the tales written down from verbal narration, to be accurate in details, and to convey as well as I could the quaint manner and dry humor which characterized the style of the narrator. Even white men do not tell the same story in the same way to everybody; and if Tomahquah and others fully expressed their feelings to me, it was because they had never before met with a white man who listened to them with such sympathy. It may be observed that the Indians commonly say that wherever the bull-frog is to be found in summer there is always water. It is not to be understood, in this tale, that the bull-frog is supposed to have merely drunk up the river. It is the river which has become incarnate in him. It is the ice of winter penetrated by the spear of the sun; that is, Glooskap. Thus, in another tale, a frozen river tries, as a man, to destroy the hero, but is melted by him. The conception of *the hour* when all wishes are granted, and the abrupt termination of the whole in a grand transformation scene, are both very striking. There is something like the former in Rabelais, in his narrative of the golden hatchet; as regards the latter, it is like the ending of a Christmas pantomime. Indeed, the entire tale is perfectly adapted to such a "dramatization."

I have been told by an old Passamaquoddy woman that the name of the monster who swallowed the stream was *Hahk-lee-be-mo*.]

How the Lord of Men and Beasts strove with the Mighty Wasis, and was shamefully defeated.

(Penobscot.)

Now it came to pass when Glooskap had conquered all his enemies, even the *Kewahqu'*, who were giants and sorcerers, and the *m'teoulin*, who were magicians, and the *Pamola*, who is the evil spirit of the night air, and all manner of ghosts, witches, devils, cannibals, and goblins, that he thought upon what he had done, and wondered if his work was at an end.

And he said this to a certain woman. But she replied, "Not so fast, Master, for there yet remains One whom no one has ever conquered or got the better of in any way, and who will remain unconquered to the end of time."

"And who is he?" inquired the Master.

"It is the mighty *Wasis*," she replied, "and there he sits; and I warn you that if you meddle with him you will be in sore trouble."

Now *Wasis* was the Baby. And he sat on the floor sucking a piece of maple-sugar, greatly contented, troubling no one.

As the Lord of Men and Beasts had never married or had a child, he knew naught of the way of managing children. Therefore he was quite certain, as is the wont of such people, that he knew all about it. So he turned to Baby with a bewitching smile and bade him come to him.

Then Baby smiled again, but did not budge. And the Master spake sweetly and made his voice like that of the summer bird, but it was of no avail, for Wasis sat still and sucked his maple-sugar.

Then the Master frowned and spoke terribly, and ordered Wasis to come crawling to him immediately. And Baby burst out into crying and yelling, but did not move for all that.

Then, since he could do but one thing more, the Master had recourse to magic. He used his most awful spells, and sang the songs which raise the dead and scare the devils. And Wasis sat and looked on admiringly, and seemed to find it very interesting, but all the same he never moved an inch.

So Glooskap gave it up in despair, and Wasis, sitting on the floor in the sunshine, went *goo! goo!* and crowed.

And to this day when you see a babe well contented, going *goo! goo!* and crowing, and no one can tell why, know that it is because he remembers the time when he overcame the Master who had conquered all the world. For of all the beings that have ever been since the beginning, Baby is alone the only invincible one. [Footnote: I am indebted for this "marchen" to Maria Saksis, a very intelligent Penobscot woman, a widow of a former governor, whom I met at North Conway, in the White Mountains, N. H. In her dialect Glooskap is invariably called *Glus-gah-be*. She told it with that admirable dry drollery, characteristic of a good story-teller in a race where there are no bad ones. The exquisite humor and humanity of this little legend, placed as a pendant to the stupendous successes of the giant hero, are such as to entitle its Indian author to rank as a genius. I have frequently asserted that these Wabanaki or Northeastern Algonquin tales bore to those of the West the apparent relation of originals to poor copies. Let the reader compare this, which is given as nearly word for word as was possible from the Indian narrative, with that of Manobozho-Hiawatha's effort to compete with a baby. The Cherokee account is that, seeing an infant sucking its own toe, he tried to do the same, and failed. It is in accounting for the unaccountable crowing of Baby that the point of the Penobscot story lies. Of this there is no mention made in the Western tale, which is utterly wanting in any feeling as to the power of childhood or its charm over the strongest. A real Indian tale may always be assumed to be ancient when it is told to set forth an *origin*. This gives the origin of a baby's crowing.]

How the great Glooskap fought the Giant Sorcerers at Saco, and turned them into Fish.

(Penobscot.)

N'karnayoo, of old times: *Woodenit atok hagen Glusgahbe.* This is a story of Glooskap (P.) There was a father who had three sons and a daughter: they were *m'teoulin*, or mighty magicians; they were giants; they ate men, women, and children; they did everything that was wicked and horrible; and the world grew tired of them and of all their abominations. Yet when this family was young, Glooskap had been their friend; he had made the father his adopted father, the brothers his brothers, the sister his sister. [Footnote: The Indians make formal adoptions of relatives of every grade, and in addition to this use all the terms of relationship as friendly greetings. This is in fact made apparent in all the stories in this collection.] Yet as they grew older, and he began to hear on every side of their wickedness, he said: "I will go among them and find if this be true. And if it be so, they shall die. I will not spare one of those who oppress and devour men, I do not care who he may be."

This family was at *Samgadihawk*, or Saco, on the sandy field which is in the Intervale or the summer bed of the Saco River, in the El-now-e-bit, the White Mountains, between Geh-sit-wah-zuch [Footnote: *Geh-sit-wah-zuch*, "many mountains" (Pen.). Mount Kearsarge, so called from the several lesser peaks around it.] and K'tchee penahbesk, [Footnote: *K'tchee penabesk*, "the great rock," a much more sensible and appropriate name than that of "Cathedral Rocks," which has been bestowed upon it; also *chee penabsk*.] and near Oonahgemessuk weegeet, the Home of the Water Fairies. [Footnote: Also called from a legend, *Oonahgemessuk k'tubbee*, the Water Fairies' Spring. This appropriate and beautiful name has been rejected in favor of the ridiculously rococo term "Diana's Bath." As there is a "Diana's Bath" at almost every summer watering place in America, North Conway must of course have one. The absolute antipathy which the majority of Americans manifest for the aboriginal names, even in a translation, is really remarkable.] Now the old man, the father of the evil magicians and his adopted father, had only one eye, and was half gray. [Footnote: This would directly connect him with the beings which are half stone, like the Oonahgemessuk, or water-goblins, the dwellers in Katahdin, and the Eskimo elves. This will be referred to again.] And Glooskap made himself like him,—there was not between them the difference of a hair; and having this form, he entered the wigwam and sat down by the old man. And the brothers, who killed everybody, not sparing one living soul, hearing a talking, looked in slyly, and seeing the new-comer, so like their father that they knew not which was which, said, "This is a great magician. But he shall be tried ere he goes, and that bitterly."

Then the sister took the tail of a whale, and cooked it for the stranger to eat. But as it lay before him, on the platter and on his knees, the elder brother entered, and saying rudely, "This is too good for a beggar like you," took it away to his own wigwam. Then Glooskap spoke: "That which was given to me was mine; therefore I take it again." And sitting still he simply *wished* for it, and it came flying into the platter where it was before. So he ate it.

Then the brothers said, "Indeed, he is a great magician. But he shall be tried ere he goes, and that bitterly."

When he had eaten, they brought in a mighty bone, the jaw of a whale, and the eldest brother, with great ado, and using both his arms and all his strength, bent it a little. Then he handed it to Glooskap, who with his thumb and fingers, snapped it like a pipe-stem. And the brothers said again, "Truly, this is a great magician. But he shall for all that be tried ere he goes, and that bitterly."

Then they brought a great pipe full of the strongest tobacco; no man not a magician could have smoked it. And it was passed round: every one smoked; the brothers blew the smoke through their nostrils. But Glooskap filled it full, and, lighting it, burnt all the tobacco to ashes at one pull, and blew all the smoke through his nostrils at one puff. Then the brothers said again in anger, "This is indeed a great magician. Yet he shall be tried again ere he goes, and that bitterly." But they never said it again.

And they still tried to smoke with him, and the wigwam was closed; they hoped to smother him in smoke, but he sat and puffed away as if he had been on a mountain-top, till they could bear it no longer. And one said, "This is idle; let us go and play at ball." The place where they were to play was on the sandy plain of Samgadihawk, or Saco, on the bend of the river. [Footnote: I have an Indian stone pestle, or hominy pounder, which I picked up on the site of this ball-play.] And the game begun; but Glooskap found that the ball with which they played was a hideous skull; it was alive and snapped at his heels, and had he been as other men and it had bitten him, it would have taken his foot off. Then Glooskap laughed, and said, "So this is the game you play. Good, but let us all play with our own balls." So he stepped up to a tree on the edge of the river-bed and broke off the end of a bough, and it turned into a skull ten times more terrible than the other. And the magicians ran before it as it chased them as a lynx chases rabbits; they were entirely beaten. Then Glooskap stamped on the sand, and the waters rose and came rushing fearfully from the mountains adown the river-bed; the whole land rang with their roar. Now Glooskap sang a magic song, which changes all beings, and the three brothers and their father became the *chinahmess*, a fish which is as long and large as a man, and they went headlong down on the flood, to the deep sea, to dwell there forever. And the magicians had on, each of them, a wampum collar; wherefore the *chinahmess* has beneath its head, as one may say, round its neck, the wampum collar, as may be seen to this day. And they were mighty *m'teoulin* in their time; but they were tried before they went, and that bitterly.

Yes, *seewass*, my brother, this is a true story. For Glus-gah-be was a great man in his day, and the day will come when I shall go to him and see him. [Footnote: This legend is from a single authority, Maria Saksis.]

How Glooskap went to England and France, and was the first to make America known to the Europeans.

(Passamaquoddy.)

There was an Indian woman: she was a Woodchuck (Mon-in-kwess, P.). She had lost a boy; she always thought of him. Once there came to her a strange boy; he called her mother.

He had a pipe with which he could call all the animals. He said, "Mother, if you let any one have this pipe we shall starve."

"Where did you get it?"

"A stranger gave it to me."

One day the boy was making a canoe. The woman took the pipe and blew it. There came a deer and a *qwah-beet*,—a beaver. They came running; the deer came first, the beaver next. The beaver had a stick in his mouth; he gave it to her, and said, "Whenever you wish to kill anything, though it were half a mile off, point this stick at it." She pointed it at the deer; it fell dead.

The boy was Glooskap. He was building a stone canoe. Every morning he went forth, and was gone all day. He worked a year at it. The mother had killed many animals. When the great canoe was finished he took his (adopted) mother to see it. He said that he would make sails for it. She asked him, "Of what will you make them?" He answered, "Of leaves." She replied, "Let the leaves alone. I have something better." She had many buffalo skins already tanned, and said, "Take as many as you need."

He took his pipe. He piped for moose; he piped for elk and for bear: they came. He pointed his stick at them: they were slain. He dried their meat, and so provisioned his great canoe. To carry water he killed many seals; he filled their bladders with water.

So they sailed across the sea. This was before the white people had ever heard of America. The white men did not discover this country first at all. Glooskap discovered England, and told them about it. He got to London. The people had never seen a canoe before. They came flocking down to look at it.

The Woodchuck had lost her boy. This boy it was, who first discovered America (England?). This boy could walk on the water and fly up to the sky. [Footnote: This tale was taken down in very strange and confused English. The first part is in my notes almost unintelligible.] He took his mother to England. They offered him a large ship for his stone canoe. He refused it. He feared lest the ship should burn. They offered him servants. He refused them. They gave him presents which almost overloaded the canoe. They gave him an anchor and an English flag.

He and his mother went to France. The French people fired cannon at him till the afternoon. They could not hurt the stone canoe. In the night Glooskap drew all their men-of-war ashore. Next morning the French saw this. They said, "Who did this?" He answered, "I did it."

They took him prisoner. They put him into a great cannon and fired it off. They looked into the cannon, and there he sat smoking his stone pipe, knocking the ashes out.

The king heard how they had treated him. He said it was wrong. He who could do such deeds must be a great man. He sent for Glooskap, who replied, "I do not want to see your king. I came to this country to have my mother baptized as a Catholic." They sent boats, they sent a coach; he was taken to the king, who put many questions to him.

He wished to have his mother christened. It was done. They called her Molly. [Footnote: The Indians pronounce the word Marie Mahli or Molly. Mahlinskwess, "Miss Molly," sounds like Mon-in-kwess, a woodchuck. Hence this very poor pun.] Therefore to this day all woodchucks are called Molly. They went down to the shore; to please the king Glooskap drew all the ships into the sea again. So the king gave him what he wanted, and he returned home. Since that time white men have come to America.

* * * * *

This is an old Eskimo tale, greatly modernized and altered. The Eskimo believe in a kind of sorcerers or spirits, who have instruments which they merely point at people or animals, to kill them. I think that the Indian who told me this story (P.) was aware of its feebleness, and was ashamed to attribute such nonsense to Glooskap, and therefore made the hero an Indian named Woodchuck. But among Mr. Rand's Micmac tales it figures as a later tribute to the memory of the great hero.

One version of this story was given to me by Tomah Josephs, another by Mrs. W. Wallace Brown. In the latter Glooskap's canoe is a great ship, with all kinds of birds for sailors. In the Shawnee legend of the Celestial Sisters (Hiawatha Legends), a youth who goes to the sky must take with him one of every kind of bird. This indicates that the Glooskap voyage meant a trip to heaven.

How Glooskap is making Arrows, and preparing for a Great Battle. The Twilight of the Indian Gods.

(Passamaquoddy.)

"*Is Glooskap living yet?*" "Yes, far away; no one knows where. Some say he sailed away in his stone canoe beyond the sea, to the east, but he will return in it one day; others, that he went to the west. One story tells that while he was alive those who went to him and found him could have their wishes given to them. But there is a story that if one travels long, and is not afraid, he may still find the great sagamore (*sogmo*). Yes. He lives in a very great, a very long wigwam. He always making arrows. One side of the lodge is full of arrows now. They so thick as that. When it is all quite full, he will come forth and make war. He never allows any one to enter the wigwam while he is making these arrows."

"*And on whom will he make war?*" "He will make war on all, kill all; there will be no more world,—world all gone. Dunno how quick,— mebbe long time; all be dead then, mebbe,—guess it will be long time."

"*Are any to be saved by any one?*" "Dunno. *Me hear* how some say world all burn up some day, water all boil all fire; some good ones be taken up in good heavens, but me dunno,—me just *hear* that. Only hear so."

It was owing to a mere chance question that this account of the Last Day was obtained from an Indian. It was related to Mrs. W. Wallace Brown, of Calais, Maine, by Mrs. Le Cool, an old Passamaquoddy Indian. It casts a great light on the myth of Glooskap, since it appears that a day is to come when, like

Arthur, Barbarossa, and other heroes in retreat, he is to come forth at a new twilight of the gods, exterminate the *Iglesmani*, and establish an eternal happy hunting-ground. This preparing for a great final battle is more suggestive of Norse or Scandinavian influence than of aught else. It is certainly not of a late date, or Christian, but it is very much like the Edda and Ragnarok. Heine does not observe, in the Twilight of the Gods, that Jupiter or Mars intend to return and conquer the world. But the Norsemen expected such a fight, when arrows would fly like hail, and Glooskap is supposed to be deliberately preparing for it.

A very curious point remains to be noted in this narration. When the Indians speak of Christian, or white, or civilized teachings, they say, "I heard," or, "I have been told." This they never do as regards their own ancient traditions. When Mrs. Le Cool said that she "had heard" that some were to be taken up into *good* heavens, she declared, in her way, that this was what Christians said, but that she was not so sure of it. The Northeastern Algonquin always distinguish very accurately between their ancient lore and that derived from the whites. I have often heard French fairy tales and Aesop's fables Indianized to perfection, but the narrator always knew that they were not *N'Karnayoo*, "of the old time."

Glooskap is now living in a Norse-like Asa-heim; but there is to come a day when the arrows will be ready, and he will go forth and slay all the wicked. Malsum the Wolf, his twin brother, the typical colossal type of all Evil, will come to life, with all the giant cannibals, witches, and wild devils slain of old; but the champion will gird on his magic belt, and the arrows will fly in a rain as at Ragnarok: the hero will come sailing in his wonderful canoe, which expands to hold an army. Thus it will be on

"That day of wrath, that dreadful day,
When heaven and earth shall pass away,"

with all things, in blood and death and fire. Then there will come the eternal happy hunting-grounds.

If this was derived from Christian priests, it must be admitted that it has changed wonderfully on the way. It is to me very heathen, grimly archaic, and with the strong stamp of an original. Its resemblance to the Norse is striking. Either the Norsemen told it to the Eskimo and the Indians, or the latter to the Norsemen. None know, after all, what was going on for ages in the early time, up about Jotunheim, in the North Atlantic! Vessels came to Newfoundland to fish for cod since unknown antiquity, and, returning, reported that they had been to Tartary.

It may be assumed at once that this Indian Last Battle of the Giants, or of the good hero giants against the Evil, led by the Malsum-Fenris Wolf, was not derived from the Canadian French. The influence of, the latter is to be found even among the Chippewas, but they never dealt in myths like this.

It is very remarkable indeed that the one great principle of the Norse mythology is identical with that of the Indian. So long as man shall make war and heroism his standard, just so long his hero god exists. But there will come a day when mankind can war no more,—when higher civilization must prevail. Then there will be a great final war, and death of the heroes, and death of their foes, and after all a new world.

"Then shall another come yet mightier, although I dare not his name declare.

Few may see further forth than when Odin meets the Wolf." (Hyndluloid, 42.)

The Norsemen may have drawn this from a Christian source; but the Indian, to judge by form, spirit, and expression, would seem to have taken it from the Norse.

How Glooskap found the Summer.

In the long ago time when people lived always in the early red morning, before sunrise, before the *Squid to neck* was peopled as to-day, Glooskap went very far north, where all was ice.

He came to a wigwam. Therein he found a giant, a great giant, for he was Winter. Glooskap entered; he sat down. Then Winter gave him a pipe; he smoked, and the giant told tales of the old times.

The charm was on him; it was the Frost. The giant talked on and froze, and Glooskap fell asleep. He slept for six months, like a toad. Then the charm fled, and he awoke. He went his way home; he went to the south, and at every step it grew warmer, and the flowers began to come up and talk to him.

He came to where there were many little ones dancing in the forest; their queen was Summer. I am singing the truth: it was Summer, the inmost beautiful one ever born. He caught her up; he kept her by a crafty trick. The Master cut a moose-hide into a long cord; as he ran away with Summer he let the end trail behind him.

They, the fairies of Light, pulled at the cord, but as Glooskap ran, the cord ran out, and though they pulled he left them far away. So he came to the lodge of Winter, but now he had Summer in his bosom; and Winter welcomed him, for he hoped to freeze him again to sleep. I am singing the song of Summer.

But this time the Master did the talking. This time his *m'teoulin* was the strongest. And ere long the sweat ran down Winter's face, and then he melted more and quite away, as did the wigwam. Then every thing awoke; the grass grew, the fairies came out, and the snow ran down the rivers, carrying away the dead leaves. Then Glooskap left Summer with them, and went home.

This poem—for it is such—was related to Mrs. W. Wallace Brown by an Indian named Neptune. It appears to be the completer form of the beautiful allegory of Winter and Spring given in the Hiawatha Legends as Peboan and Seegwum (Odjibwa). The struggle between Spring and Winter, Summer and Winter, or Heat and Cold, represented as incarnate human or mythic beings, forms the subject of several Indian legends, as it does a part of the Hymiskrida, in the Edda. The German J. B. Friedreich (Symbolik der Natur, Wurzburg, 1859) remarks that in the Bible, Job xxxviii. 28, and in the Song of the Three in the Fiery Furnace, Ice and Snow are spoken of as intelligences.

Heat and cold, in classic times, were supposed to be united, yet in conflict, in the lightning and hail (Virgil, Aen, VIII. 429), the symbol for this being a twisted horn. In the legend of the *Culloo* the frost giantess can only be killed by a crooked horn thrust into her ear. The horn darts out at once into incredible, irregular length, and evidently means lightning. In the Edda the he-goat is, on account of his horns, the symbol of lightning and storm. (Schwenk, Sinnbilden der alten Volker.) The Giala-horn of the Edda (Nyerup. Dict Scan. Mythol.) is the thunder which summons the Elves. "Miolner, the hammer of Thor, with which he kills frost giants, is the lightning." (Kirchner, Thor's Donnerkeil, Neu Strelitz, 1853, p. 60.) The coincidence of the symbols in the Edda with that of the lightning horn in the Indian legend is very curious, if nothing more.

The cord which Glooskap unrolls, and with which he deceives the fairies, who think they have him fast, while he is escaping, means delusive speech or plausible talk. To "talk like paying out rope" is an old simile.

"Speech runes thou must know, If thou wilt that no one for injury with hate requite thee. Those thou must wind, Those thou must wrap round (thee), Those thou must altogether place in the assembly, where people have into full court to go." (Sigrdrifumal.)

This is a merely accidental coincidence, but it illustrates the meaning of the myth. In both cases it is "wound or wrapped around" and rapidly unrolled, and the same simile.

The following poem on Glooskap may be appropriately placed in this work. The allusion to the agates of Cape Blomidon refers to a tradition given by S. T. Rand, which states that when Glooskap would make his adopted grandmother young again he created the brilliant stones, which are still found at that place, to adorn her. [Footnote: *Youth's Companion.*]

THE LEGEND OF GLOOSKAP.

Bathed in the sunshine still as of yore
Stretches the peaceful Acadian shore;
Fertile meadows and fields of grain
Smile as they drink the summer rain.

There like a sentinel, grim and gray,
Blomidon stands at the head of the bay,
And the famous Fundy tides, at will,
Sweep into Minas Basin still.

With wondrous beauty the Gaspereanx
Winds its way to the sea below,
And the old Acadian Grand Pre
Is the home of prosperous men to-day.

The place where Basil the blacksmith wrought,
In the glow of his forge, is a classic spot,
And every summer tourists are seen
In the fairy haunts of Evangeline.

But the old Acadian woods and shores,
Rich in beautiful legend stores,
Were once the home of an older race,
Who wore their epics with untaught grace.
Long ere the dikes that guard for aye
From the merciless tides the old Grand Pre,
Built by the Frenchman's tireless hands,
Grew round the rich Acadian lands.

The Micmac sailed in his birch canoe
Over the Basin, calm and blue;
Speared the salmon, his heart's desire,
Danced and slept by his wigwam fire;

Far in the depth of the forest gray
Hunted the moose the livelong day,
While the mother sang to her Micmac child
Songs of the forest, weird and wild.

Over the tribe, with jealous eye,
Watched the Great Spirit from on high,
While on the crest of Blomidon
Glooskap, the God-man, dwelt alone.

No matter how far his feet might stray
From the favorite haunts of his tribe away,

Glooskap could hear the Indian's prayer,
And send some message of comfort there.

Glooskap it was who taught the use
Of the bow and the spear, and sent the moose
Into the Indian banter's hands;
Glooskap who strewed the shining sands

Of the tide-swept beach of the stormy bay
With amethysts purple and agates gray,
And brought to each newly wedded pair
The Great Spirit's benediction fair.

But the white man came, and with ruthless hand
Cleared the forests and sowed the land,
And drove from their haunts by the sunny shore
Micmac and moose, forevermore.

And Glooskap, saddened and sore distressed,
Took his way to the unknown West,
And the Micmac kindled his wigwam fire
Far from the grave of his child and his sire;

Where now, as he weaves his basket gay,
And paddles his birch canoe away,
He dreams of the happy time for men
When Glooskap shall come to his tribe again.

ARTHUR WENTWORTH EATON.

THE MERRY TALES OF LOX, THE MISCHIEF MAKER,

COMMONLY KNOWN AS THE INDIAN DEVIL.

Of the Surprising and Singular Adventures of two Water Fairies who were also Weasels, and how they each became the Bride of a Star. Including the Mysterious and Wonderful Works of Lox, the Great Indian Devil, who rose from the Dead.

(Micmac and Passamaquoddy.)

Wee-zig-yik-keseyook. "Of old times." Far back in the forest, by a brook, dwelt two young men, Abistanooch, the Marten, and Team, the Moose. Of these each had a wigwam, and therewith a grandmother who kept house. And Team hunted and worked industriously, but Master Marten was greatly *moalet* (M.), which signifies one who liveth upon his neighbors, depending on their good nature, even as he that planteth corn and beans depends upon the pleasant smiles of the sun; whence it came to pass that wherever victuals were in store there too his presence did greatly abound.

Now it happened that one day Team, the Moose, had killed a bear, and brought home a single load of the meat, leaving the rest to be looked after anon. And being thrifty, and not caring to feed those who fed him not, neither did they thank, he said unto himself, and also to his grandmother, "Truly, the eyes of Marten shall not see this thing, his nose shall not smell thereof, neither shall his tongue taste it; so let not the tidings of our good luck go forth from the wigwam." "Yes," replied the old woman, "and well and wisely thou speakest, my son. But we have this day broken our kettle, while Marten has brought in a new one. Behold, I will go and borrow it, and having cooked in it I will wash and wipe it, so that there shall be no sign of what we did therewith, and so return it."

Now, this was done, but he who is *moalet* and a haunter of feasts is like a hunter of beasts: he knows well from a small sign where there is a large load, and the borrowing of kettles means the boiling of victuals therein. So having in him somewhat of sorcery, he did but step to his friend's wigwam, and, peeping through a crevice, saw a great store of bear's meat. And when the grandmother of Moose came unto him to return the kettle, just as she entered the lodge there arose from it a savory steam, and looking in it was full of well-cooked food. And Marten thanked her greatly, yet she, being put to shame, fled to her own home. But Moose said it was no matter, so the next day they went to the woods together, and all was well.

Now it befell Marten, as it might have befallen any other man, that one day he came to a distant and lonely lake in the mountains. Yet there, stepping softly as a cat behind the rocks bung with grapevines, he heard laughing and splashing, and a pleasant sound as of girls' voices. So, peeping carefully, he saw many maids merrily bathing in the lake: and these were of the fairy race, who dwell in deep waters and dark caves, and keep away from mankind. And seeing their garments lying on the shore, and beholding among the damsels one whom he desired to obtain, [Footnote: There are many of these stories which indicate passionate and deeply seated attachment, but I never once heard a real Indian say that man or woman loved, though they have words which fully express it. "He wanted her" is the nearest approach to tenderness which I have ever heard from them. This is not the result of a want of feeling, but of the suppression of all manifestation of it, to which every red man is trained from earliest infancy.] Marten quietly slipped along unseen, as all of his species can do, till he had the clothes in his hands. For being tinctured with magic and learned in the lore of all kind of goblins, elves, and witches, Master Marten knew that when Naiads are naked and a man has their garments he holds them at his mercy. For in the apparel lies their fairy power; and if you doubt it, do but give it a trial and see for yourself!

And having done this, the merry fellow ran inland with a brave whoop, which the fairies hearing, they in a great rage ran after the ravisher of their robes. But she whom he desired outstripped the rest, and when she approached him he did but tap her lightly on the head with a small stick, according to a certain ancient prescription followed in Fairy-land, which makes of a woman a wife; whereupon she, according to the antique rite, being astonished to find herself so, suddenly married, fainted dead away, and was carried off in peace. And as for the clothes of the others, the Marten gave them back without taking fee or rewards.

Then Team, the Moose, who was a good soul, but not wise above all the world, coming home and finding Marten married, wished also for a wife. And having heard all the tale, he said, "Well, if it is no harder than that, 'tis as easy as sucking a honeysuckle, and I am as good as married." And going to the pond in the mountains, among the rocks and behind the grapevines, he too beheld the virgins jumping, flapping, splashing, and mischieving merrily, like mad minxes, in the water; whereat he, being all of a rage, as it were, caught up the clothes of these, poor maids and ran; she whom he most admired catching up with him. And being resolved to do the thing thoroughly, he grappled up a great club and gave her a bang on her small head, which stunned her indeed, and that forever, inasmuch as she was slain outright. So the Moose remained unmarried.

Now Team was one of the kind not uncommon, in this world, who hold that if any other man has or gets more than they have, then they are deeply wronged. And it had come to pass that Master Marten, finding that his wife yearned greatly for the society of her sisters, offered to take yet another of them in marriage, merely to oblige his wife; for in such a kind of benevolence he was one of the best souls that ever lived, and rather than have trouble in the family he would have wedded all the pretty girls in the country. So going as before to the pond in the mountains, among the rocks and behind the grapevines, he, by the same device, captured yet another fairy, whom, taking home, he wedded.

Yet Team took this sadly to heart, and willed that Marten should give him this last spouse, to which Marten would in nowise agree. Truly, Team argued earnestly that as he had no wife, and no wisdom wherewith to win one, of course he must have one of Marten's, or that Marten should go and get him one. To which Marten replied that Moose might skin his own skunks, and fish for his own minnows, and also paddle his own canoe to the devil, if it so pleased him,—all of these being approved Indian sayings of high and racy antiquity. Whereupon Team sought to persuade Marten with a club, who gave a soft answer by shooting a flint-headed arrow through Team's scalp-lock; and this friendship they continued for many days, passing their evenings in manufacturing missiles, and the mornings in sending them one at the other.

Now the fairy water-wives, not being accustomed to this kind of intimacy, sought to subtract themselves from it. So one morning, when Marten and Team were most industriously endeavoring to effect mutual murder, the two wives of the former fled afar to seek fortune, and succeeded therein to perfection. And it came to pass when the sun had set and the voice of Bumole, the Spirit of Night, was heard afar on high, and Nibauchset (P.), the Night-Walker, shone over all, that the two brides lay in an oak opening of the forest, and looked at P'ses'muk, the Stars, and talked about them even as children might do. And one said to the other, "If those Stars be men, which would you have for a husband?" "By my faith," replied the other," it should be that little red, twinkling fellow, for I like the little stars best." "And I," said the other, "will wed the Wisawaioo P'ses'm (P.), the Great Yellow Star, for I love the large stars." And, saying this in jest, they fell asleep.

But many a word spoken in jest is recalled in earnest, as these brides learned when they awoke, and found themselves married again in the Indian manner, at only a word. For she who had wished for the Great Yellow Shining Star, as she opened her eyes, heard a man's voice say, "Take care, or you will upset my war-paint!" [Footnote: Sekroon (red ochre).] And lo, there lay by her side a great and handsome man, very noble, with large and lustrous eyes. [Footnote: In the Passamaquoddy version of this tale, given me by Tomah Josephs, the brides awake in Star-Land. The husbands are both elderly men, and he who is the Yellow Star has bright yellow corners to his eyes, while the other has red. In another the Yellow Star is called Wobeyu, the White. While they are all distinctly forms of one tale, the three differ so much that I have had great difficulty in reconstituting what appears to be the Original legend.]

Then the other, as she awoke and stirred, heard a little feeble, cracked voice crying, "Take care, or you will spill my eye-water!" [Footnote: *Nebijegwode* (eye medicine, M.)] And by her was the smaller star, whom she had chosen; but he was a weak-looking old fellow, with little red, twinkling eyes. And as they had chosen so it came unto them.

But yellow or red, young or old, in a few days they both grew a-weary of the star country to which they were taken, and wished to return to the earth. And then that came to pass which made them yearn with tenfold longing; for their husbands, who were absent all day hunting, had pointed out to them a large flat stone, which they were on no account to lift; which they obeyed in this wise, that they did not both lift the stone, but only the younger, who, as soon as the Stars had gone to the greenwood, rushed to the slab, and, lifting it up, gazed greedily down into the hole beneath. And what she saw was wonderful, for it was the sky itself, and directly under them was the world in which they had lived, and specially in sight was the home of their childhood, with all its woods and rivers. And then the elder having looked, both almost broke their hearts with weeping.

Now the Stars were by no means such evil-minded men as you may have deemed; for having perceived by magic that their wives had looked through the hole in the sky, and knowing that they were lying when they denied it, they gave them leave to go back to earth. Yet there were conditions, and those not easy to such fidgety damsels as these; for they said, "Ye shall lie together all this night, and in the morning when ye awake ye shall be in no haste to open your eyes or to uncover your faces. Wait until ye shall have heard the song of the *Ktsee-gee-gil-laxsis* (P.), or chick-a-dee-dee. And even then ye shall not arise, but be quiet until the song of the red squirrel shall be heard. And even then ye must wait and keep your faces covered and your eyes closed until ye hear the striped squirrel sing. And then ye may leave your bed and look around."

Now the younger wife was ever impatient, and when the chick-a-dee-dee sang she would have leaped up at once, but the elder restrained her. "Wait," she said, "my sister, until we hear the *Abalkakmooech*." [Footnote: Ground squirrel] And she lay still till the *Adoo-doo-dech* [Footnote: Red squirrel] began his early chatter and his morning's work. Then, without waiting, she jumped up, as did the elder, when they found themselves indeed on earth, but in the summit of a tall, spreading hemlock-tree, and that in such a manner that they could not descend without assistance. And it had come to pass in this wise: for as each song was sung by the bird and the squirrels, they had come nearer and nearer to the earth; even as the light of day drew near, but as they could not delay they had been deserted. [Footnote: A want of patience or of dignity, and restlessness, are more scorned by every Indian than any other fault. This is not the only story in which people are represented as being punished for being unable to bide their time. Glooskap was specially severe on all such sinners.]

And as they sat there and day dawned, men of the different Indian families went by, and unto all of these they cried for help. It is true that their star husbands had made for them in the tree, a bed of moss, but they cared not to rest in the hemlock, for all that. [Footnote: In another very full version of this legend (M.), the water-wives are called Weasels (*Uskoolsh*), "from their great whiteness." This, however, indicates supernatural fairness or beauty. In the same story the tree is a pine, not a hemlock. Insignificant as these differences may appear, they are of primary importance in the elucidation of a myth.] And of all the beasts of the forest or men of the clearing, who should be the first to appear but Team, or Master Moose, himself. And to him they cried, "*N'sesenen-apkwahlin, n'sesenen*!" "Oh, our elder brother, let us free; take us down, and we will be your two dear little wives, and go home with you." But he, looking up scornfully, said, "I was married this autumn." And so he went his way.

And he who next came was the shaggy Bear, or *mooin*, to whom they made the same request, offering themselves for no higher price than to be taken down safely out of their nest. But he growled out that he had been married in the spring, and that one wife was enough for any man. So he went his way. [Footnote: N. B.—There is a joke here. The animals who pass by the tree each mate at the season of the year when they declare that they were married. The White Ladies, weasels or ermines, therefore, came at the wrong time. The fickle, variable nature ascribed to woman, *varium et mutabile semper femina*, is supposed to be most decidedly expressed by such slender, slippery, active little animals.]

And then who should come along but Marten himself, even the Abistanooch, whom they had deserted! And they cried out for joy, begging him to take them back. But he, behaving as if they were utter strangers, replied that he had been married in the early spring to one of his own tribe, and unto a damsel whose name was Marten, and that it was not seemly for animals to wed out of their own land. So he scampered off, leaving the little Weasels all alone.

And last of all came Lox, whom hunters call the Indian Devil, [Footnote: In the Micmac it is the Badger, Keekwajoo, who is the rogue and teaser of the tale. But in the Passamaquoddy versions it is the dreaded and mysterious Lox, who appears to be a species of Lynx or Wolverine. The Lox is said, by trustworthy white travelers as well as Indians, to follow hunting parties for weeks, inspired apparently only by an incredible mania for mischief, much like that of a monkey or a revengeful savage, but guided by remarkable intelligence. He will find his way into a camp and destroy every object made by the hand of man with a thoroughness akin to genius, and what he cannot destroy he will carry to a great distance and carefully conceal. As his ferocity is equal to his craftiness, he is very appropriately termed the Indian Devil.] and others the Wolverine, who is exceeding subtle above the beasts of the forest, and who is gifted with more evil mischief than all of them in one. And when the Weasels called to him for help he tarried, for it came into his heart that he might in some way torment and tease them. But verily he had to deal with those who were not much more virtuous than himself, and quite as cunning, for what with traveling from the earth to the heavens and changing husbands, these fair minevers were learning wisdom rapidly. So the elder sister, who had not the least idea of keeping her promise unless it suited her fancy, played a trick, and that quickly anon. For she at once took off her hair-string [Footnote: The Hair-String, *Saggalobee* (M), occurs very often in Indian legends, generally as gifted with magic. The Indian women allowed their hair to grow long, then doubled it upon the back of the head, often making additions of something to enlarge the roll. It was then bound in a bunch with the string.] and tied it into a few less than a hundred knots among the twigs of the trees, tangling it so that you would have deemed it a week's work before a man could loosen it again without injury.

Now Master Lox, having taken down the younger sister with all the politeness in the world, came for the other, and aided her also to descend. And when on the ground she indeed said, "*Willcr-oon*" "I thank you" (P.), but begged him to go up the tree again and bring down a great treasure which she had left there, her hair-string: beseeching him for all their lives not to break or injure it in any way, but to most carefully untie every knot, for thus doing it would bring untold felicity on them all; and that they, the Weasels, would meantime build a beautiful bridal bower, or a wigwam, and that so furnished as he had never seen the like before,—in which verily they kept their word.

For they speedily built the wigwam, but the furniture thereof was of this rare kind. The Weasels had, it seems, certain sworn friends,—for birds of a feather flock together,—and these were not far to seek, as they were the Thorns, Burrs, and Briers of all kinds, Hornets and other winged and stinged insects, besides the Ants. And they were, moreover, intimate with all the sharp-edged Flints in the land, which was a goodly company. So when the bower was built it had therein a hornet's nest for a bridal bed, thorns for a carpet, flints for a floor, and an ant's nest for a seat, which for a bare-footed and bare-breeched Indian is indeed a sore essay. Now it had taken Master Lox the entire day to untie the hair-string, so when he came down it was dark, and he was glad when he saw the hut and thought of resting therein.

But, as he entered, he ran among the Thorns, which pierced his nose, and Flints, which cut his feet, so that he roared aloud. Then he heard a voice, which seemed to be that of the younger Miss Weasel, crying "*Names-cole*" (M.), "Go to my sister, yonder!" So he went, and trod in an ant-hill, and this was worse than the Briers. And then he heard another voice on that side which cried, laughing, "*N'kwech-kale*!" (M.), "Go to my sister, who is younger than I." And plunging furiously through the darkness, he fell on the hornet's nest; and verily the last state of that Indian was worst of all. Thus, seeing himself mocked, he became furious; so that he who has by nature the very worst temper of all beasts or men was never so angry before, and, seeking the tracks of the Weasels, he pursued them as they fled in the night and through the thick forest.

Now it came to pass that by daybreak the two girls, even the Misses Weasel, had come to a broad river which they could not cross. But In The edge of the water stood a large Crane, motionless, or the *Tum-gwo-lig-unach*, who was the ferryman. Now truly this is esteemed to be the least beautiful of all the birds, for which cause he is greedy of good words and fondest of flattery. And of all beings there were none who had more bear's oil ready to anoint every one's hair with—that is to say, more compliments ready for everybody—than the Weasels. So, seeing the Crane, they sang:—

"Wa wela quis kip pat kasqu',
Wa wela quis kip pat kasqu'." (P.)

The Crane has a very beautiful long neck,
The Crane has a very beautiful long neck.

This charmed the old ferryman very much, and when they said, "Please, grandfather, hurry along," he came quickly. Seeing this, they began to chant in chorus, sweetly as the Seven Stars themselves:—

"Wa wela quig nat kasqu',
Wa wela quig nat kasqu'." (P.)

The Crane has very beautiful long legs,
The Crane has very beautiful long legs.

Hearing this, the good Crane wanted more; so when they asked him to give them a lift across, he answered slowly that to do so he must be well paid, but that good praise would answer as well. Now they who had abundance of this and to spare for everybody were these very girls. "Have I not a beautiful form?" he inquired; and they both cried aloud, "Oh, uncle, it is indeed beautiful!" "And my feathers?" "Ah, *pegeakopchu*" (M.), "Beautiful and straight feathers indeed!" "And have I not a charming long, straight neck?" "Truly our uncle has it straight and long." "And will ye not acknowledge, oh, maidens, that my legs are fine?" "Fine! oh, uncle, they are perfection. Never in this life did we see such legs!" So being well pleased, the Crane put them across, and then the two little Weasels scampered like mice into the bush.

And scarcely were they concealed, or the Crane well again in his place, ere Master Lox appeared. And being in no good temper he called to Uncle Crane to set him across, and that speedily. Now the Crane had been made mightily pleased and proud by the winsome words of the Weasels, and was but little inclined to be rudely addressed. So he said to Lox, "I will bear thee over the river if thou wilt bear witness to my beauty. Are not my legs straight?" "Yea" replied the Lox, "and beautifully painted, too." Now the color thereof was little pleasing to poor Uncle Crane. "Are not my feathers very smooth and fine?" "Yea, smooth and fine; what a pity, though, that they are mildewed and dusty!" "And my straight neck?" "Yes, wonderfully straight,—straight as *this*" said Lox to himself, taking up a crooked stick. And then he sang:—

"Mecha guiskipat kasqu',
Mecha quig nat kasqu'."

The Crane has a very ugly neck,
The Crane has dirty, ugly legs.

"Come, *mooso me* (grandfather), hurry up!"

Oh, the Crane has a very ugly neck,
The Crane has dirty, ugly legs.

"I wish you to be quick, *mooso me*. Hurry up, I say!" [Footnote: This dialogue, including the songs, is from a very curious Passamaquoddy version of the tale, sent to me by Louis Mitchell. As in all such cases, there is far more humor in the Passamaquoddy narratives than in the Micmac or Eskimo.]

And all of this ill-temper and insincerity was deeply and inwardly detected by Uncle Crane, but he said not a word, and only meekly bent him down to take the traveler on his back. But when in the stream, and where it was deepest and most dangerous, he gave himself a shake, and in another instant Lox was whirling round and round like a chip in the rapids. And yet a little time he was dashed against the rocks, and then anon was thrown high and dry on the shore, but dead as a seven-year-old cedar cone.

Now the Lox is a great magician at certain times and seasons, albeit his power fails at others. [Footnote: From this point of the legend onward there is an inextricable confusion as regards the four different versions. While the hero is decidedly a Badger in the Micmac, I regard the great ferocity, craft, and above all the vitality which he displays as far more characteristic of the Lox or Wolverine of the Passamaquoddy. What is almost decisively in favor of the latter theory is that in all the stories, despite his craft and power, he is always getting himself into trouble through them. This is eminently characteristic of the Lox, much less so of the Badger.] And he is one of those who rise from the dead. Now it came to pass that some days after two boys of the Kwedech or Mohawk race found the Lox lying dead on a rock in the sunshine, and the worms were crawling from him. But when they touched him he arose as if from sleep, and stood before them as a proud and fierce warrior. But he was scarce alive ere he sought to do them who had roused him to life a mischief; for having noted that they had fine bows, he got them into his hands, and broke them, yet all as if he meant it not. [Footnote: In the Passamaquoddy version of this tale, when Lox is thus dismembered, the ants, pitying him, bring his scattered members together. As soon as he recovers, the Wolverine, with characteristic ingratitude, amuses himself by trampling his benefactors to death beneath his feet.] And then by magic making a sound as of many children at play, afar off across the next point of land by the river, he bade them run and join the pleasant games. And when he had got them a space onward, lo, the sound seemed ever farther on, mingled with the murmur of the stream; and so they went without him, seeking it, and yet it wandered ever far away.

Now he had learned from the boys that they were of a *Cullo* family; and the Culloos are certain monstrous birds, exceeding fierce. But Master Lox, having seen in the cabin plenty of fine meat, desired greatly to become one of the family, and having been much about in life knew something of the ways of every one. So putting on the Culloo style, he, seeing a babe, began to sing with the most natural air in the world a Culloo nursery-song:—

"Agoo ge abeol,
Wetkusanabeol."
[Footnote: Micmac.]

A seal-skin strap,
A shoulder-strap.

Now it costs very little to fall into the humor of a man; but this the woman would not do, and told him plainly that he could not deceive her. On hearing which Master Lox, in a great rage, seized his tomahawk and slew her. Then seeing a kettle boiling on the fire, he cut off her head and put it into the pot, hiding the body. And this was a merry jest after his own heart, so that it greatly solaced him. But after a time, the two boys, returning, missed their mother, and looking into the kettle, found her head. Then they knew well who had done this. And, being fearless, they pursued him, but having no bows they could do him no harm; however, they took from him his gloves, and with these they returned.

And anon there came also an uncle of the boys, or *Kah-kah-goos* (P.), the Crow. So he gave chase to Lox, yet all that he could do was to snatch away his cap as he ran. Yet without shame he cried aloud, "Well, my head was getting warm, and now I am cooler. Thank you!"

[Illustration: LOX CARRIED OFF BY CULLOO]

Then came another relative, *Kitpoo*, the Eagle (M.). And he, pursuing Lox, took from him his coat. Yet all unabashed he replied, "Thanks unto you also; for I was just wishing that my younger brother were here to carry my coat for me." But he who now arrived, hearing of the deadly deed, was the great Culloo himself, the most terrible of all created creatures, and he, pursuing Lox, caught him up, and carrying him in his claws, even to the summit of the sky itself, let him drop, and he was a whole day in falling; even from the first dawn unto sunset he went down ere he touched the earth. But before he was let drop, and when on high, he burst into a mocking song on what he saw, and the words were as follows:—

"Kumut kenovek,
Telap tumun ek,
Stugach' kesenagasikel,
  Yog wa egen'
  Yog wa egeno
Telap tumen ek
Kumut ken ooik'
Stuga 'mkudomoos koon."

Our country all lost
Seems clearly to us
As though it were all spread with boughs.
  Heigh ho, hay hum!
  Heigh ho, hay hum!
Our country now lost
Seems now unto us
To be blue like the clear blue sky.
  Hum, hum—tol de rol!

And when let fall, this graceless jackanapes in nowise ceased his ribaldry; for while pretending to flap with his arms as if they were wings, he imitated with his mouth, mockingly, the *wish! wish!* of the wide wings of the Culloo. Yet ere he touched the earth he uttered one little magic spell, "Oh, spare my poor backbone!" And with that all the trouble of all the birds went for nothing. Truly he was mashed to a batter, and his blood and brains flew in every direction, like raspberry pudding; but among the remains his backbone lay whole, and this was his life.

And in a few days after his younger brother came by, who, seeing the dire mess, exclaimed, "Hey, what is all this?" [Footnote: The dead body of a sorcerer must lie until addressed by some human being. Then it revives. This is suggestive of vampirism, which is well known to the Indians. There is something strangely ghastly in the idea of the Voice calling separately to each dead limb to come to it. The Culloo is an emblem of the cloud, and Lox let fall from one probably signified fire, or the lightning.] Whereupon a Voice came from the bone, crying, "*Nuloogoon, ba ho*!" "Ho, my leg, come hither!" and a leg came unto the spine. Then the Voice cried," *N'petunagum, ba ho*!" "Ho, my arm, come hither!" And when the last fragment had come he arose, the same indomitable Lox as ever, even the Indian Devil, or Wolverine, who never says Die, and whom nothing can kill, and who is hard to put away.

Now the two brothers went on till they came to the top of a high mountain, where there lay a very great round rock, or a mighty boulder. And being full of fun, they turned it over with great sticks, saying to it, "Now let us run a race!" Then it rolled downhill till it stopped at the foot, they rushing along by it all the time. And when it rested they jeered it, and bade it race with them again, when it so listed.

And truly they had not long to wait, for soon after, as they sat cooking their food, they heard a mighty commotion as of something coming with dreadful speed through the forest. And lo! it was the stone in dire wrath, which, having rested a little while, came rushing through the forest, crashing the mighty trees like grass, with a roar like thunder, leaving a smooth road behind it in the roughest wilderness. Up and after the sorcerers flew the stone, and the younger slipped aside like a snake, but the elder had scarcely time to utter his magic charm, "*Noo-goon ooskudeskuch*!" "Let my backbone remain uninjured!" ere the awful rock rolled down upon him, crushing his bones and mashing his flesh. Yet the spine was unhurt; it remained sound as ever.

And the stone went on and ever on, till the sound of its roar died away in the breeze and afar in the wilderness.

Then the younger brother turned to the Backbone and said, "*Cagooee wejismook' tumun*?" (M.) "Why are you lying there?" And hearing this charm the Bone called aloud, "*Ntenin ba ho*!" "My body, ho!" and "*Nuloogoon ba ho*!" "My leg, ho!" and so with the rest of the members as before, until he that was decomposed was now recomposed; yes, and composed perfectly. And then he that was dead, but was now alive, arose, and said as one awaking, "What have I been doing?" So his brother told him all.

Then he was greatly angered, and when the Wolverine is angry it is not a little. And he said in his wrath, "Shall I that am the devil of the woods himself be slain by birds and stones, and not be revenged?" So they went onwards through the woods till they found the Great Rock: they followed in the path of the broken trees; even by the trees did they track it. Which having found, they built a fire around it; with great stones for hammers they broke it, and ever more and still smaller, till it was all mere dust, for their souls were sore for revenge.

When lo, a great wonder! For the Spirit of the Old Rock, even that which was itself, turned all the dust to black flies, into the stinging and evil things which drive men and beasts mad, so that its hatred and spite might be carried out on all living creatures unto the end of time.

And having had their ill-will of the Rock and seen it become Flies, the two went through the forest, and so on till they came to a village of good, honest folk; and knowing what manner of men they were, Lox resolved to forthwith play them an evil trick, for in all life there was nothing half so dear to him as to make mischief, the worse the better.

And this time it came into his head that it would be a fine piece of wit to go into the town as a gay girl and get married, and see what would come of it, trusting to luck to fashion a sad fool out of somebody. So having made himself into a delicate young beauty, richly attired, he entered the place; and truly the town was soon agog over the new guests. And the young chief of the tribe, wanting her, won her without waste of time. Truly there lieth herein some mystery. I know not what, only this I know: that there are in all towns certain folk who, by means of magic or meddling, always find out everything about everybody, and then tittle-tattle thereof. Now, albeit Lox had utterly abjured all the sinfulness of manhood, and had made a new departure in an utterly new direction, saying not a word thereof to any one, yet in a brief measure of time, one here, another there, Jack in a corner and Jane by the bush, began to whisper of a strange thing, and hint that all was not as it should be, and, whatever the chief might think, that in their minds matters were going wrong in his wigwam.

Now Lox, knowing all this thread as soon as it was spun, began to think it high time to show his hand in the game. And what was the amazement of all the town to hear, one fine evening, that the chief's wife would soon be a mother. And when the time came Dame Lox informed her husband that, according to the custom of her people, she must be left utterly alone till he was a father and the babe born. And when in due time the cry of a small child was heard in the lodge the women waiting ran in, and received from the mother the little one, abundantly rolled in many wrappers, which they took to the chief. But what was his amazement, when having unrolled the package, he found under one skin after another, tied up hard, yet another sewed up, and yet again, as the inmost kernel of this nut, the little withered, wizened, dead, and dried shrivelment of an unborn moose calf. Which pleased the chief so much that, dashing Master Moose into the fire, he seized his tomahawk and ran to his lodge to make his first morning call on the mother.

But Master Lox was now a man again, and expecting this call, and not wishing to see visitors, had with his brother fled to the woods, and that rapidly. And in the rush he came to a river, and, seeing a very high waterfall, thought of a rare device whereby he might elude pursuit. For he with his brother soon built a dam across the top with trees and earth, so that but little water went below. And lying in a cave, concealed with care, he imitated the *boo-oo-oo* of a falling stream with quaint and wondrous skill. And there he lay, and no man wist thereof.

But verily the wicked one is caught in his own snare, and even so it befell Master Lox. For as he hid, the water above, having gathered to a great lake, burst the dam, so that it all came down upon him at once and drowned him; nor was there any great weeping for him that ever I heard of. So here he passes out of this story, and does not come into it again. But whether he went for good and all out of this life is doubtful, since I find him living again in so many rare, strange histories that it has become a proverb that Lox never dies.

Now the tale returns to the two little Weasels, or Ermines, or Water-Maids, poor souls, who had such a hard life! And it happened that, fleeing from Master Lox, they came at evening to a deserted village, and entered a wigwam to pass the night. But the elder, being the wiser, and somewhat of a witch in the bud, mistrusted the place, deeming it not so empty as it seemed. And beholding by the door, lying on the ground, the Neckbone of a man or some other animal, she warned her sister that she should in nowise offend it or treat it lightly, to which the younger replied by giving it a kick which sent it flying, and by otherwise treating it with scorn and disdain.

Then they laid them down to sleep; but before their slumber came they heard a doleful, bitter voice chanting aloud and shouting, and it was *Chamach keg wech*, or the Neckbone, bewailing the scorn that had been put upon him, and reviling them with all manner of curses. Then the elder said, "There, truly, I said it. I knew you would be our death if you did not mind me:" it being in all cases an esteemed solace for every woman and most men to say, "I told you so!" But the younger, being well-nigh frightened to a corpse, in a soft whisper implored the elder to let her hide herself in her roll of hair, [Footnote: That is, the elder should retain the human form, and the younger become a weasel.] which the Voice, mocking her, repeated; adding thereto all the reviling and railing that Mitche-hant, the devil, himself ever yet invented, and abusing her so for her past life, and exhorting her so for all the sins, slips, and slaps therein (of which there were many), that even the impenitent little Weasel repented and wept bitterly. Howbeit no further harm came to them beyond this, so that the next morning they went their way in peace; and I warrant you Master Neckbone got no kicks that day from them, departing. [Footnote: This incident of the Neckbone is very much like the common nursery tale of Teeny Tiny, in which an old woman takes home a human bone and puts it in the cupboard. It torments her all night by its cries.]

Then, coming to a river, they saw on the other side a handsome young man holding a bow, and to him they called, making their usual offer to become his wives, and all for no greater thing than to carry them over the ferry. And this man's name was See-witch, [Footnote: A kind of small sea-duck.] and to please them he did indeed pass them over in his canoe; but as for taking them home, he said that he had housekeepers in store, and as many as he needed just then, and that of a kind who kept him very busy. So they went their way onwards.

And coming anon to the great sea, they beheld yet another canoe with two men therein, and these were Kwe-moo, the Loon, and Mahgwis, the Scapegrace. And embarking with them, Loon soon began to admire the girls greatly. And saying many sweet things, he told them that he dwelt in the Wigem territory, or in the land of the Owealkesk, [Footnote: A very beautiful species of sea-duck.] of which he himself was one. But the Mahgwis whispered to them aside that they should put little trust in what he told them, for Loon was a great liar. Now when they came to the land of the Owealkesk, they were amazed at the beauty of the people, and saw that all in that land was lovely, nor did they themselves seem less marvelously fair to the men therein. Indeed, the poor little Weasels began to see the end of their sorrows, for, being water-fairies, these sea-birds were nigh akin to them. And there was a great feast, a great dance, and great games held in honor of their arrival, and the two finest young Sea-Duck men, utterly unheeding the old Loon, who believed indeed that they were his own wives, carried them off, and nothing loath wedded them.

And it was in this wise. There was a canoe-race, and Kwee-moo, being bitterly angry that he was held of so little account in the Sea-Duck land, went forth with the rest, and, paddling far outside, upset his canoe, and making as if he were drowning called to the Weasels to come and save him. But the Sea-Ducks laughed, and said, "Let him alone. Truly he will never drown. We know him." And the race ended they went ashore in peace. [Footnote: Here the Micmac narrative ends. The rest is as it was given to me by Noel Josephs, or *Chi gatch gok*, the Raven, a Passamaquoddy. It would not be a complete Indian tale if a man having received a slight or injury did not take a bloody revenge for it.]

And that night they danced late, and the Weasels, being better pleased with the two handsome Sea-Ducks than with Loon, forthwith divorced themselves out of hand, and at once married them, going to where their canoe lay, to pass the bridal night. Now Loon had not gone to the dance, but sat at home nursing his vengeance till he was well-nigh mad. And as the Weasels did not return, he went forth and sought them; and this he did so carefully that at last he found all four by the sea, sound asleep. Whereupon he, with his knife, slew the young men, and being in great fear of their friends took his canoe and went down the river to kill a deer. But not daring to return, and being mad for loss of the Weasels, and fearing to fall into the hands of the enemy, he in despair took his knife and killed himself.

Yet the Weasels, who had seen the deed done, did not betray him, for there was at least so much truth left in them. And they lived with the Sea-Ducks, and I doubt me not went on marrying and mischief-making after their wont even unto the end of their days. And their kind are not dead as yet in any land.

* * * * *

This is a fair specimen of many Indian legends. So much of it as is Micmac was told to Mr. Rand by a highly intelligent Indian, named Benjamin Brooks, who was certain that the story was of great antiquity. As I at first heard it, it was limited to the adventure with the Stars, but I was told that this formed only a part of an extremely long narrative. It consists, in fact, of different parts of other tales connected, and I doubt not that there is much more of it. It cannot escape the reader versed in fairy-lore that the incident of the water-maiden captured by her clothes is common to all European nations, but that it is especially Norse; while the adventures of the Wolverine, and indeed his whole character, are strangely suggestive of Loki, the Spirit of mere Mischief, who becomes evil. The fact that both Loki and Lox end their earthly career at a waterfall is very curious. The two also become, in wizard fashion, women at will. But it is chiefly in the extreme and wanton devilishness of their tricks that they are alike. Many other resemblances will suggest themselves to those who know the Eddas.

In the Passamaquoddy version of this tale, it is Seewitch, and not the Loon, who plays the part of the jealous husband at the end. The career of the Weasels *seems* to set forth the adventures of a couple of Indian Becky Sharps, very much in the spirit of an Indian Thackeray. The immorality of these damsels, the sponging of Marten, the deviltry of Lox, the servile follies and ferocious vindictiveness of the Loon, all seem to impress the composer of the tale as so many bubbles rising and falling on the sea of life, only remarkable for the sun-gleam of humor which they reflect. Outside these tales I know of nothing which so resembles the inner spirit of Aristophanes, Rabelais, and Shakespeare. I do not say that the genius of these great masters is in them, but their manner of seeing humor and wickedness combined. The cause of this lies in the cultivated stoicism with which every Indian trains himself to regard life. The inevitable result of such culture is always in some way a kind of humor, either grim or gay.

A re-perusal of the Eddas has impressed me with the remarkable resemblance of Lox, the Wolverine, to Loki. The story begins with the incident of a bird maiden caught by a trick, and married. This is distinctly Scandinavian. It is known in all lands, but the Norse made the most of it. Then the two girls sit and choose the kind of stars they will have. In the Eskimo (Rink, No. 8), two girls sitting on a beach, talking in the same way, seeing eagles' and whales' bones by them, declare that they would like to marry, the one an eagle, the other a whale, and both get their wishes. In the Norse legends stars are like human beings. Lox is pursued by a giant bird; Loki is chased by Thiassi, the giant, in eagle plumage. Again, in the Edda a giant eagle drags and trails Loki over woods and mountains, till he screams for pity. The Wolverine's race with a stone giant also recalls this race, the eagle being really one of the Jotuns, who were also all mountains and rocks. The Wolverine wizard becomes a girl, merely to make mischief. Loki took the form of a woman in Fensal, where he schemed to kill Balder. This is certainly a strange coincidence; for as in the Edda, Loki's becoming a woman led to all the subsequent tragedy and to his own doom, so in the Indian tale the very same thing caused the Wolverine to be chased to the high waterfall, where, owing to his own tricks, he perished, just as Loki came to grief in Franangursfors, the bright and glistening cataract. But the most remarkable point is that the general immoral character of the Lox, [Footnote: The coincidence of name amounts to nothing, as Lox is not, I believe, an Indian word.] or Wolverine, is so much like that of Loki, consisting of evil or mischief of the worst kind, always tempered by humor, which provokes a laugh. Now to find a similar and very singular character supported by several coincidences of incident is, if nothing more, at least very remarkable.

Loki is fire, and Lox, when killed in another tale, is revived by heat. He is carried off by the Culloo, or cloud, and let fall, typifying fire or lightning coming from a cloud. Again, in another story he dies for want of fire. And he twice dies by drowning; that is, the fire is quenched by water.

In one of the Passamaquoddy versions of this tale, which is, though less detailed, far superior in humor to the Micmac, the Loon is cheated by his two nephews, the *Assoops*, a species of loon, who steal the Weasels from him. He revenges himself, not by murdering, but by merely frightening them. He fills a bladder with blood, puts it under his shirt, and then stabs himself. They, thinking he is killed, lament, when he grandly comes to life, and is regarded as a great magician.

Of the Wolverine and the Wolves, or how Master Lox Froze to Death.

(Passamaquoddy.)

Of old times it came to pass that Master Lox, the Wolverine, or Indian Devil, he who was slain many times and as often rose from the dead, found himself deeply down in luck; for he was crossing a wide and dismal heath in winter-time, being but poorly provided in any way for travel. The wind blew like knives; the snow fell; sleet, frost, hail, and rain seemed to come all together in bad company, and still Lox was not happy, although he had no blanket or fur coat beyond his own. Yet this evil-minded jolly companion with every vice had one virtue, and that was that of all the beasts of the forest or devils in *P'lamkik'* he was the hardest hearted, toughest, and most unconquerable, being ever the first to fight and the last to give in, which even then he did not, never having done it and never intending to; whence it happened that he was greatly admired and made much of by all the blackguardly beasts of the backwoods,—wherein they differed but little from many among men.

Now as of all rowdies and rascals the wolves are the worst, we may well believe that it was with great joy Lox heard, as the darkness was coming on, a long, sad howl, far away, betokening the coming of a pack of these pleasant people; to which he raised his own voice in the wolf tongue,—for he was learned in many languages,—and soon was surrounded by some fifteen or sixteen lupine land loafers, who danced, rolling over, barking and biting one another, all for very joy at meeting with him. And the elder, he who was captain, or the sogmo, [Footnote: *Sogmo*, sagamore, a chief; the word corrupted into sachem.] said, "Peradventure thou wilt encamp with us this night, for it is ill for a gentleman to be alone, where he might encounter vulgar fellows." And Lox thanked him as if he were doing him a favor, and accepted the best of their dried meat, and took the highest place by their fire, and smoked the chief's choicest *tomawe* out of his best pipe, and all that with such vast condescension that the wolves grinned with delight.

And when they laid them down to sleep he that was the eldest, or the sogmo, bade the younger cover their guest Lox over very carefully. Now the tail of the wolf has broad-spreading, shaggy hair, and Lox, being sleepy, really thought it was a fur blanket that they spread, and though the night was cold enough to crack the rocks he threw the covering off; twice he did this, and the chief who looked after him, with all the rest, admired him greatly because he cared so little for the cold or for their care.

And having eaten after they arose, when in the morning they would wend away, the Wolf Chief said unto Lox, "Uncle, thou hast yet three days' hard travel before thee in a land where there is neither home, house, nor hearth, and it will be ill camping without a fire. Now I have a most approved and excellent charm, or spell, by which I can give thee three fires, but no more; yet will they suffice, one for each night, until thou gettest to thy journey's end. And this is the manner thereof: that thou shalt take unto thee dry wood, even such as men commonly burn, and thou shalt put them together, even as boys build little wigwams for sport, and then thou shalt jump over it. And truly, uncle, this is an approved and excellent charm of ripe antiquity, kept as a solemn secret among the wolves, and thou art the first not of our holy nation to whom it hath been given." So they parted.

Now Lox trudged on, and as he went westwards kept thinking of this great secret of the pious and peculiar people, and wondering if it were even as the Wolf said, or only a deceit; for however kindly he was treated by people, he always suspected that they mocked him to scorn, or were preparing to do so; for as he ever did this thing himself to every condition of mankind or beasts, he constantly awaited to have it done to him. And being curious withal, and anxious to see some new thing, he had not walked half an hour ere he said, "Tush! let me try it. Yea, and I will!" So building up the sticks, he jumped over them, and at once they caught fire and blazed up, and it came to pass even as the Wolf had prophesied.

Now having solaced himself by the heat, Lox went on. And anon it grew cold again, and he began to think how pleasant it was to be warm; and being, like most evil people, wanting in a corner of wisdom, he at once put the sticks together again and jumped over them, and as before there rose a blaze, and he was happy. And this was the second fire, and he had still three cold nights before him before he could reach his home.

And yet this Wolverine, who was so wise in all wickedness and witty in evil-doing, had not walked into the afternoon before he began to think of the third fire. "Truly," he said to himself, "who knows but the weather may take a turn to a thaw, and give us a warm night? Hum! ha! methinks by the look of the clouds the wind will soon be southwesterly. Have I not heard my grandmother say that such a color, even the red, meant something? I forget what, but it might be a warm change. Luck be on me, I will risk the odds." And, saying this, he set up the sticks again; and this was the last fire, though it was not even the first night.

And when he came after dark to the first camping place it grew cold in earnest. Howbeit Lox, thinking that what was good for once must be good forever, made him his little pile of sticks and jumped over them. It was of no avail. Finally, when he had jumped twenty or thirty times more, there arose a little smoke, and, having his heart cheered by this, he kept on jumping. Now it is said that there can be no smoke without fire, but this time it went not beyond smoke. Then Lox jumped again, and this time the Indian Devil came up within him, and he swore by it that he would jump till it blazed or burst. So he kept on, and yet there came no comfort, not even a spark; and being at last aweary he fell down in a swoon, and so froze to death. And so the Devil was dead, and that was the last of him for that turn; but I think he got over it, for he has been seen many a time since.

In two stories Lox (once as the *loup cervier*) is intimate with the wolves. Loki was the father of the wolves. Loki is fire: here Lox dies for want of fire. Since I wrote the foregoing, Mrs. W. Wallace Brown has learned that Lox is definitely the king or chief of the wolves, and that many Indians deny that he is really an animal at all, though he assumes the forms of certain animals. He is a spirit, and the Mischief Maker. It will be admitted that this brings the Lox much nearer to Loki.

It is said that when Glooskap left the world, as he took away with him the kings of all the animals, Lox went with him as king of the Wolves. This is an identification of him with Malsum, the Wolf, himself.

How Master Lox played a Trick on Mrs. Bear, who lost her eyesight and had her eyes opened.

(Micmac.)

Don't live with mean people if you can help it. They will turn your greatest sorrow to their own account if they can. Bad habit gets to be devilish second nature. One dead herring is not much, but one by one you may make such a heap of them as to stink out a whole village.

As it happened to old Mrs. Bear, who was easy as regarded people, And thought well of everybody, and trusted all. So she took in for A house-mate another old woman. Their wigwam was all by itself, and the next neighbor was so far off that he was not their neighbor at all, but that of some other folks.

One night the old women made up a fire, and lay down and went to sleep Indian-fashion,—*witkusoodijik*,—heads and points, so that both could lie with their back to the fire.

Now while they were sound asleep, Lox, the Wolverine, or Indian Devil, came prowling round. Some people say it was Hespuns, the Raccoon; and it is a fact that Master Coon can play a very close game of deviltry on his own account. However, this time it must have been Lox, as you can see by the tracks.

While they were both sound asleep Lox looked in. He found the old women asleep, heads and points, and at once saw his way to a neat little bit of mischief. So, going into the woods, he cut a fine long sapling-pole of *ow-bo-goos*, and poked one end of it into the fire till it was a burning coal. Then he touched the soles of Mrs. Bear; and she, waking, cried out to the other, "Take care! you are burning me!" which the other denied like a thunder-clap.

Then Master Lox carefully applied the end of the hot pole to the feet of the other woman. First she dreamed that she was walking on hot sand and roasting rocks in summer-time, and then that the Mohawks were cooking her at the death-fire; and then she woke up, and, seeing where she was, began to blame Mrs. Bear for it all, just as if she were a Mohawk.

Ah, yes. Well, Master Lox, seeing them fighting in a great rage, burst out laughing, so that he actually burst himself, and fell down dead with delight. It was a regular side-splitter. When my grandfather said *that* we *always* laughed.

In the morning, when the women came out, there lay a dead devil at the door. He must indeed have looked like a Raccoon this time; but whatever he was, they took him, skinned him, and dressed him for breakfast. Then the kettle was hung and the water boiled, and they popped him in. But as soon as it began to scald he began to come to life. In a minute he was all together again, alive and well, and with one good leap went clear of the kettle. Rushing out of the lodge, he grabbed his skin, which hung on a bush outside, put it on, and in ten seconds was safe in the greenwood. He just saved himself with a whole skin.

Now Master Lox had precious little time, you will say, to do any more mischief between his coming to life and running away; yet, short as the allowance was, he made a great deal of it. For even while jumping out his wits for wickedness came to him, and he just kicked the edge of the pot, so that it spilled all the scalding hot water into the fire, and threw up the ashes with a great splutter. They flew into the eyes of Dame Bear and blinded her.

Now this was hard on the old lady. She could not go out hunting, or set traps, or fish any more; and her partner, being mean, kept all the nice morsels for herself. Mrs. Bear only got the leanest and poorest of the meat, though there was plenty of the best. As my grandfather used to say, Mrs. Bear might have fared better if she had used her eyes earlier.

One day, when she was sitting alone in the wigwam, Mrs. Bear began to remember all she had ever heard about eyes, and it came into her head that sometimes they were closed up in such a way that clever folk could cut them open again. So she got her knife and sharpened it, and, carefully cutting a little, saw the light of day. Then she was glad indeed, and with a little more cutting found that she could see as well as ever. And as good luck does not come single, the very first thing she beheld was an abundance of beautiful fat venison, fish, and maple-sugar hung up overhead.

Dame Bear said nothing about her having recovered her eyesight. She watched all the cooking going on, and saw the daintiest dinner, which all went into one platter, and a very poor lot of bones and scraps placed in another. Then, when she was called to eat, she simply said to the other woman, who kept the best, "Well, you have done well for yourself!"

The other saw that Mrs. Bear had recovered her sight. She was frightened, for Dame Bear was by far the better man of the two. So she cried out, "Bless me! what a mistake I've made! Why, I gave you the wrong dish. You know, my dear sister, that I always give you the best because you are blind."

My grandfather said that after this Mrs. Bear kept her eyes open on people in two ways. And it always made us laugh, *that* did.

The Spirit of Mischief in these stories is sometimes Lox, the Wolverine; at others the Raccoon, or the Badger. Their adventures are interchangeable. But the character is always the same, and it is much like that of Loki. Now Loki is Fire; and it may be observed in this legend that the wolverine or raccoon comes to life when thrown into scalding water, and that in another narrative Lox dies for want of fire; in another he is pricked by thorns and stung by ants. "We must," says C. F. Keary, in his Mythology of the Eddas, "admit that the constant appearance of thorn-hedges, pricking with a sleep-thorn (Lox's thorns are his bed), in German and Norse legends, is a mythical way of expressing the idea of the funeral *fire*."

The first thing that the Lox-Raccoon does in this tale, on coming to life, is to upset a pot into the ashes for mischief's sake. And the very first exploit of the magic deer, made by the evil spirits and sorcerers in the Kalevala (Runes XIII.), is thus set forth:—

> "Then the Husi stag went bounding,
> Bounding to the land of Pohja,
> Till he reached the fields of Lapland.
> Passing there before a cabin (*goatte*),
> With a single kick while running
>
> He upset the boiling kettle,
> So that all the meat went rolling,
> Rolling ruined in the ashes,
> And the soup upon the hearth-stone."

This is, in both cases, the very first act of an animal, created and living only for mischief, on coming to a magic or artificial life.

The legends of Finland and Lapland are as important as the Norse to explain the origin of our Indian mythology.

How Lox came to Grief by trying to catch a Salmon.

(Passamaquoddy.)

Kusk, the Crane, had two brothers. One of these was Lox, the Wolverine, or Indian Devil. And his other brother was Koskomines, the Blue Jay.

Kusk was very lazy, and one day, being hungry, thought he would go and get a dinner from Lox. Lox served him a kind of pudding-soup in a broad, flat platter. Poor Kusk could hardly get a mouthful, while Lox hipped it all up with ease.

Soon after, Kusk made a fine soup, and invited Lox to dinner. This he served up in a jug, a long cylinder. None of it had Lox. Kusk ate it all.

The next day the pair went to dine with Blue Jay. Blue Jay said, "Wait till I get our food." Then he ran out on a bough of a tree which spread over a river, and in a minute fished out a large salmon. "Truly," thought Lox, "that is easy to do, and I can do it."

So the next day he invited the Blue Jay and Crane to feed with him. Then he, too, ran down to the river and out on a tree, and, seeing a fine salmon, caught at it with his claws. But he had not learned the art, and so fell into the river, and was swept away by the rushing current.

This is one of AEsop's fables Indianized and oddly eked out with a fragment from a myth attributed to both Manobozho and the Wabanaki Rabbit. As the Wolverine has a great resemblance to Loki, it may be here observed that, while he dies in trying to catch a salmon, "Loki, in the likeness of a salmon, cast himself into the waterfall of Franangr." which was effectively his last act in life before being captured by the gods, as told in the Edda. Otter, in the Edda, caught a salmon, and was then caught by Loki. There is, of course, great confusion here, but the Indian tale is a mere fragment, carelessly pieced and indifferently told. Lox is, like Loki, *fire* and perishes by water.

How Master Lox as a Raccoon killed the Bear and the Black Cats and performed other Notable Feats of Skill, all to his Great Discredit.

(Passamaquoddy.)

Now of old time there is a tale of Hespuns, the Raccoon, according to the Passamaquoddy Indians, but by another record it is Master Lox, to whom all Indian deviltry truly belongs. And this is the story. One fine morning Master Lox started off as a Raccoon; [Footnote: The same stories are attributed to the Wolverine, Badger, and Raccoon.] for he walked the earth in divers disguises, to take his usual roundabouts, and as he went he saw a huge bear, as the manuscript reads, "right straight ahead of him."

Now the old Bear was very glad, to see the Raccoon, for he had made up his mind to kill him at once if he could: firstly, to punish him for his sins; and secondly, to eat him for breakfast. Then the Raccoon ran into a hollow tree, the Bear following, and beginning to root it up.

Now the Coon saw that in a few minutes the tree would go and he be gone. But he began to sing as if he did not care a bean, and said, "All the digging and pushing this tree will never catch me. Push your way in backwards, and then I must yield and die. But that you cannot do, since the hole is too small for you." Then Mooin, the Bruin, hearing this, believed it, but saw that he could easily enlarge the hole, which he did, and so put himself in arrear; upon which the Raccoon seized him, and held on till he was slain. [Footnote: As Reynard, the Fox, won the victory in the famous tale versified by Goethe. Vide *Reinecke Fuchs*.]

Then he crawled out of the tree, and, having made himself a fine pair Of mittens out of the Bear's skin, started off again, and soon saw a wigwam from which rose a smoke, and, walking in, he found a family of *Begemkessisek*, or Black Cats. So, greeting them, he said, "Young folks, comb me down and make me nice, and I will give you these beautiful bear-skin mittens." So the little Black Cats combed him down, and parted his hair, and brushed his tail, and while they were doing this he fell asleep; and they, being very hungry, took the fresh bear-skin mitts, and scraped them all up, and cooked and ate them. Then the Coon, waking up, looked very angry at them, and said in an awful voice, "Where are my bear-skin mitts?" And they, in great fear, replied, "Please, sir, we cooked and ate them." Then the Coon flew at them and strangled them every one, all except the youngest, who, since he could not speak as yet, the Raccoon, or Lox, thought could not tell of him. Then, for a great joke, he took all the little dead creatures and set them up by the road-side in a row; as it was a cold day they all froze stiff, and then he put a stick across their jaws, so that the little Black Cats looked as if they were laughing for joy. Then he made off at full speed.

Soon the father, the old Black Cat, came home, and, seeing his children all grinning at him, he said, "How glad the dear little things are to see me." But as none moved he saw that something was wrong, and his joy soon changed to sorrow. [Footnote: This trick is so precisely in the style of Lox that it seems a gross mistake to attribute it to the Raccoon. Those who have seen a wild cat grin will appreciate the humor of Lox on this occasion.]

Then the youngest Black Cat, the baby, came out of some hole where he had hid himself. Now the baby was too young to speak, but he was very clever, and, picking up a piece of charcoal, he made a mark from the end of his mouth around his cheek. [Footnote: The reader cannot fail to recall the peculiar mustache of the Raccoon so well indicated by the infant artist.] Then the father cried, "Ah, *now* I know who it was,—the Raccoon, as sure as I live!" And he started after him in hot pursuit.

Soon the Raccoon saw the fierce Black Cat, as an Indian, coming after him with a club. And, looking at him, he said, "No club can kill me; nothing but a bulrush or cat-tail can take my life." Then the Black Cat, who knew where to get one, galloped off to a swamp, and, having got a large cat-tail, came to the Coon and hit him hard with it. It burst and spread all over the Raccoon's head, and, being wet, the fuzz stuck to him. And the Black Cat, thinking it was the Coon's brains and all out, went his way.

The Raccoon lay quite still till his foe was gone, and then went on his travels. Now he was a great magician, though little to other folks' good. And he came to a place where there were many women nursing their babes, and said, "This is but a slow way you have of raising children." To which the good women replied, "How else should we raise them?" Then he answered, "I will show you how we do in our country. When we want them to grow fast, we dip them into cold water over night. Just lend me one, and I will show you how to raise them in a hurry." They gave him one: he took it to the river, and, cutting a hole in the ice, put the child into it. The next morning he went to the place, and took out a full-grown man, alive and well. The women were indeed astonished at this. All hastened to put their babes that night under the ice, and then the Raccoon rushed away. So they all died.

Then he came to another camp, where many women with fine stuff and furs were making bags. "That is a very slow way you have of working," he said to the goodwives. "In our country we cook them under the ashes. Let me see the stuff and show you how!" They gave him a piece: he put it under the hot coals and ashes, and in a few minutes drew out from them a beautiful bag. Then they all hurried to put their cloth under the fire. Just then he left in haste. And when they drew the stuff out it was scorched or burned, and all spoiled.

Then he came to a great river, and did not know how to get across. He saw on the bank an old *Wiwillmekq'*, a strange worm which is like a horned, alligator; but he was blind. "Grandfather," said the Raccoon, "carry me over the lake." "Yes, my grandson," said the Wiwillmekq', and away he swam; the Ravens and Crows above began to ridicule them. "What are those birds saying?" inquired the Old One. "Oh, they are crying to you to hurry, hurry, for your life, with that Raccoon!" So the Wiwillmekq', not seeing land ahead, hurried with such speed that the Raccoon made him run his head and half his body into the bank, and then jumped off and left him. But whether the Wiwillmekq' ever got out again is more than he ever troubled himself to know.

So he went on till he came to some Black Berries, and said, "Berries, how would you agree with me if I should eat you?" "Badly indeed, Master Coon," they replied, "for we are Choke-berries." "Choke-berries, indeed! Then I will have none of you." And then further he found on some bushes, Rice-berries. "Berries," he cried, "how would you agree with me if I should eat you?" "We should make you itch, for we are Itch-berries." "Ah, that is what I like," he replied, and so ate his fill. Then as he went on he felt very uneasy: he seemed to be tormented with prickles, he scratched and scratched, but it did not help or cure. So he rubbed himself on a ragged rock; he slid up and down it till the hair came off.

Now the Raccoon is bare or has little fur where he scratched himself, to this very day. This story is at an end.

This story is from the Passamaquoddy Indian-English collection made for me by Louis Mitchell. In the original, the same incident of boiling the hero in a kettle and of his springing out of it occurs as in the tale of Mrs. Bear and the Raccoon. This I have here omitted. The Mephistophelian and mocking character of Lox is strongly shown when he says, "Nothing but a cat-tail or bulrush can kill me," this being evidently an allusion to Glooskap. This is to an Indian much like blasphemy. Lox, or Raccoon, or Badger,—for they are all the same,—in his journeyings after mere mischief reminds us of an Indian Tyl Eulenspiegel. But the atrocious nature of his jokes is like nothing else, unless it be indeed the homicide Punch. It is the indomitable nature of both which commends them respectively to the Englishman and to the Red Indian. In this tale Lox appears as the spirit of fire by drawing a bag from it. The itching or pricking from which he suffers is also significant of that element, as appears, according to Keary, in many Norse, etc., legends.

In the Seneca tale of the Mischief Maker, the Berries are distinctly declared to have souls.

How Lox deceived the Ducks, cheated the Chief, and beguiled the Bear.

(Micmac and Passamaquoddy.)

Somewhere in the forest lived Lox, with a small boy, his brother. When winter came they went far into the woods to hunt. And going on, they reached at last a very large and beautiful lake. It was covered with water-fowl. There were wild geese and brant, black ducks and wood-ducks, and all the smaller kinds down to teal and whistlers.

The small boy was delighted to see so much game. He eagerly asked his brother how he meant to catch them. He answered, "We must first go to work and build a large wigwam. It must be very strong, with a heavy, solid door." This was done; and Lox, being a great magician, thus arranged his plans for taking the wild-fowl. He sent the boy out to a point of land, where he was to cry to the birds and tell them that his brother wished to give them a kingly reception. (*Nakamit*, to act the king.) He told them their king had come. Then Lox, arraying himself grandly, sat with dignity next the door, with his eyes closed, as if in great state. Then the little boy shouted that they might enter and hear what the great sagamore had to say. They flocked in, and took their seats in the order of their size. The Wild Geese came nearest and sat down, then the Ducks, and so on to the smallest, who sat nearest the door. Last of all came the boy, who entering also sat down by the door, closed it, and held it fast. So the little birds, *altumabedajik* (M.), sat next to him.

Then they were all told "*Spegwedajik!*" "Shut your eyes!" and were directed to keep them closed for their very lives, until directed to open them again. Unless they did this first, their eyes would be blinded forever when they beheld their king in all his magnificence. So they sat in silence. Then the sorcerer, stepping softly, took them one by one, grasping each tightly by the wings, and ere the bird knew what he was about it had its head crushed between his teeth. And so without noise or fluttering he killed all the Wild Geese and Brant and Black Ducks. Then the little boy began to pity the poor small wild-fowl. He thought it was a shame to kill so many, having already more than they needed. So stooping down, he whispered to a very little bird to open its eyes. It did so, but very cautiously indeed, for fear of being blinded.

Great was his horror to see what Lox was doing! He screamed, "*Kedumeds'lk!*" "We are all being killed!" Then they opened their eyes, and flew about in the utmost confusion, screaming loudly in terror. The little boy dropped down as if he had been knocked over in the confusion, so that the door flew wide open, and the birds, rushing over him, began to, escape, while Lox in a rage continued to seize them and kill them with his teeth. Then the little boy, to avoid suspicion, grasped the last fugitive by the legs and held him fast. But he was suspected all the same by the wily sorcerer, who caught him up roughly, and would have beaten him cruelly but that he earnestly protested that the birds knocked him down and forced the door open, and that he could by no means help it: which being somewhat slowly believed, he was forgiven, and they began to pluck and dress the game. The giblets were preserved, the fowls sliced and dried and laid by for the winter's store.

Then having plenty of provisions, Lox gave a feast. Among the guests were Marten and Mahtigwess, the Rabbit, who talked together for a long time in the most confidential manner, the Rabbit confiding and the Marten attending to him.

Now while this conversation had been going on, Lox, who was deeply addicted to all kinds of roguery and mischief, had listened to it with interest. And when the two little guests had ceased he asked them where their village was, and who lived in it. Then he was told that all the largest animals had their homes there: the bear, caribou or reindeer, deer, wolf, wild cat, to say nothing of squirrels and mice. And having got them to show him the way, he some time after turned himself into a young woman of great beauty, or at least disguised himself like one, and going to the village married the young chief. And having left little Marten alone in a hollow tree outside the village, the boy, getting hungry, began to howl for food; which the villagers hearing were in a great fright. But the young chiefs wife, or the magician Lox, soon explained to them what it meant. "It is," she-he said, "*Owoolakumooejit*, the Spirit of Famine. He is grim and gaunt; hear how he howls for food! Woe be unto you, should he reach this village! Ah, I remember only too well what happened when he once came among us. Horror! starvation!"

"Can you drive him back?" cried all the villagers.

"Yes, 'tis in my power. Do but give me the well-tanned hide of a yearling moose and a good supply of moose-tallow, [Footnote: A great delicacy among these semi-Arctic Indians.] then the noise will cease." And seizing it, and howling furiously the name of his brother after a fashion which no one could understand,—*Aa-chowwa'n*!—and bidding him begone, he rushed out into the night, until he came to Marten, to whom he gave the food, and, wrapping him up well in the moose-skin, bade him wait a while. And the villagers thought the chief's wife was indeed a very great conjurer.

And then she-he announced that a child would soon be born. And when the day came Badger handed out a bundle, and said that the babe was in it. "*Noolmusugakelaimadijul*," "They kiss it outside the blanket." But when the chief opened it what he found therein was the dried, withered embryo of a moose-calf. In a great rage he flung it into the fire, and all rushed headlong in a furious pack to catch Badger. They saw him and Marten rushing to the lake. They pursued him, but when he reached the bank the wily sorcerer cast in a stick; it turned into a canoe, and long ere the infuriated villagers could reach them they were on the opposite shore and in the woods.

Now it came to pass one day that as Lox sat on a log a bear came by, who, being a sociable fellow, sat down by him and smoked a pipe. While they were talking a gull flew over, and inadvertently offered to Lox what he considered, or affected to consider, as a great insult. And wiping the insult off, Lox cried to the Gull, "Oh, ungrateful and insolent creature, is this the way you reward me for having made you white!"

Now the Bear would always be white if he could, for the White Bear (*wabeyu mooin*) is the aristocrat of Beardom. So he eagerly cried, "Ha! did you make the Gull white?"

"Indeed I did," replied Lox. "And this is what I get for it."

"Could you, my dear friend,—could you make *me* white?"

Then Lox saw his way, and replied that he could indeed, but that it would be a long and agonizing process; Mooin might die of it. To be sure the Gull stood it, but could a Bear?

Now the Bear, who had a frame as hard as a rock, felt sure that he could endure anything that a gull could, especially to become a white bear. So, with much ceremony, the Great Enchanter went to work. He built a strong wigwam, three feet high, of stones, and having put the Bear into it he cast in red-hot stones, and poured water on them through a small hole in the roof. Erelong the Bear was in a terrible steam.

"Ah, Doctor Lox," he cried, "this is awfully hot! I fear I am dying!"

"Courage," said Lox; "this is nothing. The Gull had it twice as hot."

"Can't stand it any more, doctor. *O-o-o-oh*!"

Doctor Lox threw in more hot stones and poured more water on them. The Bear yelled.

"Let me out! *O-o-h*! let me out! *O-o-o-oh*!"

So he came bursting through the door. The doctor examined him critically.

Now there is on an old bear a small white or light spot on his upper breast, which he cannot see. [Footnote: This is very white on the Japanese bears.] And Doctor Lox, looking at this, said,—

"What a pity! You came out just as you were beginning to turn white. Here is the first spot. Five minutes more and you'd have been a white bear. Ah, you haven't the pluck of a gull; that I can see."

Now the Bear was mortified and disappointed. He had not seen the spot, so he asked Lox if it was really there.

"Wait a minute," said the doctor. He led the Bear to a pool and made him look in. Sure enough, the spot was there. Then he asked if they could not begin again.

"Certainly we can," replied the doctor. "But it will be much hotter and harder and longer this time. Don't try it if you feel afraid, and don't blame *me* if you die of it."

The Bear went in again, but he never came out alive. The doctor had roast bear meat all that winter, and much bear's oil. He gave some of the oil to his younger brother. The boy took it in a measure. Going along the creek, he saw a Muskrat (*Keuchus*, Pass.). He said to the Muskrat, "If you can harden this oil for me, I will give you half." The Muskrat made it as hard as ice. The boy said, "If my brother comes and asks you to do this for him, do you keep it all." And, returning, he showed the oil thus hardened to his brother, who, taking a large measure of it, went to the Muskrat and asked him to harden it. The Muskrat indeed took the dish and swam away with it, and never returned.

Then the elder, vexed with the younger, and remembering the ducks in the wigwam, and believing now that he had indeed been cheated, slew him.

[Illustration: THE INDIAN BOY AND THE MUSK-RAT. SEEPS, THE DUCK.]

This confused and strange story is manifestly pieced together out of several others, each of which have incidents in common. A part of it is very ancient. Firstly, the inveigling the ducks into the wigwam is found in the Eskimo tale of Avurungnak (Rink, p. 177). The Eskimo is told by a sorcerer to let the seabirds into the tent, and not to begin to kill them till the tent is full. He disobeys, and a part of them escape. In Schoolcraft's Hiawatha Legends, Manobozho gets the mysterious oil which ends the foregoing story from a fish. He fattens all the animals in the world with it, and the amount which they consume is the present measure of their fatness. When this ceremony is over, he inveigles all the birds into his power by telling them to shut their eyes. At last a small duck, the diver, suspecting something, opens one eye, and gives the alarm.

The sorcerer's passing himself off for a woman and the trick of the moose abortion occurs in three tales, but it is most completely given in this. To this point the narrative follows the Micmac, Passamaquoddy, and Chippewa versions. After the tale of the chief is at an end it is entirely Passamaquoddy; but of the latter I have two versions, one from Tomah Josephs and one from Mrs. W. Wallace Brown.

I can see no sense in the account of the bear's oil hardened by ice, but that oil is an essential part of the duck story appears from the Chippewa legend (Hiawatha L. p. 30). In the latter it is represented as giving size to those who partake of it.

The Mischief Maker. A Tradition of the Origin of the Mythology of the Senecas. A Lox Legend.

(Seneca.)

An Indian mischief maker was once roving about. He saw that he was approaching a village, and said, "How can I attract attention?"

Seeing two girls coming from the wigwams, he pulled up a wild plum-bush and placed it upon his head, the roots clasping about his chin.

It will be strange to see a plum-tree on my head, bearing ripe fruit. These girls will want trees also. So he thought. The tree shook as he walked, and many plums fell to the ground.

The girls wondered greatly at the strange man with the tree. They admired it, and said they, too, would like to be always supplied with fruit in such a manner.

"I can manage that," he replied. So he pulled up a bush for each, and planted them on their heads. The plums were delicious, and grew as fast as they were plucked; and the girls stepped along proudly, for they had something which certainly no girls ever had before.

The Mischief Maker went on to the village. On the way he reflected, "There is no such thing in the world as a plum-tree growing on a man's head. I will take this off." He did so, and, on entering the village, gave a loud signal (a whoop). All the people listened, and the chiefs sent messengers to inquire what news he brought.

He said, "I have seen a very strange sight. As I was coming hither I saw two girls walking. Trees grew on their heads; the boughs were covered with plums, and the roots, which came through their hair, were fastened about their necks. They were beautiful, and seemed to be very happy."

"We will go and see them!" cried the women.

They had not gone far before they saw one of the girls lying on the ground, while the other pulled at the tree on her head. The roots gave way and the tree came out, but all the hair came with it also. Then the other lay down, and her friend in turn pulled the tree from her head. They were very angry, and said, "If we meet with the man who played us this trick we will punish him."

When the women who had gathered round them learned how the trees had been fastened by magic upon the girls' heads, they returned to the village, resolved to chastise the man who had played the trick. But when they reached home he was gone.

Gone far and away to another town. Before reaching it he sat down, and said, "Now I will show these people also what I can do." He went a little distance into the woods, where he found a wigwam. A woman with a bucket in her hand came from it. He saw that as she passed along she reached high with one hand, and felt her way by a thong which ran from tree to tree till it ended at a spring of cold water. She went on, filled her bucket, and so returned. Then another woman after her did the same.

"They must be blind," said the Mischief Maker. "I will have some fun with them." And so it was. There lived in that wigwam five blind sisters.

Then he untied the thong from the tree near the spring and fastened it to another, where there was no water. Then a third blind woman came with a bucket, and followed the line to the end, but found no water. She returned to the wigwam, and said, "The spring is dried up."

"No, it isn't," replied one of the sisters, who was stirring pudding over the fire. "You say that because you are too lazy to bring water; you never work. Here, do you stir the pudding, and let me go for water."

The Mischief Maker heard all this, and made haste to tie the end of the thong where it belonged. The blind woman filled her bucket, and when she returned said to her sister, "There, you lazy creature, I found the water!"

By this time the Mischief Maker was in the house, and slipping quietly up to the fire he dipped out some of the pudding and threw it, scalding hot, into the face of the scolding woman, who cried in a rage,—

"You throw hot pudding at me, do you?"

"No, I did not throw any at you," replied the sister.

Then the Mischief Maker threw some into *her* face. She screamed, being very angry.

"You mean thing! You threw hot pudding at me, when I did you no harm."

"I didn't throw any!" said the other, in a rage.

"Yes, you *did*, you mean thing!"

"Stop! stop!" cried the others. Just then hot pudding flew in all their faces; they had a terrible quarrel, and the Mischief Maker left them to settle it among themselves as they could.

He entered the village near by, and gave the usual signal for news. The runners came out and met him; the chiefs and all the people assembled, lining the path on both sides for a long way. They asked, "What news do you bring?"

He replied, "I come from at village where there is great distress. A pestilence visited the people. The medicine man could not cure the sick; till I came there was no remedy; the tribe was becoming very small. But I told them the remedy, and now they are getting well. I have come to tell you to prepare for the pestilence: it will soon be here; it is flying like the wind, and there is only one remedy."

"What is it? what is it? what is it?" interrupted the people.

He answered, "Every man must embrace the woman who is next to him at this very instant; kiss her, quick, immediately!"

They all did so on the spot, he with the rest.

As he was leaving them an elderly man came to him and whispered, "Are you going to do this thing again at the next village? If you are I should like to be on hand. I didn't get any girl myself here. The woman I went for dodged me, and said she had rather have the pestilence, and death too, than have me kiss her. Is the operation to be repeated?"

The Mischief Maker said that it certainly would be, about the middle of the morrow forenoon.

"Then I will start now," said the middle-aged man, "for I am lame, and it will take me all night to get there."

So he hurried on, and at daylight entered the village. He found a wigwam, by which several beautiful Indian girls were pounding corn in a great wooden mortar. He sat down by them. He could hardly take his eyes from them, they were so charming, and they wondered at his strange behavior.

He talked with them, and said, "My eyelids quiver, and by that I know that some great and strange news will soon be brought to this tribe. Hark!"—here he moved up towards the one whom he most admired,—"did you not hear a signal?"

"No," they replied.

The middle-aged man became very uneasy. Suddenly the girls gave a cry, and dropped their corn pestles. A voice was heard afar; the runners leaped and flew, the chiefs and people went forth. With them went the girls and the middle-aged man, who took great pains to keep very near his chosen one, so as to lose no time in applying the remedy for the pestilence when the Mischief Maker should give the signal. He was determined that a life should not be lost if he could prevent it.

The Stranger went through his story as at the other village. The people became very much excited. They cried, out to know the remedy, and the old bachelor drew nearer to the pretty girl.

"The only remedy for the pestilence is for every woman *to knock down the man who is nearest her.*"

The women began to knock down, and the first to fall was the too familiar old bachelor. So the Mischief Maker waited no longer than to see the whole town in one general and bitter fight, tooth and nail, tomahawk and scalper, and then ran at the top of his speed far away and fleet, to find another village. Then the people, finding they had been tricked, said, as people generally do on such occasions, "If we had that fellow here, wouldn't we pay him up for this?"

The Mischief Maker was greatly pleased at his success. It was nearly dark when he stopped, and said, "I will not enter the next village to-night; I will camp here in the woods." So he had piled up logs for a fire, and was just about to strike a light, when he saw a stranger approaching. "Camp with me here over night," said the Mischief Maker, "and we will go to the village in the morning."

So they ate and smoked their pipes, and told stories till it was very late. But the stranger did not seem to tire; nay, he even proposed to tell stories all night long. The Mischief Maker looked at him aslant.

"My friend," he said, "can you tell me of what wood my back-log is?"

"Hickory?" inquired the stranger.

"No, not hickory."

"Maple?"

"No, not maple."

"White oak?"

"No, not white oak."

"Black walnut?"

"No, not black walnut."

"Moosewood?"

"No, not moosewood."

"Ash?"

"No, not ash."

"Pine?"

"No, not pine."

"Cedar?"

"No, not cedar."

"Birch?"

The stranger began to yawn, but he kept on guessing. Then his head nodded. By the time he had found out that it was slippery elm he was sound asleep.

"This fellow deserves punishment," remarked the Mischief Maker. "He is an enemy to mankind." Here he adroitly put some sticky clay on the sleeper's eyes, and departed. When the stranger awoke he thought himself still fast asleep in darkness, and then that he was blind.

"If ever I meet with that fellow again," he said, "I'll punish him!"

The Mischief Maker played so many pranks that all the tribes sent out runners to catch him. He heard their whoops in every forest. He knew that he was being hunted down. He hurried on, and once at night hid in a cave under a rock. The runners did not quite overtake him, but they saw that his tracks were fresh, and thought they might catch him in the morning. In the morning he was up and far away long before they awoke. The next night he hid again in a hollow log. In the middle of the afternoon of the next day he heard the whoops of the pursuers very near, and knew that they were gaining fast on him. He climbed a thickly limbed tree, and hid in the top. Here the runners lost his track, because he had broken the weeds and bushes down beyond the tree, as if he had gone further on. They ran for a long distance. Then they returned, and camped and built a fire under the tree.

The smoke crept up among the branches and curled above, and rose in a straight column to the sky. The fugitive sailed away on the smoke, going up and up,—past beautiful lakes and hunting-grounds stocked with deer, large fields of corn and beans, tobacco and squashes; past great companies of handsome Indians, whose wigwams were hung full of dried venison and bear's meat. And so he went on and up to the wig-wam of the Great Chief.

Here he rested. He remained for a hundred moons observing the customs of the people and learning their language. One morning the Great Chief told him that he must return to his own people. He disliked to do this, for he was very happy in the new place. The Chief said, "These are the happy hunting grounds. We have admitted you that you may know how and what to teach your people, that they may get here. Go, and if you do what I tell you, you may return to remain forever. You have not been allowed to come here to remain, but only to observe. When you come again, you shall join us in all things. You shall hunt and fish then, and have whatever you wish. But return now, and teach what you have learned here."

A cloud of smoke in the form of a great eagle came to him, and, seated on its back, he was borne down to the top of the tree from which he had risen. He opened his eyes. The sun was shining. His pursuers had gone away. He descended and traveled on. His mind was filled with what he had seen. He said, "I will no longer play tricks, but tell the people about what I learned in the happy hunting-grounds."

After a long journey he drew near a village. He gave the common signal. Runners came to meet him. The head chief and all the people came to hear. He was asked, "What news do you bring us?"

He said, "I that was the Mischief Maker am the Peace Maker now. The Great Spirit took me to the happy hunting-grounds, and I am sent back to tell you how to get there." Then the Peace Maker described all he had seen. The people built a great fire and danced around it, and shouted as they had never done before. Then he said, "This is the message I bring you."

So the people sat in a great circle round the fire and listened. He spoke:—

"The Great Spirit is unseen, but he is about us. He will not forsake us. He rules all things for us. He will take care of us. He told me that we should return thanks to him, for he changes the seasons, and makes corn and beans and squashes grow for us. He is displeased when we kill our brothers. He hopes that we will not forget him. He will never die. His name is *Ha-wen-ni-yu,*—the Ruler. He bids us keep away from his wicked brother, whose name is *Ha-ne-go-ate-geh*, the Evil-Minded. He is very bad. He brings pestilence and fevers, and lizards and poisonous weeds. He destroys peace, and brings war. Ha-wen-ni-yu will care for us if we trust in him. Obey his words, and Ha-ne-go-ate-geh will never harm us.

The Great Spirit, has messengers, who aid him in his work. They watch over the people. They take care of the mother and her new-born babe, that they receive no harm; they watch over those whom the Evil-Minded has troubled with disease. The Evil-Minded has messengers who do his work. They scatter pestilence, and whisper in our ears, and tell us to go against Ha-wen-ni-yu.

The Great Spirit has messengers. Heno has a pouch filled with thunderbolts. Heno gathers the clouds and sends the rain. He is a friend to the corn and beans and squashes. He also punishes witches and evil persons. Pray to Heno when you plant, and thank him when you gather your crop. Pray also to Ha-wen-ni-yu, who will send Heno to care for you. Let Heno be called Grandfather.

Ga-oh is the Spirit of the Winds. He moves the winds, but he is chained to a rock. The winds trouble him, and he tries very hard to get free. When he struggles the winds are forced away from him, and they blow upon the earth. Sometimes he suffers terrible pain, and then his struggles are violent. This makes the winds wild, and they do damage on the earth. Then he feels better and goes to sleep, and the winds become quiet also.

There is a spirit for the corn, another for beans, another for squashes. They are sisters, and are very kind to each other. They dwell together, and live in the fields. They shall be known as *De-o-ha-ka*,—the keepers of our life.

There are spirits in the water, in fire, in all the trees and berries, in herbs and in tobacco, in the grass. They assist the Great Spirit.

Always return thanks to *Ho-noh-che-noh-keh*, the Guardian Spirits.

Ha-ne-go-ate-geh has messengers. These are the spirits of disease, of fever, of witches, weeds, and murder. But the Great Spirit will keep them away from his children.

This is the message I bring from the happy hunting-grounds. Obey these words, and the Great Spirit will give you a place there."

So Peace Maker taught the people. They threw tobacco on the fire, according to his instructions, and on the column of its smoke he was borne away to the happy hunting-grounds. And the people danced and sang around the dying embers of the council fire.

This is probably an ancient legend with a modern moral. The idea of an Indian Tyl Eulenspiegel going about the country making mischief recalls a great part of the adventures of Hiawatha or Manobozho; in fact, it could not fail to suggest itself to a believer in Shamanism, or pow-wow, according to which evil spirits and men like them are continually teasing mankind, out of sheer malice. The reform of the wicked man, under the influence of the "Great Spirit," is of later days. I do not believe that the idea of a Great Spirit, in the sense in which it is generally used by Indians, or is attributed to them, was ever known till learned from the whites. Nothing is more natural than that during the two hundred years past intelligent Indians, who felt that there were many evils in the old barbaric state, yet who were still under the influence of its myths and poetry, should have made up legends like this purporting to be revelations. There is one of the kind given in the Hiawatha Legend, as "Eroneniera, an Indian visit to the Great Spirit," which bears on its face every mark of modern manufacture for a purpose. For these very reasons, however, the tale here given is of great interest to the impartial historian. I am indebted for it to the kindness of Colonel T. Wentworth Higginson. This is the only story in my collection of which I cannot give the name and residence of the original Indian narrator.

In the first part we have in the *Mischief Maker* the same character or principle who appears as Lox, the Wolverine, the Raccoon, and Badger among the Wabanaki. The setting the blind women together by the ears, and the dashing of hot pudding, soup, or water in their faces, is another form of a Lox story, which occurs again in the Kalevala. But the entire spirit of the tricks is that of Lox, as those of Lox are like those of Loki. The Rev. D. Moncure Conway once said to me, as Miss E. Robins has also said in an article in the Atlantic Monthly, that it is only in the Norse mythology that the Evil One, or devil, is represented as growing up from or inspired solely by reckless wanton *mischief*,—the mischief of a bad boy or a monkey. But the very same is as true of so much of a devil as there is in the Wabanaki mythology. It is as a grotesque shadow of Loki, but still it is his. The Germans say the devil is God's ape; the Indian Lox is the Norse devil's.

How Lox told a Lie.

(Passamaquoddy.)

Lox had a brother, who had married a red squaw. When she was touched the red color rubbed off. The brother kept this wife in a box.

One day, returning, the brother saw that Lox had red fingers. "Aha!" he cried, in a rage, "you have taken my wife out of the box." But Lox denied it, so that his brother believed him.

The next time the husband returned, Lox's fingers were again red. And again he was accused, and once more he denied it. But as he swore with all his might that he was innocent, something, as if on the floor, laughed, and said, "You lie. I was with you; I helped you."

Lox thought it was his right foot. So he cut off the toes, and then the foot, but the accusation continued. Thinking it was the other foot, he cut that off; yet as the testimony was continued, he found that it was *Taloose*, even he himself, the bodily offender in person, testifying against his lying soul. So in a rage he struck himself such a blow with his war-club that he fell dead. I cannot give in full all the adventures of Lox. I may, however, observe one thing of great importance. Lox, in these tales, is the Evil Principle, that is, a giant by birth. His two feet in this story are male and female; they talk as if they were human. In the Edda, a giant's two feet beget together a six-headed son (Vafthrudnismal):—

"Foot with foot begot
Of that wise Jotun,
A six-headed son."

This six-headed son reappears as a demon in the Passamaquoddy tale of the Three Strong Men.

Tuloose, literally translated, is the phallus. The red squaw refers to the Newfoundland Indians, covered with red ochre. They are believed to be now extinct.

THE AMAZING ADVENTURES OF MASTER RABBIT

WITH THE OTTER, THE WOODPECKER GIRLS, AND MOOIN THE BEAR

ALSO A FULL ACCOUNT OF THE FAMOUS CHASE, IN WHICH HE FOOLED LUSIFEE, THE WILD CAT

I. How Master Rabbit sought to rival Keeoony, the Otter.

Of old times, *Mahtigwess*, the Rabbit, who is called in the Micmac tongue *Ableegumooch*, lived with his grandmother, waiting for better times; and truly he found it a hard matter in midwinter, when ice was on the river and snow was on the plain, to provide even for his small household. And running through the forest one day he found a lonely wigwam, and he that dwelt therein was *Keeoony*, the Otter. The lodge was on the bank of a river, and a smooth road of ice slanted from the door down to the water. And the Otter made him welcome, and directed his housekeeper to get ready to cook; saying which, he took the hooks on which he was wont to string fish when he had them, and went to fetch a mess for dinner. Placing himself on the top of the slide, he coasted in and under the water, and then came out with a great bunch of eels, which were soon cooked, and on which they dined.

"By my life," thought Master Rabbit, "but that is an easy way of getting a living! Truly these fishing-folk have fine fare, and cheap! Cannot I, who am so clever, do as well as this mere Otter? Of course I can. Why not?" Thereupon he grew so confident of himself as to invite the Otter to dine with him—*adamadusk ketkewop*—on the third day after that, and so went home.

"Come on!" he said to his grandmother the next morning; "let us remove our wigwam down to the lake." So they removed; and he selected a site such as the Otter had chosen for his home, and the weather being cold he made a road of ice, or a coast, down from his door to the water, and all was well. Then the guest came at the time set, and Rabbit, calling his grandmother, bade her get ready to cook a dinner. "But what am I to cook, grandson?" inquired the old dame.

"Truly I will see to that," said he, and made him a *nabogun*, or stick to string eels. Then going to the ice path, he tried to slide like one skilled in the art, but indeed with little luck, for be went first to the right side, then to the left, and so hitched and jumped till he came to the water, where he went in with a bob backwards. And this bad beginning had no better ending, since of all swimmers and divers the Rabbit is the very worst, and this one was no better than his brothers. The water was cold, he lost his breath, he struggled, and was well-nigh drowned.

"But what on earth ails the fellow?" said the Otter to the grandmother, who was looking on in amazement.

"Well, he has seen somebody do something, and is trying to do likewise," replied the old lady.

"Ho! come out of that now," cried the Otter, "and hand me your *nabogun*!" And the poor Rabbit, shivering with cold, and almost frozen, came from the water and limped into the lodge. And there he required much nursing from his grandmother, while the Otter, plunging into the stream, soon returned with a load of fish. But, disgusted at the Rabbit for attempting what he could not perform, he threw them down as a gift, and went home without tasting the meal.

II. How Mahtigwess, the Rabbit dined with the Woodpecker Girls, and was again humbled by trying to rival them.

Now Master Rabbit, though disappointed, was not discouraged, for this one virtue he had, that he never gave up. [Footnote: It will be seen in the end that this great Indian virtue of never giving in eventually raised Rabbit to power and prosperity. *Il y a de morale ici.*] And wandering one day in the wilderness, he found a wigwam well filled with young women, all wearing red head-dresses; and no wonder, for they were Woodpeckers. Now, Master Rabbit was a well-bred Indian, who made himself as a melody to all voices, and so he was cheerfully bidden to bide to dinner, which he did. Then one of the red-polled pretty girls, taking a *woltes*, or wooden dish, lightly climbed a tree, so that she seemed to run; and while ascending, stopping here and there and tapping now and then, took from this place and that many of those insects called by the Indians *apchel-moal-timpkawal*, or rice, because they so much resemble it. And note that this rice is a dainty dish for those who like it. And when it was boiled, and they had dined, Master Rabbit again reflected, "La! how easily some folks live! What is to hinder me from doing the same? Ho, you girls! come over and dine with me the day after to-morrow!"

And having accepted this invitation, all the guests came on the day set, when Master Rabbit undertook to play woodpecker. So having taken the head of an eel-spear and fastened it to his nose to make a bill, he climbed as well as he could—and bad was the best—up a tree, and tried to get his harvest of rice. Truly he got none; only in this did he succeed in resembling a Woodpecker, that he had a red poll; for his pate was all torn and bleeding, bruised by the fishing-point. And the pretty birds all looked and laughed, and wondered what the Rabbit was about.

"Ah!" said his grandmother, "I suppose he is trying again to do something which he has seen some one do. 'T is just like him."

"Oh, come down there!" cried Miss Woodpecker, as well as she could for laughing. "Give me your dish!" And having got it she scampered up the trunk, and soon brought down a dinner. But it was long ere Master Rabbit heard the last of it from these gay tree-tappers.

III. Of the Adventure with Mooin, the Bear; it being the Third and Last Time that Master Rabbit made a Fool of himself.

Now, truly, one would think that after all that had befallen Master *Mahtigwess*, the Rabbit, that he would have had enough of trying other people's trades; but his nature was such that, having once set his mighty mind to a thing, little short of sudden death would cure him. And being one day with the Bear in his cave, he beheld with great wonder how *Mooin* fed his folk. For, having put a great pot on the fire, he did but cut a little slice from his own foot and drop it into the boiling water, when it spread and grew into a mess of meat which served for all. [Footnote: Mr. Rand observes that this is evidently an allusion to the bear's being supposed to live during the winter by sucking his own paws.] Nay, there was a great piece given to Rabbit to take home to feed his family.

"Now, truly," he said, "this is a thing which I can indeed do. Is it not recorded in the family wampum that whatever a Bear can do well a Rabbit can do better? "So, in fine, he invited his friend to come and dine with him, *Kothoowopk'*, the day after to-morrow.

And the Bear being there, Rabbit did but say, "*Noogume' kuesawal' wohu*!" "Grandmother, set your pot to boiling!" And, whetting his knife on a stone, he tried to do as the Bear had done; but little did he get from his small, thin soles, though he cut himself madly and sadly.

"What can he be trying to do?" growled the guest.

"Ah!" sighed the grandmother, "something which he has seen some one else do."

"Ho! I say there! Give me the knife," quoth Bruin. And, getting it, he took a slice from his sole, which did him no harm, and then, what with magic and fire, gave them a good dinner. But Master Rabbit was in sad case, and it was many a day ere he got well.

IV. Relating how the Rabbit became Wise by being Original, and of the Terrible Tricks which he by Magic played Loup-Cervier, the Wicked Wild Cat.

There are men who are bad at copying, yet are good originals, and of this kind was Master Rabbit, who, when he gave up trying to do as others did, succeeded very well. And, having found out his foible, he applied himself to become able in good earnest, and studied *m'teoulin*, or magic, so severely that in time he grew to be an awful conjurer, so that he could raise ghosts, crops, storms, or devils whenever he wanted them. [Footnote: The three previous chapters of the Rabbit legend are from the Micmac. The rest is Passamaquoddy, as told by Tomah Josephs, who in his narration not only often interpolated jocose remarks, but was wont to ejaculate "By Jolly!" especially in the most striking scenes. I think that with him the interjection had become refined and dignified.] For he had perseverance, and out of this may come anything, if it be only brought into the right road.

Now it came to pass that Master Rabbit got into great trouble. The records of the Micmacs say that it was from his stealing a string of fish from the Otter, who pursued him; but the Passamaquoddies declare that he was innocent of this evil deed, probably because they make great account of him as their ancestor and as the father of the Wabanaki. Howbeit, this is the way in which they tell the tale.

Now the Rabbit is the natural prey of the Loup-Cervier, or Lusifee, who is a kind of wild cat, none being more obstinate. And this Wild Cat once went hunting with a gang of wolves, and they got nothing. Then Wild Cat, who had made them great promises and acted as chief, became angry, and, thinking of the Rabbit, promised them that this time they should indeed get their dinner. So he took them to Rabbit's wigwam; but he was out, and the Wolves, being vexed and starved, reviled Wild Cat, and then rushed off howling through the woods.

Now I think that the Rabbit is *m'teoulin*. Yes, he must be, for when Wild Cat started to hunt him alone, he determined with all his soul not to be caught, and made himself as magical as he could. So he picked up a handful of chips, and threw one as far as possible, then jumped to it,—for he had a charm for a long jump; and then threw another, and so on, for a great distance. This was to make no tracks, and when he thought he had got out of scent and sight and sound he scampered away like the wind.

[Illustration: THE RABBIT MAGICIAN.]

Now, as I said, when the wolves got to Master Rabbit's house and found nothing, they smelt about and left Wild Cat, who swore by his tail that he would catch Rabbit, if he had to hunt forever and run himself to death. So, taking the house for a centre, he kept going round and round it, all the time a little further, and so more around and still further. [Footnote: While telling this, Tomah described a spiral line. It is evident that if the volute were only continued long enough it must inevitably end in finding any trail, if the point of departure be only known. This device is familiar to all Indians, and it is mentioned in other stories.] Then at last having found the track, he went in hot haste after Mr. Rabbit. And both ran hard, till, night coming on, Rabbit, to protect himself, had only just time *to trample down the snow a little, and stick up a spruce twig on end and sit on it.* But when Wild Cat came up he found there a fine wigwam, and put his head in. All that he saw was an old man of very grave and dignified appearance, whose hair was gray, and whose majestic (*sogmoye*) appearance was heightened by a pair of long and venerable ears. And of him Wild Cat asked in a gasping hurry if he had seen a Rabbit running that way.

"Rabbits!" replied the old man. "Why, of course I have seen many. They abound in the woods about here. I see dozens of them every day." With this he said kindly to Wild Cat that he had better tarry with him for a time. "I am an old man," he remarked with solemnity,—"an old man, living alone, and a respectable guest, like you, sir, comes to me like a blessing." And the Cat, greatly impressed, remained. After a good supper he lay down by the fire, and, having run all day, was at once asleep, and made but one nap of it till morning. But how astonished, and oh, how miserable he was, when he awoke, to find himself on the open heath in the snow and almost starved! The wind blew as if it had a keen will to kill him; it seemed to go all through his body. Then he saw that he had been a fool and cheated by magic, and in a rage swore again by his teeth, as well as his tail, that the Rabbit should die. There was no hut now, only the trampled snow and a spruce twig, and yet out of this little, Rabbit had conjured up so great a delusion.

Then he ran again all day. And when night came, Master Rabbit, having a little more time than before, again trampled down the snow, but for a greater space, and strewed many branches all about, for now a huge effort was to be made. And when Wild Cat got there he found a great Indian village, with crowds of people going to and fro. The first building he saw was a church, in which service was being held. And he, entering, said hastily to the first person he saw, "Ha! ho! have you seen a Rabbit running by here?"

"Hush—sh, sh!" replied the man. "You must wait till meeting is over before asking such questions." [Footnote: Though this story is very old, the incident of the church (*sogmoye wigwam*, or chief house) is manifestly modern.] Then a young man beckoned to him to come in, and he listened till the end to a long sermon on the wickedness of being vindictive and rapacious; and the preacher was a gray ancient, and his ears stood up over his little cap like the two handles of a pitcher, yet for all that the Wild Cat's heart was not moved one whit. And when it was all at an end he said to the obliging young man, "But *have* you seen a Rabbit running by?"

"Rabbits! Rabbits!" replied the young man. "Why, there are hundreds racing about in the cedar swamps near this place, and you can have as many as you want." "Ah!" replied Wild Cat, "but they are not what I seek. Mine is an entirely different kind." The other said that he knew of no sort save the wild wood-rabbits, but that perhaps their Governor, or Chief, who was very wise, could tell him all about them. Then the Governor, or Sagamore, came up.

Like the preacher, he was very remarkable and gray, with the long locks standing up one on either side of his head. And he invited the stranger to his house, where his two very beautiful daughters cooked him a fine supper. And when he wished to retire they brought out blankets and a beautiful *white bear's skin*, and made up a bed for him by the fire. Truly, his eyes were closed as soon as he lay down, but when he awoke there had been a great change. For now he was in a wet cedar swamp, the wind blowing ten times worse than ever, and his supper and sleep had done him little good, for they were all a delusion. All around him were rabbits' tracks and broken twigs, but nothing more.

Yet he sprang up, more enraged than ever, and swearing more terribly by his tail, teeth, and claws that he would be revenged. So he ran on all day, and at night, when he came to another large village, he was so weary that he could just gasp, "Have—you—seen a Rab—bit run this way?" With much concern and kindness they all asked him what was the matter. So he told them all this story, and they pitied him very much; yea, one gray old man,—and this was the Chief,—with two beautiful daughters, shed tears and comforted him, and advised him to stay with them. So they took him to a large hall, where there was a great fire burning in the middle thereof. And over it hung two pots with soup and meat, and two Indians stood by and gave food to all the people. And he had his share with the rest, and all feasted gayly.

Now, when they had done eating, the old Governor, who was very gray, and from either side of whose head rose two very venerable, long white feathers, rose to welcome the stranger, and in a long speech said it was, indeed, the custom of their village to entertain guests, but that they expected from them a song. Then Wild Cat, who was vain of his voice, uplifted it in vengeance against the Rabbits:—

"Oh, how I hate them!
How I despise them!
How I laugh at them!
May I scalp them all!"

Then he said that he thought the Governor should sing. And to this the Chief consented, but declared that all who were present should bow their heads while seated, and shut their eyes, which they did. Then Chief Rabbit, at one bound, cleared the heads of his guests, and drawing his *timheyen*, or tomahawk, as he jumped, gave Wild Cat a wound which cut deeply into his head, and only fell short of killing him by entirely stunning him. When he recovered, he was again in snow, slush, and filth, more starved than ever, his head bleeding from a dreadful blow, and he himself almost dead. Yet, with all that, the Indian devil was stronger in him than ever, for every new disgrace did but bring more resolve to be revenged, and he swore it by his tail, claws, teeth, and eyes.

So he tottered along, though he could hardly walk; nor could he, indeed, go very far that day. And when, almost broken down with pain and weariness, he came about noon to two good wigwams. Looking into one, he saw a gray-haired old man, and in the other a young girl, apparently his daughter. And they received him kindly, and listened to his story, saying it was very sad, the old man declaring that he must really remain there, and that he would get him a doctor, since, unless he were well cared for at once, he would die. Then he went forth as if in great concern, leaving his daughter to nurse the weary, wounded stranger.

Now, when the Doctor came, he, too, was an old gray man, with a scalp-lock strangely divided like two horns. But the Wild Cat had become a little suspicious, having been so often deceived, for much abuse will cease to amuse even the most innocent; and truly he was none of these. And, looking grimly at the Doctor, [Footnote: This cross-examination of the Doctor is taken from an Abenaki version, narrated by a St. Francis Indian to Miss Alger. This Indian is the well-known Josep Cappino.] he said: "I was asking if any Rabbits are here, and truly you look very much like one yourself. How did you get that split nose?" "Oh, that is very simple," replied the old man. "Once I was hammering wampum beads, and the stone on which I beat them broke in halves, and one piece flew up, and, as you see, split my nose." "But," persisted the Wild Cat, "why are the soles of your feet so yellow, even like a Rabbit's?" "Ah, that is because I have been preparing some tobacco, and I had to hold it down with my feet, for, truly, I needed both my hands to work with. So the tobacco stained them yellow." Then the Wild Cat suspected no more, and the Doctor put salve on his wound, so that he felt much better, and, ere he departed, put by him a platter of very delicate little round biscuits, or rolls, and a beautiful pitcher full of nice wine, and bade him refresh himself from these during the night, and so, stealing away softly, he departed.

But oh, the wretchedness of the awaking in the morning! For then Wild Cat found himself indeed in the extreme of misery. His head was swollen and aching to an incredible degree, and the horrible wound, which was gaping wide, had been stuffed with hemlock needles and pine splinters, and this was the cool salve which the Doctor had applied. And as a last touch to his rage and shame, thinking in his deadly thirst of the wine, he beheld on the ground, still left in the snow, a last summer's pitcher-plant, half full of what might indeed pass for wine by the mere sight thereof, though hardly to the taste. While seeking for the biscuits on a platter, he found only certain small pellets, such as abound about a rabbit warren. And then he swore by all his body and soul that he would slay the next being he met, Rabbit or Indian. Verily this time he would be utterly revenged.

Now Mahtigwess, the Rabbit, had almost come to an end of his *m'teoulin*, or wizard power, for that time, yet he had still enough left for one more great effort. And, coming to a lake, he picked up a very large chip, and having seamed it with sorcery and magnified it by magic threw it into the water, where it at once seemed to be a great ship, such as white men build. And when the Wild Cat came up he saw it, with sails spread and flags flying, and the captain stood so stately on the deck, with folded arms, and he was a fine, gray-haired, dignified man, with a cocked hat, the two points of which were like grand and stately horns. But the Wild Cat had sworn, and he was mindful of his great oath; so he cried, "You cannot escape me this time, Rabbit! I have you now!" Saying this he plunged in, and tried to swim to the ship. And the captain, seeing a Wild Cat in the water, being engaged in musket drill, ordered his men to fire at it, which they did with a bang! Now this was caused by a party of night-hawks overhead, who swooped down with a sudden cry like a shot; at least it seemed so to Wild Cat, who, deceived and appalled by this volley, deeming that he had verily made a mistake this time, turned, tail and swam ashore into the dark old forest, where, if he is not dead, he is running still. [Footnote: This expression, very common among the Indians, appears to have been taken from the Canadians, *Il court encore* ends many of their stories. This was related to me by Tomah Josephs, September 2, 1882. I have four versions of it. In one, the Chippewa, given by Schoolcraft, the wretched efforts to rival the woodpeckers and bear are attributed to a no less personage than Hiawatha, or Manobozho, himself, when under a cloud. But Hiawatha as a poem deals only with the better part of the hero's character. In the Rand manuscript, the most amusing portion of the adventures of the Rabbit, or those with the Wild Cat, are much abbreviated. Tomah's tale supplies this missing portion, but consists of nothing else. The Abenaki tale is slightly different in its beginning: "Rabbit was making maple-sugar in the woods, but he was very pious, and rested on the Sabbath. While praying on this day by his hearth, there came a great black fierce man, who glared at him, but Mahtigwess kept saying 'Peace! peace! peace!' for that is the way the Rabbit prays. Then the stranger was angry because he would not cease praying and talk to him, but the Rabbit said, 'Would you have me break the Sabbath?' Then he went and brought the stranger, who was a Wild Cat, refreshments." These refreshments were the same as those given by the Doctor. Here the chase begins.

There is probably much more of this story.]

V. How Master Rabbit went to a Wedding and won the Bride.

(Passamaquoddy.)

Chee mahtigwess, or the Great Rabbit, was once very stout or large of body, having a very long tail. And one day in the old times, as he sat on the rock, with his fine long tail trailing afar into the bushes, an old man came by who asked the way. And Master Rabbit, being as usual obliging, offered to show it to him. So they talked together and grew intimate, but as the old man went very slowly, while Rabbit was always running, he said, "Go on before, and I will follow." So the guide was soon out of sight, and then the old man, hurrying without heeding, fell down into a deep pit or chasm, where he cried out aloud for help, but was not heard. After a time, Rabbit, missing his follower, turned back and tracked him till he found the pit. Yet they could not between them manage to bring the traveler up again, until Rabbit said, "Catch hold of my tail;" and when this was done he gave a jump, but alas! the fine tail broke off short within an inch of the root.

One would think that by this time Master Rabbit must have had enough of helping, but all the stories of him show that he never gave up anything which he had once begun. So he simply said to the old man, "Catch hold of me round the waist;" and when this was done he gave another leap, and brought the prisoner out. But the man, being heavy, had slipped down, and almost broken Rabbit's back. So it came to pass that since that day Master Rabbit has had a very short tail and a slender waist.

The old man was on his way to marry a young girl. But she was in love with Mikumwess, the forest fairy. However, the old man married her, and invited Master Rabbit to the dance, which in old times made the ceremony. And the guest dressed for the occasion by putting ear-rings on his heels—for Rabbits or Hares dance on their tip-toes—and a beautiful bangle round his neck, and he danced opposite the bride. Now the bride had on only a very short skirt, and in crossing a brook it had got wet. So that as she danced, it began to shrink and shrink, until Master Rabbit, pitying the poor girl, ran out and got a deer-skin, and hastily twisted a cord to tie it with. But it seemed as if Master Rabbit's efforts to oblige people always got him into trouble, for he twisted this string so rapidly and earnestly, holding one end of it in his teeth as he did so, that he cut his upper lip through to the nose, for which reason his descendants all have hare-lips to this day.

Now having dressed the bride, she was so grateful to Rabbit that she danced with him all the night. The old man, seeing this, was so angry at her fickleness that, without saying a word, he walked away, and left her to Mahtigwess, with whom she lived very happily until she ran away with Mikumwess; with whom, if she has not run away again, she is living yet. This story is at an end.

VI. How Master Rabbit gave himself Airs.

(Micmac.)

It happened once that Lox was living in great luxury. He had a wigwam full of hundreds of dried sea-ducks, moose meat, maple sugar, and corn. He gave a dinner, and among the guests invited Marten and Mahtigwess, the Rabbit.

Now it is a great weakness of Master Rabbit that he is much given to hinting at one minute, and saying pretty plainly the next, that he has been in better society than that around him, and has lived among great people, and no one was quicker than the Marten to find out that wherein any one was foolish or feeble. So when Master Rabbit, smoothing down his white fur, said it was the only kind of a coat worn by the aristocracy, Marten humbly inquired, "if that were so, how he came by it."

"It shows," replied Master Rabbit, "that I have habitually kept company with gentlemen."

"How did you get that slit in your lip?" inquired Marten, who knew very well what this Indian really was.

"Ah!" replied the Rabbit, "where *I* live they use knives and forks. And one day, while eating with some great sagamores, my knife slipped, and I cut my lip."

"And why are your mouth and whiskers always going when you are still? Is that high style?"

"Yes; I am meditating, planning, combining great affairs; talking to myself, you see. That's the way *we* do."

"But why do you always hop? Why don't you sometimes walk, like other people?"

"Ah, that's *our* style. We gentlemen don't run, like the vulgar. *We* have a gait of our own, don't you know?"

"Indeed! Well, if you don't mind a question, I would like to know why you always scamper away so suddenly, and jump so far and so rapidly when you run."

"Aw! don't you know? I used to be employed in very genteel business; public service,—in fact, diplomatic. I carried dispatches (*weegadigunn*, Micmac; *wighiggin*, Pass.)—books, letters, papers, and so I got in the way of moving nimbly. Now it comes naturally to me. One of my old aristocratic habits." [Footnote: This droll dialogue occurs in the middle of the Micmac story of Lox, or Badger, and the Ducks and Bear, where it evidently does not belong, or has been interpolated to make length. In the original, Marten carries his inquiries much further into certain physiological details, all of which Master Rabbit naively explains as the result of the delicate diet and the wine to which he as a gentleman had been accustomed.]

Upon this Marten gave it up. He had seen something of good society himself, as he lived habitually with Glooskap, but Master Rabbit was too much for him.

VII. The Young Man who was Saved by a Rabbit and a Fox.

(Passamaquoddy.)

There dwelt a couple in the woods, far away from other people,—a man and his wife. They had one boy, who grew up strong and clever. One day he said, "Father and mother, let me go and see other men and women." They grieved, but let him go.

He went afar. All night he lay on the ground. In the morning he heard something coming. He rose and saw it was a Rabbit, who said, "Ha, friend, where go you?" The boy answered, "To find people." "That is what I want," replied the Rabbit. "Let us go together."

So they went on for a long time, till they heard voices far off, and walking quietly came to a village. "Now," said the Rabbit, "steal up unseen, and listen to them!" The boy did so, and heard the people saying that a *kewahqu'*, a cannibal monster, was to come the next day to devour the daughter of their sagamore. And having returned and reported this to the Rabbit, the latter said to the boy, "Have no fear; go to the people and tell them that you can save her." He did so, but it was long before they would listen to him. Yet at last it came to the ears of the old chief that a strange young man insisted that he could save the girl; so the chief sent for him, and said, "They tell me that you think you can deliver my daughter from death. Do so, and she shall be yours."

Then he returned to the Rabbit, who said, "They did not send the girl far away because they know that the demon can follow any track. But I hope to make a track which he cannot follow. Now do you, as soon as it shall be dark, bring her to this place." The young man did so, and the Rabbit was there with a sled, and in his hand he had two squirrels. These he smoothed down, and as he did so they grew to be as large as the largest sled-dogs. Then all three went headlong, like the wind, till they came to another village.

The Rabbit looked about till he found a certain wigwam, and then peered through a crevice into it. "This is the place," he said. "Enter." They did so; then the Rabbit ran away. They found in the cabin an old woman, who was very kind, but who, on seeing them, burst into tears. "Ah, my dear grandchildren," [Footnote: The terms grandchildren, grandmother, etc., do not here signify actual relationship, but only friendship between elderly and young people.] she cried, "your death is following you rapidly, for the kewahqu' is on your track, and will soon be here. But run down to the river, where you will find your grandfather camping."

They went, and were joined by the Rabbit, who had spent the time in making many divergent tracks in the ground. The kewahqu' came. The tracks delayed him a long time, but at last he found the right one. Meanwhile the young couple went on, and found an old man by the river. He said, "Truly you are in great danger, for the kewahqu' is coming. But I will help you." Saying this, he threw himself into the water, where he floated with outstretched limbs, and said, "Now, my children, get on me." The girl feared lest she should fall off, but being reassured mounted, when he turned into a canoe, which carried them safely across. But when they turned to look at him, lo! he was no longer a canoe, but an old Duck. "Now, my dear children," he said, "hasten to the top of yonder old mountain, high among the gray rocks. There you will find your friend." They fled, to the old gray mountain. The kewahqu' came raging and roaring in a fury, but however he pursued they were at the foot of the precipice before him.

There stood the Rabbit. He was holding up a very long pole; no pine was ever longer. "Climb this," he said. And, as they climbed, it lengthened, till they left it for the hill, and then scrambled up the rocks. Then the kewahqu' came yelling and howling horribly. Seeing the fugitives far above, he swarmed up the pole. With him, too, it grew, and grew rapidly, till it seemed to be half a mile high. Now the kewahqu' was no such sorcerer that he could fly; neither had he wings; he must remain on the pole; and when he came to the top the young man pushed it afar. It fell, and the monster was killed by the fall thereof.

They went with the squirrel-sledge; they flew through the woods on the snow by the moonlight; they were very glad. And at last they came to the girl's village, when the Rabbit said, "Now, friend, good-by. Yet there is more trouble coming, and when it is with you I and mine will aid you. So farewell." And when they were home again it all appeared like a dream. Then the wedding feast was held, and all seemed well.

But the young men of the village hated the youth, and desired to kill him, that they might take his wife. They persuaded him to go with them fishing on the sea. Then they raised a cry, and said, "A whale is chasing us! he is under the canoe!" and suddenly they knocked him overboard, and paddled away like an arrow in flight.

The young man called for help. A Crow came, and said, "Swim or float as long as you can. I will bring you aid." He floated a long time. The Crow returned with a strong cord; the Crow made himself very large; he threw one end of the cord to the youth; by the other he towed him to a small island. "I can do no more," he said; "but there is another friend." So as the youth sat there, starving and freezing, there came to him a Fox. "Ha, friend," he said, "are you here?" "Yes," replied the youth, "and dying of hunger." The Fox reflected an instant, and said, "Truly I have no meat; and yet there is a way." So he picked from the ground a blade of dry grass, and bade the youth eat it. He did so, and found himself a moose (or a *horse*). Then he fed richly on the young grass till he had enough, when the Fox gave him a second straw, and he became a man again. "Friend," said the Fox, "there is an Indian village on the main-land, where there is to be a great feast, a grand dance. Would you like to be there?" "Indeed I would," replied the youth. "Then wait till dark, and I will take you there," said the Fox. And when night came he bade the youth close his eyes and enter the river, and take hold of the end of his tail, while he should draw. So in the tossing sea they went on for hours. *Thought* the youth, "We shall never get there." *Said* the Fox, "Yes, we will, but keep your eyes shut." So it went on for another hour, when the youth *thought* again, "We shall never reach land." *Said* the Fox, "Yes, we shall." However, after a time he opened his eyes, when they were only ten feet from the shore, and this cost them more time and trouble than all the previous swim ere they had the beach under foot.

It was his own village. The festival was for the marriage of his own wife to one of the young men who had pushed him overboard. Great was his magic power, great was his anger; he became strong as death. Then he went to his own wigwam, and his wife, seeing him, cried aloud for joy, and kissed him and wept all at once. He said, "Be glad, but the hour of punishment for the men who made these tears is come." So he went to the sagamore and told him all.

The old chief called for the young men. "Slay them all as you choose," he said to his son-in-law; "scalp them." But the youth refused. He called to the Fox, and got the straws which gave the power to transform men to beasts. He changed his enemies into bad animals,—one into a porcupine, one into a hog,—and they were driven into the woods. Thus it was that the first hog and the first porcupine came into the world.

This story, narrated by Tomah Josephs, is partly old Indian and partly European, but whether the latter element was derived from a French Canadian or a Norse source I cannot tell, since it is common to both. The mention of the horse and the hog, or of cattle, does not prove that a story is not pre-Columbian. The Norsemen had brought cattle of various descriptions even to New England. It is to be very much regretted that the first settlers in New England took no pains to ascertain what the Indians knew of the white men who had preceded them. But modern material may have easily been added to an old legend.

THE CHENOO LEGENDS.

I. The Chenoo, or the Story of a Cannibal with an Icy Heart.

(Micmac and Passamaquoddy.)

Of the old time. An Indian, with his wife and their little boy, went one autumn far away to hunt in the northwest. And having found a fit place to pass the winter, they built a wigwam. The man brought home the game, the woman dressed and dried the meat, the small boy played about shooting birds with bow and arrow; in Indian-wise all went well.

One afternoon, when the man was away and the wife gathering wood, she heard a rustling in the bushes, as though some beast were brushing through them, and, looking up, she saw with horror something worse than the worst she had feared. It was an awful face glaring at her,—a something made of devil, man, and beast in their most dreadful, forms. It was like a haggard old man, with wolfish eyes; he was stark naked; his shoulders and lips were gnawed away, as if, when mad with hunger, he had eaten his own flesh. He carried a bundle on big back. The woman had heard of the terrible Chenoo, the being who comes from the far, icy north, a creature who is a man grown to be both devil and cannibal, and saw at once that this was one of them.

Truly she was in trouble; but dire need gives quick wit, as it was with this woman, who, instead of showing fear, ran up and addressed him with fair words, as "My dear father," pretending surprise and joy, and, telling him how glad her heart was, asked where he had been so long. The Chenoo was amazed beyond measure at such a greeting where he expected yells and prayers, and in mute wonder let himself be led into the wigwam.

She was a wise and good woman. She took him in; she said she was sorry to see him so woe-begone; she pitied his sad state; she brought a suit of her husband's clothes; she told him to dress himself and be cleaned. He did as she bade. He sat by the side of the wigwam, and looked surly and sad, but kept quiet. It was all a new thing to him.

She arose and went out. She kept gathering sticks. The Chenoo rose and followed her. She was in great fear. "Now," she thought, "my death is near; now he will kill and devour me."

The Chenoo came to her. He said, "Give me the axe!" She gave it, and he began to cut down the trees. Man never saw such chopping! The great pines fell right and left, like summer saplings; the boughs were hewed and split as if by a tempest. She cried out, "*Noo, tabeagul boohsoogul!*" "My father, there is enough!" [Footnote: The tremendous pine chopper is a character in another Indian tale.] He laid down the axe; he walked into the wigwam and sat down, always in grim silence. The woman gathered her wood, and remained as silent on the opposite side.

She heard her husband coming. She ran out and told him all. She asked him to do as she was doing. He thought it well. He went in and spoke kindly. He said, "*N'chilch*," "My father-in-law," and asked where he had been so long. The Chenoo stared in amazement, but when he heard the man talk of all that had happened for years his fierce face grew gentler.

They had their meal; they offered him food, but he hardly touched it. He lay down to sleep. The man and his wife kept awake in terror. When the fire burned up, and it became warm, the Chenoo asked that a screen should be placed before him. He was from the ice; he could not endure heat.

For three days he stayed in the wigwam; for three days he was sullen and grim; he hardly ate. Then he seemed to change. He spoke to the woman; he asked her if she had any tallow. She told him they had much. He filled a large kettle; there was a gallon of it. He put it on the fire. When it was scalding hot he drank it all off at a draught.

He became sick; he grew pale. He cast up all the horrors and abominations of earth, things appalling to every sense. When all was over he seemed changed. [Footnote: The Chenoo is not only a cannibal, but a ghoul. He preys on nameless horrors. In this case, "having yielded to the power of kindness, he has made up his mind to partake of the food and hospitality of his hosts,"" to change his life; but to adapt his system to the new regimen, he must thoroughly clear it of the old."—Rand manuscript. This is a very *naive* and curious Indian conception of moral reformation. It appears to be a very ancient Eskimo tale, recast in modern time by some zealous recent Christian convert.]

He lay down and slept. When he awoke he asked for food, and ate much. From that time he was kind and good. They feared him no more.

They lived on meat such as Indians prepare. [Footnote: That is, cured, dried, smoked, and then packed and pressed in large blocks.] The Chenoo was tired of it. One day he said, "*N'toos*" (my daughter), "have you no *pela weoos*?" (fresh meat). She said, "No." When her husband returned the Chenoo saw that there was black mud on his snow-shoes. He asked him if there was a spring of water near. The friend said there was one half a day's journey distant. "We must go there to-morrow," said the Chenoo.

And they went together, very early. The Indian was fleet in such running. But the old man, who seemed so wasted and worn, went on his snow-shoes like the wind. They came to the spring. [Footnote: "The Micmacs have two words for a spring of water: one for summer, *utkuboh*, which means that the water is cool; the other for winter, *keesoobok*, indicating that it is warm."—S.T.

Rand.] It was large and beautiful; the snow was all melted away around it; the border was flat and green. [Footnote: Not uncommon round warm springs even in midwinter, and among ice and snow.]

[Illustration: THE CHENOO AND THE LIZARD.]

Then the Chenoo stripped himself, and danced around the spring his magic dance; and soon the water began to foam, and anon to rise and fall, as if some monster below were heaving in accord with the steps and the song. The Chenoo danced faster and wilder; then the head of an immense *Taktalok*, or lizard, rose above the surface. The old man killed it with a blow of his hatchet. Dragging it out he began again to dance. He brought out another, the female, not so large, but still heavy as an elk. They were small spring lizards, but the Chenook had conjured them; by his magic they were made into monsters.

He dressed the game; he cut it up. He took the heads and feet and tails and all that he did not want, and cast them back into the spring. "They will grow again into many lizards," he said. When the meat was trimmed it looked like that of the bear. He bound it together with withes; he took it on his shoulders; he ran like the wind; his load was nothing.

The Indian was a great runner; in all the land was not his like; but now he lagged far behind. "Can you go no faster than that?" asked the Chenoo. "The sun is setting; the red will be black anon. At this rate it will be dark ere we get home. Get on my shoulders."

The Indian mounted on the load. The Chenoo bade him hold his head low, so that he could not be knocked off by the branches. "Brace your feet," he said, "so as to be steady." Then the old man flew like the wind,— *ne[original illegible] sokano'v'jal samastukteskugul chel wegwasumug wegul*; the bushes whistled as they flew past them. They got home before sunset.

The wife was afraid to touch such meat. [Footnote: "The Indians are much less particular than white men as to food, but they avoid *choojeeck*, or reptiles."—Rand manuscript.] But her husband was persuaded to eat of it. It was like bear's meat. The Chenoo fed on it. So they all lived as friends.

Then the spring was at hand. One day the Chenoo told them that something terrible would soon come to pass. An enemy, a Chenoo, a woman was coming like wind, yes—on the wind—from the north to kill him. There could be no escape from the battle. She would be far more furious, mad, and cruel than any male, even one of his own cruel race, could be. He knew not how the battle would end; but the man and his wife must be put in a place of safety. To keep from hearing the terrible war-whoops of the Chenoo, which is death to mortals, their ears must be closed. They must hide themselves in a cave.

Then he sent the woman for the bundle which he had brought with him, and which had hung untouched on a branch of a tree since he had been with them. And he said if she found aught in it offensive to her to throw it away, but to certainly bring him a smaller bundle which was within the other. So she went and opened it, and that which she found therein was a pair of human legs and feet, the remains of some earlier horrid meal. She threw them far away. The small bundle she brought to him.

The Chenoo opened it and took from it a pair of horns,—horns of the *chepitchcalm*, or dragon. One of them has two branches; the other is straight and smooth. [Footnote: In the winter of 1882-1883, Tomah Josephs killed a deer whose horns were precisely like those of the chepitchcalm as regarded shape.] They were golden-bright. He gave the straight horn to the Indian; he kept the other. He said that these were magical weapons, and the only ones of any use in the coming fight. So they waited for the foe.

And the third day came. The Chenoo was fierce and bold; he listened; he had no fear. He heard the long and awful scream—like nothing of earth—of the enemy, as she sped through the air far away in the icy north, long ere the others could hear it. And the manner of it was this: that if they without harm should live after hearing the first deadly yell of the enemy they could take no harm, and if they did but hear the answering shout of their friend all would be well with them. [Footnote: In all this we clearly perceive the horrible scream of the *angakok*, or Eskimo shaman, trained through years and generations to utter sounds which terrify even brave men.] But he said, "Should you hear me call for help, then hasten with the horn, and you may save my life."

They did as he bade: they stopped their ears; they hid in a deep hole dug in the ground. All at once the cry of the foe burst on them like screaming thunder; their ears rang with pain: they were well-nigh killed, for all the care they had taken. But then they heard the answering cry of their friend, and were no longer in danger from mere noise.

The battle begun, the fight was fearful. The monsters, by their magic with their rage, rose to the size of mountains. The tall pines were torn up, the ground trembled as in an earthquake, rocks crashed upon rocks, the conflict deepened and darkened; no tempest was ever so terrible. Then the male Chenoo was heard crying: "*N'loosook! choogooye! abog unumooe!*" "My son-in-law, come and help me!"

He ran to the fight. What he saw was terrible! The Chenoos, who upright would have risen far above the clouds as giants of hideous form, were struggling on the ground. The female seemed to be the conqueror. She was holding her foe down, she knelt on him, she was doing all she could to thrust her dragon's horn into his ear. And he, to avoid death, was moving his head rapidly from side to side, while she, mocking his cries, said, "You have no son-in-law to help you." *Neen nabujjeole,* "I'll take your cursed life, [Footnote: It is generally said that there can be no swearing in Indian, but Mr. Rand corrects this gross error. "It is a mistake," he writes, "to suppose that the red man cannot swear in his own tongue." It cannot, of course, be expected that simple savages can swear like cultivated Christians, but they do the best they can. They introduce the venom into their speech by inserting an extra syllable. Thus *nabole* or *nabol'* means, "I will kill you," but *nabujeol'* is the equivalent of "I'll take your cursed life," though it has not that literal meaning. Having only one small syllable to swear with, the Indians are, however, not so profuse and wasteful of profanity as their more gifted and pious white brethren.] and, eat your liver."

The Indian was so small by these giants that the stranger did not notice him. "Now," said his friend, "thrust the horn into her ear!" He did this with a well-directed blow; he struck hard; the point entered her head. At the touch it sprouted quick as a flash of lightning, it darted through the head, it came out of the other ear, it had become like a long pole. It touched the ground, it struck downward, it took deep and firm root.

The male Chenoo bade him raise the other end of the horn and place it against a large tree. He did so. It coiled itself round the tree like a snake, it grew rapidly; the enemy was held hard and fast. Then the two began to dispatch her. It was long and weary work. Such a being, to be killed at all, must be hewed into small pieces; flesh and bones must all be utterly consumed by fire. Should the least fragment remain unburnt, from it would spring a grown Chenoo, with all the force and fire of the first. [Footnote: The idea is common to both Eskimo and Indian that so long as a fragment of a body remains unburned, the being, man or beast, may, by magic, be revived from it. It was probably suggested by observing the great vitality and power of self-production inherent in many lower forms of life, and may have given rise to the belief in vampires.]

The fury of battle past, the Chenoos had become of their usual size. The victor hewed the enemy to small pieces, to be revenged for the insult and threat as to eating his liver. He, having roasted that part of his captive, ate it before her; while she was yet alive he did this. He told her she was served as she would have served him.

But the hardest task of all was to come. It was to burn or melt the heart. It was of ice, and more than ice: as much colder as ice is colder than fire, as much harder as ice is harder than water. When placed in the fire it put out the flame, yet by long burning it melted slowly, until they at last broke it to fragments with a hatchet, and then melted these. So they returned to the camp.

Spring came. The snows of winter, as water, ran down the rivers to the sea; the ice and snow which had encamped on the inland hills sought the shore. So did the Indian and his wife; the Chenoo, with softened soul, went with them. Now he was becoming a man like other men. Before going they built a canoe for the old man: they did not cover it with birch bark; they made it of moose-skin. [Footnote: "The Indians have several names for a canoe: *Kwedun* (M.); *A'kweden* (P.); *N'tooal* (M.), my canoe or my water-craft of any kind; *Mooseoolk*, a canoe covered with moose-skin (M.); *Skogumoolk* (M..), a new canoe; *N'canoolk* (M.), an old canoe."—Rand manuscript. To these may be added the different patterns of canoes peculiar to different tribes, as for instance the Mohawk, which is broad, with peculiar ends, etc.] In it they placed a part of their venison and skins. The Chenoo took his place in it; they took the lead, he followed.

And after winding on with the river, down rapids and under forest-boughs, they came out into the sunshine, on a broad, beautiful lake. But suddenly, when midway in the water, the Chenoo laid flat in the canoe, as if to hide himself. And to explain this he said that be had just then been discovered by another Chenoo, who was standing on the top of a mountain, whose dim blue outline could just be seen stretching far away to the north. "He has seen me," he said, "but he cannot see you. Nor can he behold me now; but should he discover me again, his wrath will be roused. Then he will attack me; I know not who might conquer. I prefer peace."

So he lay hidden, and they took his canoe in tow. But when they had crossed the lake and come to the river again, the Chenoo said that he could not travel further by water. He would walk the woods, but sail on streams no more. So they told him where they meant to camp that night. He started over mountains and through woods and up rocks, a far, round-about journey. And the man and his wife went down the river in a spring freshet, headlong with the rapids. [Footnote: One should be familiar with the almost impassable forests of Maine and Canada, even as they are at the present day, to properly appreciate the Chenook's journey. As for the speed of the canoe, I have myself gone down the Kenawha River (Va.), in a dug-out, at the rate of one hundred miles in a day.] But when they had paddled round the point where they meant to pass the night, they saw smoke rising among the trees, and on landing they found the Chenoo sleeping soundly by the fire which had been built for them.

This he repeated for several days. But as they went south a great change came over him. He was a being of the north. Ice and snow had no effect on him, but he could not endure the soft airs of summer. He grew weaker and weaker; when they had reached their village he had to be carried like a little child. He had grown gentle. His fierce and formidable face was now like that of a man.

His wounds had healed; his teeth no longer grinned wildly all the time. The people gathered round him in wonder.

He was dying. This was after the white men had come. They sent for a priest. He found the Chenoo as ignorant of all religion as a wild beast. At first he would repel the father in anger. Then he listened and learned the truth. So the old heathen's heart changed; he was deeply moved. He asked to be baptized, and as the first tear which he had ever shed in all his life came to his eyes he died. [Footnote: This strange and touching tale was told to Mr. Rand by a Micmac Indian, Louis Brooks, who heard it from his grandfather, Samuel Paul, a chief, who died in 1843, at the age of eighty. He was a living chronicle of ancient traditions. The Chenoo can be directly identified with the so-called Inlander of the Greenland Eskimo. He is a cannibal, a giant, a mysterious being who haunts the horrible and almost unexplored interior. He assumes different forms; in one shape he is supposed to be a man who has become a recluse and a misanthrope. But no such being as a Chenoo could ever have been imagined out of an arctic country. The conception of the heart of hardest ice and the gradual civilization of the savage by kindness; the tact with which this is done, as only a woman could do it; the indication of the old nature, as shown by eating the liver of his conquered foe, and his final conversion, display a genius which is greatly heightened by the simplicity of the narrative.]

As there is actually a tribe of Indians in the Northwest called Chenoo, there can be little doubt as to the derivation of the name. Such a character could have originated, as I have said, only in the icy north; it could never have grown in the milder regions of the west and south. But the Chenoo, the monstrous, ferocious cannibal giant, with an icy heart, is the central figure of the evil supernatural beings of the north. The Schoolcraft traditions and Hiawatha have little to say of Titans whose heads top the clouds, who tear up forests and rend rocks, and change the whole face of Nature in their hideous battles or horrible revels. But such scenes are continually described by the Passamaquoddy and Micmac story-tellers, and they would be natural enough to Greenlanders, familiar with whales, icebergs, frozen wastes, long winter nights, and all the frozen desolation of the north.

There is a mystery connected with the *eating of the liver*, which is to be explained, like many other Indian mysteries, by having recourse to the Eskimo Shamanism. "In Greenland a man who has been murdered can revenge himself by *rushing into* him," that is, entering his soul, "which can only be prevented by eating a piece of his liver." (Rink, T. and T. of the Eskimo, page 45.) The Chenoo is in all essentials identical with the *Kivigtok* of Greenland, "a man who has fled mankind, and acquired extraordinary mental and physical powers." The story which I have here given is probably that of the Eskimo tale of the Blind Man who recovered his sight (Rink, page 99), in which a *Kivigtok*, after becoming incredibly old, returns to mankind to seek a Shaman priest and repent. In both stories there is a "Chenoo," and in both there is atonement with mankind and the higher powers.

It may be observed that while the Chenoo is a giant with a heart of ice as hard as stone, the giant Hrungnir, of the Edda, has a heart of stone. The Chenoo agrees with the Jotuns in many respects.

The Story of the Great Chenoo, as told by the Passamaquoddies.

(Passamaquoddy.)

What the Micmacs call a Chenoo is known to the Passamaquoddies as a *Kewahqu'* or *Kewoqu'*. And this is their origin. When the *k'tchi m'teoulin*, or Great Big Witch, [Footnote: When legends from the Anglo-Indian manuscript collection of Mitchell are given, many of the phrases or words in the original are retained, without regard to style or correctness. Wizard is here placed for witch.] is conquered by the smaller witches, or *M'teoulinssisk*, they can kill him or turn him into a *Kewahqu'*. He still fights, however, with the other *Kewaquiyck*. When they get ready to fight, they suddenly become as tall as the highest trees; their weapons are the trees themselves, which they uproot with great strength. And this strength depends upon the quantity or size of the piece of ice which makes the heart of the *Kewahqu'*. This piece of ice is like distance. "There is a great female Kewahqu' coming to fight me. In the struggle I may not know you, and may hurt you." So they went away as fast and as far as they could, but they heard the fighting, the most frightful noises, howls, yells, thundering and crashing of wood and rocks. After a time the man determined to see the fight. When he got to the place he saw a horrible sight: big trees uprooted, the giants in a deadly struggle. Then the Indian, who was very brave, and who was afraid that his father-in-law would be killed, came up and helped as much as he could, and in fact so much that between them they killed the enemy. The old Kewahqu' was badly but not fatally hurt, and the woman was very glad her father came off victorious. She had always heard that a Kewahqu' had a piece of ice for a heart. If this can be taken out, the Kewahqu' can be tamed and cured. So she made a preparation or medicine, and offered it to him. He did not know what it was, nor its strength, so he swallowed it, and it gave him a vomit. She saw something drop, so quietly picked it up: it was the figure of a man of ice; it was the Kewahqu's heart. She, not being seen or noticed, put it in the fire, when he cried," Daughter, you are killing me now; you destroy my strength." Yet she made him take more of the medicine, and a second heart came out. This she also put on the fire. But when a third came he grabbed it from her hand, and swallowed it. However, he was almost entirely cured.

Another time an Indian village was visited by a Kewahqu', but he was driven away by magic. The people marked *crosses* on the trees where they expected the Kewahqu' to come. There was a great excitement among the Indians, expecting to hear their strange visitor with his frightful noises. It was the old people who gave the advice to mark crosses on the trees.

Another time an Indian of either the Passamaquoddy or Mareschite tribe was turned to a Kewahqu'. The last time he was seen was by a party of Indian hunters, who recognized him. He had only small strips of clothing. "This country,'" he said," is too warm for me. I am going to a colder one."

This story from the Passamaquoddy Anglo-Indian, manuscript of Mitchell supplies some very important deficiencies in the preceding Micmac version. We are told that the *heart* of the Chenoo is of ice in human figure. This human figure is that of the Kewahqu' himself, or rather his very self, or microcosm. It is this, and not the liver, which is swallowed by the victor, who thus adds another frozen "soul" to his own. Of the three vomited by the Kewahqu', two were the hearts of enemies whom he had conquered. He could not give up his own, however. It is much more according to common sense that the woman should have given the cannibal the magic medicine which made him yield his heart than that he should voluntarily have purged himself. In the Micmac tale he merely relieves his stomach; in the Passamaquoddy version he, by woman's influence, loses his icy *heart*. It is interesting to observe that the use of the Christian cross is in the additional anecdote described as *magic*.

It is the main point in the Chenoo stories that this horrible being, this most devilish of devils, is at first human; perhaps an unusually good girl, or youth. From having the heart once chilled, she or he goes on in cruelty, until at last the sufferer eats the heart of another Chenoo, especially a female's. Then utter wickedness ensues. It is more than probable that this leads us back to some dark and terrible Shaman superstition, older than we can now fathom. There is a passage in the Edda which its translator, Thorpe, thinks can never be explained. "I believe," he writes, "the difficulty is beyond help." The lines are as follows:—

"Loki scorched up [Footnote: The *Edda*, p. 112.] In his heart's affections, Had found a half-burnt Woman's heart. Loki became guileful from that wicked woman: thence in the world are all giantesses come."

Of which Thorpe writes, "The sense of this and the following line is not apparent. They stand thus in the original: *Loki of hiarta lyrdi brendu, fann hann halfsvidthin hugstein konu*, for which Grimm (Myth. Vorrede 37) would read *Loki at hiarta lundi brenda*, etc., *Lokius comedit cor in nemore assum, invenit semiustum mentis lapidem mulieris*." Whatever obscurity exists here, it is evident that it means that Loki, having become bad, grew worse after having got the half-burnt stone of a woman's soul. That is, his own heart, half ruined, became utterly so after he had added to it the demoralized *hugstein*, soul-stone, thought-stone, or *heart* of a woman. If we assume that stone and heart are the same, the difficulty vanishes. And they are one in the Chenoo, who, like Loki, illustrates or symbolizes the passage from good to evil, which a German writer declares is quicker than thought, or that very same *Ilugi* which the Norse myth puts forwards as swiftest of all runners. Loki, not as yet lost, gets the stone heart of a giantess, and becomes an utter devil at once. The Chenoo becomes an utter devil when he has swallowed the *thought-stone* of a giantess, and so does Loki.

The Girl-Chenoo.

(Micmac.)

Of the old time. Far up the Saguenay River a branch turns off to the north, running back into the land of ice and snow. Ten families went up this stream one autumn in their canoes, to be gone all winter on a hunt. Among them was a beautiful girl, twenty years of age. A young man in the band wished her to become his wife, but she flatly refused him. Perhaps she did it in such a way as to wound his pride; certainly she roused all that was savage in him, and he gave up all his mind to revenge. He was skilled in medicine, or in magic, so he went into the woods and gathered an herb which makes people insensible. Then stealing into the lodge when all were asleep, he held it to the girl's face, until she had inhaled the odor and could not be easily awakened. Going out he made a ball of snow, and returning placed it in the hollow of her neck, in front, just below the throat. Then he retired without being discovered. So she could not awake, while the chill went to her heart. [Footnote: The Eskimo Shamans and the Indian *boo-oin* are familiar with many very ingenious and singular ways of producing prolonged illness and death. There is one known to a very few old gypsies, of gradually inducing insanity and death, which I have never seen noted in any work on toxicology. In a work which I lately read, it was positively denied that there was any such thing as a "lingering poison"!]

When she awoke she was chilly, shivering, and sick. She refused to eat. This lasted long, and her parents became alarmed. They inquired what ailed her. She was ill-tempered; she said that nothing was the matter. One day, having been sent to the spring for water, she remained absent so long that her mother went to seek her. Approaching unseen, she observed her greedily eating snow. And asking her what it meant, the daughter explained that she felt within a burning sensation, which the snow relieved. More than that, she craved the snow; the taste of it was pleasant to her.

After a few days she began to grow fierce, as though she wished to kill some one. At last she begged her parents to kill her. Hitherto she had loved them very much. Now she told them that unless they killed her she would certainly be their death. Her whole nature was being changed.

"How can we kill you?" her mother asked.

"You must shoot at me," she replied, "with seven arrows. [Footnote: The Micmac version gives *guns*. But the Chenoo stories are evidently very ancient, and refer to terrors of the olden time.] And if you can kill me with seven shots, all will be well. But if you cannot, I shall kill you."

Seven men shot at her, as she sat in the wigwam. She was not bound. Every arrow struck her in the breast, but she sat firm and unmoved. Forty-nine times they pierced her; from time to time she looked up with an encouraging smile. When the last arrow struck she fell dead.

Then they burned the body, as she had directed. It was soon reduced to ashes, with the exception of the heart, which was of the hardest ice. This required much time to melt and break. At last all was over.

She had been brought under the power of an evil spirit; she was rapidly being changed into a Chenoo a wild, fierce, unconquerable being. But she knew it all the while, and it was against her will. So she begged that she might be killed.

The Indians left the place; since that day none have ever returned to it. They feared lest some small part of the body might have remained unconsumed, and that from it another Chenoo would rise, capable of killing all whom she met. [Footnote: Mr. Rand (manuscript) gives a detailed account of an Indian who went mad during the winter, ran away naked into the wilderness among the snows, and was unanimously declared to have turned into a Chenoo. I agree with Mr. Rand that "the historical basis of these tales, if they have any, may be the same,—a case of lunacy; fiction and figure adding the incredible details."]

THUNDER STORIES

Of the Girl who married Mount Katahdin, and how all the Indians brought about their own Ruin.

(Penobscot.)

Of the old time. There was once an Indian girl gathering blueberries on Mount Katahdin. And, being lonely, she said, "I would that I had a husband!" And seeing the great mountain in all its glory rising on high, with the red sunlight on the top, she added, "I wish Katahdin were a man, and would marry me!"

All this she was heard to say ere she went onward and up the mountain, but for three years she was never seen again. Then she reappeared, bearing a babe, a beautiful child, but his little eyebrows were of stone. For the Spirit of the Mountain had taken her to himself; and when she greatly desired to return to her own people, he told her to go in peace, but forbade her to tell any man who had married her.

Now the boy had strange gifts, and the wise men said that he was born to become a mighty magician. For when he did but point his finger at a moose, or anything which ran, it would drop dead; and when in a canoe, if he pointed at the flocks of wild ducks or swans, then the water was at once covered with the floating game, and they gathered them in as they listed, and through that boy his mother and every one had food and to spare.

Now this was the truth, and it was great wonder, that Katahdin had wedded this girl, thinking with himself and his wife to bring up a child who should build up his nation, and make of the Wabanaki a mighty race. And he said, "Declare unto these people that they are not to inquire of thee who is the father of thy child; truly they will all know it by seeing him, for they shall not grieve thee with impertinence." Now the woman had made it known that she would not be questioned, and she gave them all what they needed; yet, for all this, they could not refrain nor restrain themselves from talking to her on what they well knew she would fain be silent. And one day when they had angered her, she thought, "Truly Katahdin was right; these people are in nowise worthy of my son, neither shall he serve them; he shall not lead them to victory; they are not of those who make a great nation." And being still further teased and tormented, she spake and said, "Ye fools, who by your own folly will kill yourselves; ye mud-wasps, who sting the fingers which would pick ye out of the water, why will ye ever trouble me to tell you what you well know? Can you not see who was the father of my boy? Behold his eyebrows; do ye not know Katahdin by them? But it shall be to your exceeding great sorrow that ever ye inquired. From this day ye may feed yourselves and find your own venison, for this child shall do so no more for you."

And she arose and went her way into the woods and up the mountain, and was seen on earth no more. And since that day the Indians, who should have been great, have become a little people. Truly it would have been wise and well for those of early times if they could have held their tongues.

This remarkable legend was related to me by Mrs. Marie Sakis, a Penobscot, a very clever story-teller. It gives the Fall of Man from a purely Indian standpoint. Nothing is so contemptible in Indian eyes as a want of dignity and idle, loquacious teasing; therefore it is made in the myth the sin which destroyed their race. The tendency of the lower class of Americans, especially in New England, to raise and emphasize the voice, to speak continually in italics and small and large capitals, with a wide display, and the constant disposition to chaff and tease, have contributed more than any other cause to destroy confidence and respect for them among the Indians.

Since writing the foregoing paragraph, I have read The Abnakis, by Rev. Eugene Vetromile. In his chapter on the Religion and Superstition of these Indians he gives this story, but, as I think, in a corrupted form. Firstly, he states that Pamola (that is, Bumole), who is the evil spirit of the night air, was the Spirit of Mount Katahdin. Now these are certainly *at present* two very distinct beings, which are described as being personally quite unlike. Secondly, in Vetromile's story the mother and child disappear in consequence of the child having *inadvertently* killed an Indian by pointing at him. It will be seen that this feeble, impotent conclusion utterly spoils the manifest meaning of the whole legend.

Of this story Vetromile remarks that "it is, of course, a superstitious tale, made up by the prolific imagination of some Indians, yet we can perceive in it some vestiges of the fall of the first man in having transgressed the command of God, and how it could be repaired only by God. We can also trace some ideas of the mystery of the Incarnation of the Son of God in the womb of the Blessed Virgin Mary, mixed with fables, superstitions, and pagan errors. The appearance of God to Moses in the Burning Bush may be glimpsed in Pamole appearing to the Indian on Mount Katahdin, and so forth."

The pilgrims in Rabelais did not point out scriptural coincidences with greater ingenuity than this. It is deeply to be regretted that the reverend father's entire knowledge of the mythology of the Abenakis was limited to this single story. (Vide Bumole, in chapter on Supernatural Beings.) It may be, however, observed, that if the name Bumole or Pamola really means "he curses on the mountain," or curse on mountain, it was natural that the evil spirit should be supposed to be on the mountain. Pamola was perhaps at an early period the spirit of lightning, and might thus be very easily confused with Katahdin.

How a hunter visited the Thunder Spirits who dwell in Mount Katahdin.

(Passamaquoddy.)

N'karnayoo. Of old times. Once an Indian went forth to hunt. And he departed from the east branch of the Penobscot, and came to the head of another branch that leads into the east branch, and this he followed even to the foot of Mount Katahdin. [Footnote: This minuteness of needless detail is very characteristic of Indian tales. I do not think that it is introduced for the sake of local color, or to give an air of truthful seeming, because the Indian simply believes the whole, as it is. I think the reason may be that, owing to their love of adventure, they enjoy the mere recitation of topographical details.] And there he hunted many a day alone, and met none, till one morning in midwinter he found the track of snow-shoes. So he returned to his camp; but the next day he met with it again in a far-distant place. And thus it was that, wherever he went, this track came to him every day. Then noting this, as a sign to be observed, he followed it, and it went up the mountain, Katahdin, which, being interpreted, means "the great mountain," until at last it was lost in a hard snow-shoe road made by many travelers. And since it was hard and even, he took off his *agahmook* (P.), or snow shoes, and went ever on and up with the road; and it was a strange path and strange was its ending, for it stopped just before a high ledge, like an immense wall, on a platform at its foot. And there were many signs there, as of many people, yet he saw no one. And as he stayed it seemed to grow stranger and stranger. At last he heard a sound as of footsteps coming, yet within the wall, when lo! a girl stepped directly out of the precipice upon the platform. But though she was beautiful beyond belief, he was afraid. And to his every thought she answered in words, and that so sweetly and kindly and cleverly that he was soon without fear, though he saw that she had powerful *m'teoulin*, or great magic power. And they being soon pleased one with the other, and wanting each other, she bade him accompany her, and that by walking directly through the rock. "Have no fear," said she, "but, advance boldly!" So he obeyed, and lo! the rock was as the air, and it gave way as he went on. And ever as they went the maiden talked to him, answering his thoughts, so that he spoke not aloud.

And anon they came to a great cavern far within, and there was an old man seated by a fire, and the old man welcomed him. And he was very kindly treated by the strange pair all day: in all his life he had never been so happy. Now as the night drew near, the old man said to his daughter, "Can you hear aught of your brothers?" Then she went out to the terrace, and, returning, said, "No." Then anon he asked her again, and she, going and returning as before, replied, "Now I hear them coming." Then they listened, when lo! there came, as at the door without, a crash of thunder with a flash of lightning, and out of the light stepped two young men of great beauty, but like giants, stupendous and of awful mien. And, like their father, their eyebrows were of stone, while their cheeks were as rocks.

And the hunter was told by their sister that when they went forth, which was every few days, their father said to them, "Sons, arise! it is time now for you to go forth over the world and save our friends. Go not too near the trees, but if you see aught that is harmful to those whom we love, strike, and spare not!" Then when they went forth they flew on high among the clouds; and thus it is that the Thunder and Lightning, whose home is in the mighty Katahdin, are made. And when the thunder strikes, the brothers are shooting at the enemies of their friends.

Now when the day was done the hunter returned to his home, and when there, found he had been gone seven years. All this I have heard from the old people who are dead and gone.

This tale was told me by Tomah Josephs (P.). It seems to have nothing in common with the very widely spread myth that the thunder is the flapping of the wings of a giant bird, and the lightning the flashes of its eyes. The tradition is probably of Eskimo origin, supernatural beings partially of stone being common to Greenland and Labrador. There is a strange but entirely accidental resemblance between this story and Rip Van Winkle, as in the distant sound of the nine-pins like low-muttered thunder, the hospitable entertainment, and finally the seven years as one day. Apparent resemblances are very deceptive. In the Eskimo mythology the *mersugat* or *kutadlit*, who are the higher or benevolent spirits, protecting mortals, are distinguished from the evil ones by dwelling in cliffs, to which there are invisible entrances.

There is a remarkable resemblance between Katahdin and Hrungnir of the Edda. Hrungnir has a face of stone; he is unquestionably a mountain personified, as Miss Larned declares: "His stony head pierces the blue sky." [Footnote: *Tales of the Elder Edda*, p. 235.] Both giants are the typical great mountain of their respective countries. Hrungnir has also very great affinity with the Chenoo giant. He has a *stony heart*, an insatiable appetite, and is cruel and brutal.

The Iroquois have the very stone giants—or, as Schoolcraft calls them, the stonish giants—themselves, and a very curious picture of them has been preserved. [Footnote: Vide Cusick's *Five Nations*, 2d edition, and Schoolcraft's *Indian Tribes*, vol. i p: 429.] Of them he remarks, "Who the giants are intended to symbolize is uncertain. They are represented as impenetrable by darts." The connection between the stone giants of the Indians, the Eskimo, and the

Norsemen, if not historical, is at least identical in this, that they all typify the mountains.

The Thunder and Lightning Men.

(Passamaquoddy.)

This is truly an old Indian story of old time. Once an Indian was whirled up by the roaring wind: he was taken up in a thunder-storm, and set down again in the village of the Thunders. [Footnote: This tale is transcribed, with very little alteration, from a manuscript collection of tales written in Indian-English by an Indian. I retain the word *thunders* as expressive of the beings in question. It has for title, *A Story called "An Indian transformed into a Thunder!"*] In after-times he described them as very like human beings: they used bows and arrows (*tah-bokque*), and had wings.

But these wings can be laid aside, and kept for use. And from time to time their chief gives these Thunders orders to put them on, and tells them where to go. He also tells them how long they are to be gone, and warns them not to go too low, for it is sure death for them to be caught in the crotch of a tree.

The great chief of the Thunders, hearing of the stranger's arrival, sent for him, and received him very kindly, and told him that he would do well to become one of them. To which the man being willing, the chief soon after called all his people together to see the ceremony of thunderifying [Footnote: This word is one of the Indian author's own, but as I know of no synonym for it I retain it. It is certainly not worse than "Native-Americanizing."] the Indian.

Then they bade him go into a square thing, or box, and while in it he lost his senses and became a Thunder. Then they brought him a pair of wings, and he put them on. So he flew about like the rest of the Thunders; he became quite like them, and followed all their ways. And he said that they always flew towards the *sou' n' snook*, or, south, and that the roar and crash of the thunder was the sound of their wings. Their great amusement is to play at ball across the sky. [Footnote: The Eskimo say that the lightning of the Northern Lights is caused by spirits playing at ball with the head of a walrus.] When they return they carefully put away their wings for their next flight. There is a big bird in the south, and this they are always trying to kill, but never succeed in doing so.

They made long journeys, and always took him with them. So it went on for a long time, but it came to pass that the Indian began to tire of his strange friends. Then he told the chief that he wished to see his family on earth, and the sagamore listened to him and was very kind. Then he called all his people together, and said that their brother from the other world was very lonesome, and wished to return. They were all very sorry indeed to lose him, but because they loved him they let him have his own way, and decided to carry him back again. So bidding him close his eyes till he should be on earth, they carried him down.

The Indians saw a great thunder-storm drawing near; they heard such thunder as they never knew before, and then something in the shape of a human being coming down with lightning; then they ran to the spot where he sat, and it was their long-lost brother, who had been gone seven years.

He had been in the Thunder-world. He told them how he had been playing ball with the Thunder-boys: yes, how he had been turned into a real Thunder himself.

This is why the Indians to this very day have a firm belief that the thunder and lightning we hear and see are caused by (beings or spirits) (called) in Indian *Bed-dag yek* (or thunder), [Footnote: The manuscript is here difficult to understand, but this is apparently the real meaning of it.] because they see them, and have, moreover, actually picked up the *bed-dags k'chisousan*, or thunder-bullet. [Footnote: Thunderbolt.] It is of many different kinds of stone, but always of the same shape. The last was picked up by Peter Sabattis, [Footnote: I heard of the existence of this legend a long time before I found it in the manuscript collection obtained for me by Louis Mitchell. It is very curious as being unquestionably of Eskimo origin, or common to the Eskimo; also because it speaks of the Thunders as always endeavoring to kill a great bird in the south. This is probably the thunder or storm bird, called by the Passamaquoddy Indians *Wochowsen* or *Wuchowsen*, that is, Wind-Blower. Another legend makes Thunder and Lightning the sons of Mount Katahdin.

I may here mention that I am well acquainted with old Peter Sabattis, the possessor of the "thunder-bullet."] one of the Passamaquoddy tribe. He has it yet. He found it in a crotch-root of a spruce-tree at Head Harbor, on the island of Campobello. This stone is a sign of good-luck to him who finds it.

The thunder is the sound of the wings of the men who fly above. The lightning we see is the fire and smoke of their pipes.

Of the Woman who married the Thunder, and of their Boy.

(Passamaquoddy.)

Once a woman went to the edge of a lake [Footnote: It is impossible to distinguish in any Indian story between lake and sea.] and lay down to sleep. As she awoke, she saw a great serpent, with glittering eyes, crawl from the water, and stealthily approach her. She had no power to resist his embrace. After her return to her people her condition betrayed itself, and she was much persecuted; they pursued her with sticks and stones, howling abuse.

She fled from the village; she went afar into wild places, and, sitting down on the grass, wept, wishing that she were dead. As she sat and wailed, a very beautiful girl, dressed in silver and gold, [Footnote: Both silver and gold were known in pre-Columbian, times to the Indians. I had a cousin who once found a very old stone pipe in which a small piece of gold had been set. Particles of gold are found in many mountain-streams in New England.] appeared, and after listening to her sad story said, "Follow me!"

Then they went up on high into a mountain, through three rocks, until they came into a pleasant wigwam with a very smooth floor. An old man, so old that he was all white, came to meet them. Then he, taking a short stick, bade her dance. He began to sing, and as he sang she gave birth, one by one, to twelve serpents. These the old man killed in succession with his stick as they were born. Then she had become thin again, and was in her natural form.

The old man had a son, Badawk, the Thunder, and a daughter, *Psawk-tankapic*, the Lightning, and when Thunder returned he offered to take her back to her own people, but she refused to go. Then the old man, said to his son, "Take her for your wife and be good to her." So they were married.

In time she bore a son. When the boy could stand, the old man, who never leaves the mountain, called him to stand before him, while be fastened wings to the child. He was soon able, with these wings, to make a noise, which greatly pleased the grandfather. When a storm is approaching, the distant rumbling is the muttering thunder made by the child, but it is *Badawk*, his father, who comes in the dark cloud and makes the roaring crash, while *Psawk-tankapic* flashes her lightnings.

In after days, when the woman visited her people, she told them that they never need fear the thunder or lightning.

AT-O-SIS, THE SERPENT

How Two Girls were changed to Water-Snakes, and of Two Others that became Mermaids.

(Passamaquoddy.)

Pocumkwess, or Thoroughfare, is sixty-five miles from Campobello. There was an Indian village there in the old times. Two young Indian girls had a strange habit of absenting themselves all day every Sunday. No one knew for a long time where they went or what they did. But this was how they passed their time. They would take a canoe and go six miles down the Grand Lake, where, at the north end, is a great ledge of rock and sixty feet of water. There they stayed. All day long they ran about naked or swam; they were wanton, witch-like girls, liking eccentric and forbidden ways.

They kept this up for a long time. Once, while they were in the water, an Indian who was hunting spied them. He came nearer and nearer, unseen. He saw them come out of the water and sit on the shore, and then go in again; but as he looked they grew longer and longer, until they became snakes.

He went home and told this. (But now they had been seen by a man they must keep the serpent form.) Men of the village, in four or five canoes, went to find them. They found the canoe and clothes of the girls; nothing more. A few days after, two men on Grand Lake saw the snake-girls on shore, showing their heads over the bushes. One began to sing.

"N'ktieh ieben iut,
Qu'spen ma ke owse."

We are going to stay in this lake
A few days, and then go down the river.
Bid adieu to our friends for us;
We are going to the great salt water.

After singing this they sank into the water. They had very long hair.

A picture of the man looking at the snake-girls was scraped for me by the Indian who told me this story. The pair were represented as snakes with female heads. When I first heard this tale, I promptly set it down as nothing else but the Melusina story derived from a Canadian French source. But I have since found that it is so widely spread, and is told in so many different forms, and is so deeply connected with tribal traditions and totems, that there is now no doubt in my mind that it is at least pre-Columbian.

Another and a very curious version of this story was obtained by Mrs. W. Wallace Brown, who has been the chief discoverer of curious Indian lore among the Passamaquoddies. It is called:

Ne Hwas, the Mermaid.

A long time ago there was an Indian, with his wife and two daughters. They lived by a great lake, or the sea, and the mother told her girls never to go into the water there, for that, if they did, something would happen to them.

They, however, deceived her repeatedly. When swimming is prohibited it becomes delightful. The shore of this lake *sands* away out or slopes to an island. One day they went to it, leaving their clothes on the beach. The parents missed them.

The father went to seek them. He saw them swimming far out, and called to them. The girls swam up to the sand, but could get no further. Their father asked them why they could not. They cried that they had grown to be so heavy that it was impossible. They were all slimy; they grew to be snakes from below the waist. After sinking a few times in this strange slime they became very handsome, with long black hair and large, bright black eyes, with silver bands on their neck and arms.

When their father went to get their clothes, they began to sing in the most exquisite tones:—

"Leave them there!
Do not touch them!
Leave them there!"

Hearing this, their mother began to weep, but the girls kept on:—

"It is all our own fault,
But do not blame us;
'T will be none the worse for you.
When you go in your canoe,
Then you need not paddle;
We shall carry it along!"

And so it was: when their parents went in the canoe, the girls carried it safely on everywhere.

One day some Indians saw the girls' clothes on the beach, and so looked out for the wearers. They found them in the water, and pursued them, and tried to capture them, but they were so slimy that it was impossible to take them, till one, catching hold of a mermaid by her long black hair, cut it off.

Then the girl began to rock the canoe, and threatened to upset it unless her hair was given to her again. The fellow who had played the trick at first refused, but as the mermaids, or snake-maids, promised that they should all be drowned unless this was done, the locks were restored. And the next day they were heard singing and were seen, and on her who had lost her hair it was all growing as long as ever.

We may very easily detect the hand of Lox, the Mischief Maker, in this last incident. It was the same trick which Loki played on Sif, the wife of Odin. That both Lox and Loki were compelled to replace the hair and make it grow again—the one on the snake-maid, the other on the goddess—is, if a coincidence, at least a very remarkable one. It is a rule with little exception that where we have to deal with myths which have passed into romances or tales, that which was originally one character becomes many, just as the king who has but one name and one appearance at court assumes a score when he descends to disguise of low degree and goes among the people. But when, in addition to characteristic traits, we have even a single anecdote or attribute in common, the identification is very far advanced. When not one, but many, of these coincidences occur, we are in all probability at the truth. Thus we find in the mythology of the Wabanaki, as in the Edda, the chief evil being indulging in mere wanton, comic mischief, to an extent not to be found in the devil of any other race whatever. Here, in a mythical tale, the same mischief maker steals a snake-girl's hair, and is compelled to replace it. In the Edda, the corresponding mischief maker steals the hair of a goddess, and is also forced to make restitution. Yet this is only one of many such resemblances in these tales. It will be observed that in both cases the hair of the loser is made to grow again. But while the incident has in the Edda a meaning, as appears from its context, it has none in the Indian tale. All that we can conclude from this is that the Wabanaki tale is subsequent to the Norse, or taken from it. The incidents of tales are often remembered when the plot is lost. It is certainly very remarkable that, wherever the mischief maker occurs in these Indian tales, he in every narrative does something in common with his Norse prototype.

Of the Woman who loved a Serpent who lived in a Lake.

(Passamaquoddy.)

Of old times. There was a very beautiful woman. She turned the heads of all the men. She married, and her husband died very soon after, but she immediately took another. Within a single year she had five husbands, and these were the cleverest and handsomest and bravest in the tribe. And then she married again.

This, the sixth, was such a silent man that he passed for a fool. But he was wiser than people thought. He came to believe, by thinking it over, that this woman had some strange secret. He resolved to find it out. So he watched her all the time. He kept his eye on her by night and by day.

It was summer, and she proposed to go into the woods to pick berries, and to camp there. By and by, when they were in the forest, she suggested that he should go on to the spot where they intended to remain and build a wigwam. He said that he would do so. But he went a little way into the woods and watched her.

As soon as she believed that he was gone, she rose and walked rapidly onwards. He followed her, unseen. She went on, till, in a deep, wild place among the rocks, she came to a pond. She sat down and sang a song. A great foam, or froth, rose to the surface of the water. Then in the foam appeared the tail of a serpent. The creature was of immense size. The woman, who had laid aside all her garments, embraced the serpent, which twined around her, enveloping all her limbs and body in his folds. The husband watched it all. He now understood that, the venom of the serpent having entered the woman, she had saved her life by transferring it to others, who died.

He went on to the camping ground and built a wigwam. He made up two beds; he built a fire. His wife came. She was earnest that there should be only a single bed. He sternly bade her lie by herself. She was afraid of him. She laid down, and went to sleep. He arose three times during the night to replenish the fire. Every time he called her, and there was no answer. In the morning he shook her. She was dead. She had died by the poison of the serpent. They sunk her in the pond where the snake lived.

[Illustration: THE WOMAN AND THE SERPENT]

I do not omit this ghastly and repulsive legend for the following reasons: One might hastily conclude, from its resemblance to the old legend of the origin of the Merovingian family, that this idea of the woman with the horrible water spirit for a lover was of Canadian French origin. But a story like it in the main detail is told by the Indians of Guiana, and that of the Faithless Wife, given in Rink's Tales and Traditions of the Eskimo (p. 143), is almost the same. But in the latter the husband revenges himself by stuffing the woman full of poisonous vermin. Rink says that he had five different versions of this tale, and that one was from Labrador, a country often traveled by the Micmacs, and even by the Penobscots and Passamaquoddies; I myself knowing one of the latter who has been there. I conjecture that this tale sets forth the aboriginal idea of the origin of a certain disease supposed to have come from America. It is popularly believed among the vulgar that this disease can be transferred to another person, thereby removing it from the first. Of this the Rev. Thistleton Dyer, in his Folk Lore of Shakespeare, says, "According to an old but erroneous belief, infection communicated to another left the infecter free; in allusion to which Timon of Athens (Act IV. 3) says,—

"'I will not kiss thee; then the rot returns
To thy own lips again.'"

Bonifacius, Historia Ludicra, has collected all the instances known to classical antiquity of women who had serpent lovers. The kings of the early races of Central America laid great stress on the fact that they were descendants of serpents. One could fill a volume with all the Arab, Hindoo, and other Oriental tales belonging to the beloved of "ophitic monsters."

I am indebted for this very curious and ancient tale to Governor Tomah Josephs, of Peter Dana's Point, Maine.

The Mother of Serpents.

(Passamaquoddy.)

There was once a couple well advanced in years. They were powerful and rich in the Indian fashion, but they were unhappy because they had no children. This was near the river St. John's, on the shore of a small lake.

After the woman had gone in vain to all the medicine men and *m'teoulin*, she heard of an old doctress, or witch, who lived not very far off. And though hope was almost dead, the witch was consulted.

She gave the wife some herbs, and bade her steep them in a pot out-of-doors, and then let them boil. When the vessel should dance over the flame, the propitious moment would be at hand.

Everything succeeded according to the witch's prediction. A few days after she appeared in the town. The mother, who was a very proud woman, had in advance hung up an Indian cradle with very fine ornaments. The old woman was very dirty, poor, and squalid. The proud woman was furious at the visit, which mortified her in every way. She drove the witch away with bitter words, bidding her begone with her rags. The old woman went away muttering, "That woman—too proud—too ugly proud—I'll see." [Footnote: The story was narrated in Indian-English.]

What she saw was bad for the mother. She took some more herbs from her box and threw them in the fire, crying with a loud voice, "*At-o-sis! At-o-sis!*" and imitated the motions of a snake.

When the proud woman was confined, she gave birth to two large serpents. They had each a white ring round the neck and red stripes down the sides. As soon as they were born they went rapidly to the lake, and disappeared in its water. They have been seen there, now and then, ever since.

She who gave birth, to them was a Mohawk, and she is called the Mother of Serpents.

Another Passamaquoddy tale gives the following account of the origin of the Serpent-race.

Once there was an Indian sorcerer came to a wigwam where there was a man who had a very handsome daughter.

The magician wished to win the girl; the father made up his mind that he should not have her.

The magician told them that he was very wealthy, and had a great lodge filled with furs and wampum. It was of no use.

Then he told the father that if he would go and cast his lines in a certain place he would catch as many of the finest fish as he wanted. The old man went, but took his daughter with him.

When they returned, loaded with fish, the magician, smiling, said to the girl with great mystery, "When you have cooked *these* fish, always throw away the tail, and begin by eating the head first."

He knew very well that her curiosity and perversity would make her disobey him. She waited with impatience till the man had left, when she hurried to cook and eat the fish. Thereby she became a mother, and the magician had his revenge.

Origin of the Black Snakes.

(Passamaquoddy.)

Far away, very far in the north, there dwelt by the border of a great lake a man and his wife. They had no children, and the woman was very beautiful and passionate.

The lake was frozen over during the greater part of the year. One day when the woman cut away the ice, she saw in the water a bright pair of large eyes looking steadily at her. They charmed her so that she could not move. Then she distinguished a handsome face; it was that of a fine slender young man. He came out of the water. His eyes seemed brighter and more fascinating than ever; he glittered from head to foot; on his breast was a large shining silvery plate.

The woman learned that this was At-o-sis, the Serpent, but she returned his embraces and held conversation with him, and was so charmed with her lover that she not only met him more than once every day, but even went forth to see him in the night.

Her husband, noticing these frequent absences asked her why she went forth so frequently. She replied, "To get the fresh air."

The weather grew warmer; the ice left the lake; grass and leaves were growing. Then the woman waited till her husband slept, and stole out from the man whom she kissed no more, to the lover whom she fondled and kissed more than ever.

At last the husband's suspicions being fairly aroused, he resolved to watch her. To do this he said that he would be absent for three days. But he returned at the end of the first day, and found that she was absent. As she came in he observed something like silvery scales on the logs. He asked what they were. She replied, *Brooches*. [Footnote: *Nskmahn'k* coins of all sizes hammered out by the Indians and made into pin-brooches.]

He was still dissatisfied, and said that he would be gone for one day. He went to the top of a hill not far distant, whence he watched her. She went to the shore, and sat there. By and by there rose up out of the lake, at a distance, what seemed to be a brightly shining piece of ice. It came to the strand and rose from the water. It was a very tall and very handsome man, dressed in silver. His wife clasped the bright stranger in her arms, kissing him again and again.

The husband was awed by this strange event. He went home, and tried to persuade his wife to leave the place and to return to her people. This she refused to do. He departed; he left her forever. But her father and mother came to find her. They found her there; they dwelt with her. Every day she brought to them furs and meat. They asked her whence she got them. "I have another husband," she replied; "one who suits me. The one I had was bad, and did not use me well. This one brings all the animals to me." Then she sent them away with many presents, telling them not to return until the ice had formed; that was in the autumn.

When they returned she had become white. She was with young, and soon gave birth to her offspring. It consisted of many serpents. The parents went home. As they departed she said to them, "When you come again you may see me, but you will not know me."

Years after some hunters, roaming that way, remembered the tale, and looked for the wigwam. It was there, but no one was in it. But all the woods about the place were full of great black snakes, which would rise up like a human being and look one in the face, then glide away without doing any harm.

THE PARTRIDGE

The Adventures of the Great Hero Pulowech, or the Partridge.

(Micmac.)

Wee-yig-yik-keseyook. A tale of old times. Two men once lived together in one wigwam in the woods, on the border of a beautiful lake. Many hard-wood trees made their pictures in it. One of these Indians was Pulowech, the Partridge in the Micmac tongue, but who is called by the Passamaquoddy Mitchihess; but the other was Wejek (M.), the Tree Partridge.

Now it befell that one day Pulowech was walking along the shore, when it was winter, and he beheld three girls, fair and fine, with flowing hair, sitting on the ice braiding their locks. Then he knew that they were of the fairy kind, who dwell in the water; and, verily, these were plentier of old than they are now,—to our sorrow be it said, for they were good company for the one who could get them. And Pulowech, knowing this, said, "I will essay this thing, and perchance I may catch one or two of them; which will be a great comfort, for a pretty girl is a nice thing to have about the wigwam." So he sought to secure them by stealing softly along; but one cried, "*Ne miha skedap!*" "I see a man!" P., and they all went head over heels, first best time, into the water; and verily that was a cold duck for December in the Bay of Fundy.

But though Pulowech had never hunted for sea-girls, yet he had fished for seals, who are greatly akin unto them, being almost as slippery; and wotting well that no man hath the mitten till he is refused thirty times and many more, he went about it in another wise. For this time he gat many fir boughs, strewing them about as if blown by the wind, and hiding himself behind them, again came up and made a sudden dart. Then the maids, crying as before, "*Ne miha skedap!*" "I see a, man!" went with a dive into the deep. But this time he caught, if not the hair, at least the hair-string, of the fairest, which remained in his hand. And, gazing on this, it came into his mind that he had got that which was her charm, or life, and that she could not live without it, [Footnote: The magic hair-string plays a part in many of these tales. It belongs to the sorcery of all the world in all ages.] or her cherished *sakultobee* (M.). And taking it home, he tied it to the place in the wigwam above that wherein he slept. Nor had he waited long before she came, and, with little ado, remained with him as his wife.

Now Pulowech, being himself addicted to sorcery, knew that there were divers knaves of the same stamp prowling about the woods, who would make short work of a wife if they could find a plump young one in the way,—they being robbers, ravishers, and cannibals withal. Therefore he warned his bride to keep well within doors when he was away, and to open to none, which she, poor soul, meant to obey with all her might. But being alone at midnight, and hearing a call outside, even "*Pantahdooe!*" M., "Open the door to me!" she wondered greatly who it might be. And it was a very wicked wizard, a *boo-oin*, or pow-wow; and he, being subtle and crafty, and knowing of her family, so imitated the voices of her brothers and sisters; beseeching her to let them in, that her very heart ached. "O sister, we have come from afar!" they cried. "We missed you, and have followed you. Let us in!" And yet again she heard a sad and very earnest voice, and it was that of her old mother, crying, "*N'toos', n'toos', pantahdooe!*" M., "My daughter! my daughter! open unto me!" and she verily wist that it must be so. But when she heard the voice of her dear old father, shaking and saying, "*Pantahdooe loke cyowchee!*" "Open the door, for I am very cold!" she could resist no more, and, springing up, opened it to those who were without. And then the evil sorcerers, springing on her like mad wolves, dragged her away and devoured her. They did not leave two of her little bones one with another. [Footnote: This Indian Little Red Riding-Hood story is very effective. The wolfish sorcerers bursting in at midnight are even more terrible, from a nursery melodramatic point, than the old wolf in bed.]

Now when *Wejek*, the Tree Partridge, came in and found his friend's wife gone, he was so angry that, without waiting, he set forth to seek her. And this was not wisely done, since, falling among them, he was himself slain. Then Pulowech, returning last of all, and finding no one, sought by means of magic to know where friend and wife might be. For taking a *woltes*, or a wooden dish, he filled it with water, and charmed it with a spell, and placed it in the back part of his wigwam, just opposite the door. So he laid him down to sleep, and in the morning when he arose he looked upon the dish,—even the dish of divination,—and lo! it was half full of blood. Then he knew that the twain had been murdered.

Then gathering all his arms, he went forth for revenge, and passed many days on the path, tracking the *boo-oin*; and having the eyesight of sorcery, he one day beheld very far away, upon an exceeding high cliff, the knee of a man sticking out of the stone, and knew that a sorcerer had hidden himself in the solid rock, even as a child might hide itself in a pile of feathers. Then throwing his tomahawk he cut away the knee, and the *boo-oin*, his spell broken, remained hard and fast forever in the ledge. And yet, anon, a little further on, he saw a foot projecting from a wall, and this he likewise cut off, and with that he had slain two.

And as he went further he found by the way a poor little squirrel, even *Meeko*, who was crawling along, half dead, in sorry plight. And taking her up he made her well, and placing her in his bosom, said, "Rest there yet a while, *Meeko*, for thou must fight to-day, and that fiercely. Yet fear not, for I will stand by thee, and when I tap thy back, then shalt thou bring forth thy young!"

Then going ever on, he saw from the mountains far in a lake below a flock of wild geese sporting merrily, even the *Senum-kwak'*. But he wist right well that these also were of the *boo-oin*, whom he sought, and placing a spell on his bow, and singing a charm over his arrows that they should not miss, he slew the wild fowl one by one, and tying their heads together, he carried them in a bunch upon his back. And truly he deemed it a good bag of game for one day.

And yet further on he came to a wigwam, and entering it saw a man there seated, whom he knew at once was of the enemy. For he who sat there glared at him grimly; he did not say to him, "*'Kutakumoogwal!*" "Come higher up!" as they do who are hospitable. But having cooked some meat, and given it in a dish to Pulowech's hand, he snatched it back again, and said he would sooner give it to his dog. And this he did more than once, saying the same thing. But Pulowech kept quiet. Then the rude man said, "Hast thou met with aught to-day, thou knave?" And the guest replied, "Truly I saw a fellow's knee sticking out of a stone, and I cut it off. And yet, anon, I saw a foot coming from a rock, and this I also chopped. And further on there was a flock of wild geese, and them I slew; there was not one left,—no, not one. And if you will look without there you may see them all dead, and much good may it do you!"

Then the savage sorcerer burst forth in all his rage: "Come on, then, our dogs must fight this out!" "Thou sayest well," replied Pulowech; "truly I am fond of a good dog-fight, so bring out thy pup!" And that which the man brought forth was terrible; for it was no dog, but a hideous savage beast, known to Micmacs as the *Weisum*. [Footnote: The *Amarok* of the Eskimo.]

But that which Pulowech produced was quite as different from a dog as was the *Weisum*; for it was only *Meeko*, a poor little squirrel, and half dead at that, which he laid carefully before the fire that it might revive. [Footnote: In another version of this story, the savage stranger puts up a real dog against the squirrel; and in the story of Glooskap, it is that great man who makes the squirrel great or small.] But anon it began to revive, and grew until it was well-nigh as great as the *Weisum*. And then there was indeed a battle as of devils and witches; he who had been a hundred miles away might have heard it.

But anon it seemed that the *Weisum* was getting the better of *Meeko*. Then Pulowech did but tap the squirrel on the back, when lo! she brought forth two other squirrels, and these grew in an instant to be as large as their mother, and the three were soon too many for the beast. "Ho! call off your dogs!" cried the *boo-oin*; "you have beaten. But spare mine, since, indeed, he does not belong to me, but to my grandmother, who is very fond of him." [Footnote: This trivial episode of begging a call-off seems to have deeply impressed the

Indians, who are generally sporting-men, since I find it in both the Passamaquoddy and Micmac versions of the legend.]

Pulowech, who held to his own in all things like a wolverine, was the last man alive to think of, and he encouraged the squirrels until they had torn the *Weisum* to rags.

Then he who had staked it, bitterly lamented, saying, "Alack, my poor grandmother! Alas, how she will wail when she hears that her *Weisum* is dead! Woe the day that ever I did put him up! Alas, my grandmother!" For all which the cruel Pulowech, the hard-hearted, impenitent Partridge, did not care the hair of a dead musk-rat.

Now the host, who had thus suddenly grown so tender-hearted, said, "Let us sail forth upon the river in a canoe." Then they were soon on the stream, and rushing down a rapid like a dart. And anon they came to a terribly high cliff, in which there was a narrow cavern into which the river ran. And on it, thundering through this door of death, borne on a boiling surge, the bark was forced furiously into darkness. And Pulowech sat firmly in his seat, and steered the boat with steady, certain hand; but just as he entered the horrible hole, glancing around, he saw the sorcerer leap ashore. For the evil man, believing that no one had ever come alive out of the cavern, had betrayed him into it.

Yet ever cool and calm the mighty man went on, for danger now was bringing out all the force of his magic; [Footnote: It is very characteristic of the heroes of these Indian tales that they gradually unfold or develop from small characteristics to very great ones. There is a lesson in this, and it has been perfectly appreciated by poets and similar sorcerers.] and soon the stream grew smoother, the rocks disappeared from its bed, and then from afar there was a brightness, and he was soon in the daylight and sunshine on a beautiful stream, and by the banks thereof there grew the *wabeyu-beskwan*, or water-lilies, and very pleasant it was to him to feel the wind again. So using his paddle he saw a smoke rising from a cave in the rocks, And landing and softly stepping up heard talking within.

Nor had he listened long ere he knew the voice of the man who had lured him into the canoe, and he was telling his grandmother how, one after the other, all the best *boo-oin* of their band had been slain by a mighty sorcerer. But when she heard from him how her beloved, or the one who had inspired the *Weisum*, had been beaten, her wrath burst forth in a storm, like the raving of devils, like a mad wind on the waves. And she said, "If Pulowech were but before me, were he but alive, I would roast him." The man, hearing this, cried, "Aye; but he is *not* alive, for I sent him afloat down into the dark cavern!"

And then Pulowech, stepping in before them, said, "And yet I am alive. And do thou, woman, *bak sok bok sood*!" (roast me to death). Then she scowled horribly at him, but said naught; and he, sitting down, looked at them.

This woman was of the Porcupines, who are never long without raising their quills, and they are fond of heat. Now there was in the cave much hemlock bark, and this she began to heap on the fire. Then it blazed, it crackled and roared; but Pulowech sat still, and said naught, neither did his eyes change. And he called unto himself all his might, the might of his magic did he awaken, and the spirit came unto him very terribly, so that all the *boo-oin*, with their vile black witchcraft, were but as worms before him, the Great and Terrible One. And when the fire had burned low he brought in by his will great store of bark, so that the whole cave was filled, and closing the door he lighted the fuel. Then the Porcupines, who were those who had slain his wife and friend, howled for mercy, but he was deaf as a stone to their cries. Then the roof and sides of the cavern cracked with the heat, the red-hot stones fell in heavy blocks, the red flames rose in the thickest smoke, but Pulowech sat and sang his song until the witch and wizard were burned to cinders; yea, till their white bones crumbled to ashes beneath his feet. And then he arose and went unto his home. [Footnote: In this Micmac legend, which is plainly a poem, there is one very striking and original element in the art with which the great knowledge and power of Pulowech are kept out of sight until towards the final unfolding. When he picks up the Squirrel it is with a full comprehension that he will be confronted with the *Weisum*. From the beginning to the end, he is master of the situation; all goes on with him like the unfolding of Fate in a Greek tragedy, until the end, when, stern and unpitying, he sits in the cavern of fire and sees his enemies roasted alive before him.—From the Rand Manuscript.]

In this legend the hero passes the mysterious river which separates in several Indian tales the ordinary world from that where the evil giants, Jotuns, sorcerers, or witches live. It appears to correspond exactly to "the stream called Ifing, which divides the earth between the Jotuns and the Gods." (Edda, Vafthrudnismal, 16.) The attempt by the Porcupine host to roast the guest alive and its failure bears marked likeness to the scene in the Grimnismal, in which King Geirrod vainly strives to roast his guest, Odin, and is himself slain.

"Fire, thou art hot, and much too great; flame, let us separate."

The grandeur of Odin and the behavior of the Indian are set forth in a strikingly similar manner in both narratives. If any modern poet had depicted this incident in so like a style, every critic would have cried out plagiarism!

The Story of a Partridge and his Wonderful Wigwam.

Once a man was traveling through the woods, and he heard afar off a sound as of footsteps beating the ground. So he sought to find the people that made it, and went on for a full week ere he came to them. And it was a man and his wife dancing about a tree, in the top of which was a Raccoon. They had, by their constant treading, worn a trench in the ground; indeed, they were in it up to their waists. [Footnote: To dance away the ground, or walk knee-deep in it, was characteristic of wizards. So was the hearing of any sound at an apparently incredible distance. To an Indian mind this tale is weird and wonderful from the first words thereof.] Then, being asked why they did this strange thing, they answered that, being hungry, they were trying to dance down the tree to catch the Raccoon.

Then the man who had come said, "Truly there is a newer and better way of felling trees, which has lately come into the land." As they wished to know what this might be, he showed them how to cut it down, and did so; making it a condition that if they got the game they might have the meat and he should get the skin. So when the tree fell they caught the animal, and the woman, having tanned the skin, gave it to the man, and he went his way.

And being afar, in a path in the forest, he met another man, and was greatly amazed at him because he was bearing on his head a house, or a large birch wigwam of many rooms. He was frightened at first at such a sight, but the man, putting down his house, shook hands with him, and seemed to be a right honest good fellow. Then while they smoked and talked, the Man of the House, seeing the skin of *Hespuns*, or that of the Raccoon, in the other's belt, said, "Well, that is a fine pelt! Where did you get it, brother?" And he, answering, told all the story of the Dancing Man and Wife; whereupon he of the House became mightily anxious to buy it, offering one thing after another for it, and at last the House, which was accepted. And, examining it, the buyer was amazed to find how many rooms it contained, and how full it was of good furniture. "Truly," said he, "I can never carry this as you do!" "Yes, you can," replied the *Pil-wee-mon-soo-in* (P., one who belongs somewhere else,—a stranger). "Do but try it!" So he essayed and lifted it easily, for he found it as light as any *bassinode* or basket.

So they parted and he went on carrying his cabin till night-fall, when coming to a hard-wood ridge, near a good spring of water, he resolved to settle there. [Footnote: A hard-wood ridge; that is, where there is plenty of birch, ash, and such trees as are necessary for baskets, dishes, canoes, and other Indian wants. Hence it is mentioned in many tales as a desirable place to live.] And, searching, he found a room in which there was a very fine bed, covered with a *white bear-skin*. [Footnote: A sure indication of sorcery.] And as it was very soft, and he was very weary, he slept well.

In the morning, when he awoke, what was his astonishment and delight to see above him, hanging to the beams, all kinds of nice provisions,— venison, hams, ducks, baskets of berries and of maple-sugar, with many ears of Indian corn. And as he, in his joy, stretched out his arms and made a jump towards all these dainties, behold the white bear-skin melted and ran away, for it was the snow of winter; and his arms spread forth into wings, and he flew up to the food, which was the early buds of the birch, on which they hung. [Footnote: Birch-buds are the food of the partridge. The unexpected ending of this tale signifies the sudden return of spring. As told by an Indian, it is very effective. This tale was told me by Tomah Josephs.] And he was a Partridge, who after the manner of his kind had been wintering under a snow-drift, and now came forth to greet the pleasant spring.

How the Partridge built Good Canoes for all the Birds, and a Bad One for Himself.

When a partridge beats upon a hollow log he makes a noise like an Indian at work upon a canoe, and when an Indian taps at a canoe it sounds afar off like the drumming of a partridge, even of *Mitchihess*. And this comes because that *N'karnayoo*, of ancient days, the Partridge, was the canoe builder for all the other birds. Yes, for all at once.

And on a certain day they every one assembled, and each got into his bark, and truly it was a brave sight to see. First of all *Kicheeplagon*, the Eagle, entered his great shell and paddled off, using the ends of his wings; and then came *Ko-ko-kas*, the Owl, doing the same; and, *Kosqu'*, the Crane, *Wee-sow-wee-hessis*, the Bluebird, *Tjidge-is-skwess*, the Snipe, and *Meg-sweit-tchip-sis*, the Blackbird, all came sailing proudly after. Even the tiny *A-la-Mussit*, the Humming-Bird, had a dear little boat, and for him the good Partridge had made a pretty little paddle, only that some thought it rather large, for it was almost an inch long. And *Ishmegwess*, the Fish-Hawk, who lived on the wing, cried in amazement, "*Akweden skouje!*" "A canoe is coming!" when he beheld this beautiful squadron standing out to sea.

But when *Mitchihess*, the great builder, was asked why he had not built a canoe for himself, he merely looked mysterious and drummed. And being further questioned by the birds, he shook his head, and at last hinted that when he built a canoe unto himself it would be indeed a marvel; yea, a wonder such as even birds' eyes had never beheld,—an entire novelty, and something to dream of. And this went on for many days.

But in due time it was noised abroad that the wonderful canoe had at last been really built, and would soon be shown. And at an appointed time all the birds assembled on the banks to behold this new thing. Now the Partridge had reasoned that if a boat having two ends could be rowed in two ways, one which was all ends, all round, could be rowed in every way. So he had made a canoe which was exactly like a nest, or perfectly round. And this idea had greatly amazed the honest feathered folk, who were astonished that so simple a thing had not occurred to all of them.

But what was their wonder when Partridge, having entered his canoe and proceeded to paddle, made no headway at all; for it simply turned round and round, and ever and again the same way, let him work it as he would. And after wearying himself and all in vain, he went ashore, and, flying far inland, hid himself for very shame under the low bushes, on the earth, where he yet remains. This is the reason why he never seeks the sea or rivers, and has ever since remained an inland bird. [Footnote: Having met Mr. Louis Mitchell, the Indian member of the legislature in Maine, one day in Eastport, I asked him to occupy the few minutes which would pass before I should take the steamboat for Calais by telling me a story. He complied by narrating the foregoing. It is very remarkable that the Indian story-tellers of ancient days should have taken it into their heads to satirize an idea which has been of late carried out completely by the Russian Admiral Popoff, in his celebrated circular war steamer. The story and all the Indian words in it are Passamaquoddy.]

The Mournful Mystery of the Partridge-Witch; setting forth how a Young Man died from Love.

Of the olden time. Two brothers went hunting in the autumn, and that as far as the head waters of the Penobscot, where they remained all winter. But in March their snow-shoes (*agahmook*, P.) gave out, as did their moccasins, and they wished that a woman were there to mend them.

When the younger brother returned first to the lodge, the next day,— which he generally did, to get it ready for the elder,—he was astonished to find that some one had been there before him, and that, too, in the housekeeping. For garments had been mended, the place cleaned and swept, a fire built, and the pot was boiling. He said nothing of this to his brother; but returning the next day at the same time, found that all had been attended to, as at first. And again he said nothing; but in the morning, when he went forth to hunt, he did but go a little way, and, returning, watched, from a hidden place, the door. And there came a beautiful and graceful girl, well attired, who entered the wigwam. And he, stepping softly, looking through a hole in the hut, saw her very busy with his housekeeping.

Then he entered, and she seemed to be greatly alarmed and confused; but he calmed her, and they soon became good friends, sporting together very happily all day long like children, for indeed they were both young.

When the sun's height was little and his shadows long, the girl said, "I must go now. I hear your brother coming, and I fear him. But I will return tomorrow. *Addio!*" So she went, and the elder brother knew nothing of what had happened. The next day she came again, and once more they played in sunshine and shadow until evening; but ere she went he sought to persuade her to remain always. And she, as if in doubt, answered, "Tell thy brother all, and it may be that I will stay and serve ye both. For I can make the snow-shoes and moccasins which ye so much need, and also canoes." Then she departed with the day, and the elder, returning, heard from his brother all that had happened, and said, "Truly I should be glad to have some one here to take care of the wigwam and make snow-shoes." So she came in the morning, and hearing from the younger that his brother had consented to her coming was very glad, and went away, as in haste. But she returned about noon, drawing a *toboggin* (sled) piled up with garments and arms, for she was a huntress. Indeed, she could do all things as few women could, whether it were cooking, needle-work, or making all that men need. And the winter passed very pleasantly, until the snow grew soft, and it was time for them to return. Till she came they had little luck in hunting, but since her coming all had gone well with them, and they now had a wonderful quantity of furs.

Then they returned in a canoe, going down the river to their village. But as they came near it the girl grew sad, for she had thrown out her soul to their home, though they knew it not, by *meelahbi-give*. [Footnote: Passamaquoddy: Clairvoyance, or state of vision.] And suddenly she said, as they came to a point of land, "Here I must leave. I can go no further. Say nothing of me to your parents, for your father would have but little love for me." And the young men sought to persuade her, but she only answered sorrowfully, "It cannot be." So they came home with their furs, and the elder was so proud of their luck and their strange adventure that he could not hold his peace, but told all.

Then his father was very angry, and said, "All my life have I feared this. Know that this woman was a devil of the woods, a witch of the Mitche-hant, a sister of the *Oonahgamess* [Footnote: P. Goblins and ghosts.] and of the *Ke'tahks*." And he spoke so earnestly and so long of this thing that they were afraid, and the elder, being persuaded by the sire, went forth to slay her, and the younger followed him afar. So they sought her by the stream, and found her bathing, and, seeing them, she ran up a little hill. And, as she ran, the elder shot an arrow at her. Then there was a strange flurry about her, a fluttering of scattered feathers, and they saw her fly away as a partridge. Returning, they told all this to their father, who said, "You did well. I know all about these female devils who seek to destroy men. Verily this was a she Mikumwess." [Footnote: P. The Mikumwess is a Robin Goodfellow, who plays pranks on people, or treats them kindly, according to his caprice.]

But the younger could not forget her, and longed to see her again; so one day he went into the woods, and there he indeed found her, and she was as kind as before. Then he said, "Truly it was not by my goodwill that my brother shot at you." And she answered, "Well do I know that, and that it was all by your father; yet I blame him not, for this is an affair of *N'karnayoo*, the days of old; and even yet it is not at an end, and the greatest is to come. But let the day be only a day unto itself; the things of to-morrow are for to-morrow, and those of yesterday are departed." So they forgot their troubles, and played together merrily all day long in the woods and in the open places, and told stories of old times till sunset. And as, the *Kah-kah-goos*, or Crow, went to his tree, the boy said, "I must return;" and she replied, "Whenever you would see me, come to the woods. And remember what I say. Do not marry any one else. For your father wishes you to do so, and he will speak of it to you, and that soon. Yet it is for your sake only that I say this." Then she told him word by word all that his father had said; but he was not astonished, for now he knew that she was not as other women; but he cared not. And he grew brave and bold, and then he was above all things. And when she told him that if he should marry another he would surely die, it was as nothing to him.

Then returning, the first thing his father said was, "My son, I have provided a wife for you, and the wedding must be at once." And he said, "It is well. Let it be so." Then the bride came. For four days they held the wedding dance; four days they feasted. But on the last day he said, "This is the end of it all," and he laid him down on a white bear-skin, and a great sickness came upon him, and when they brought the bride to him he was dead.

Truly the father knew what ailed him, and more withal, of which he said nothing. But he liked the place no longer, and he and his went away therefrom, and scattered far and wide.

This strange story recalls the Undine of La Motte Fouque. There is in it an element of mystery and destiny, equal in every way to anything in German literature. The family secret, touched on but never explained, which ends in such a death, is, speaking from an artistic point of view, very skillfully managed. It must be borne in mind that in this, as in most of these tales, there are associations and chords which make as gold to an Indian that which is only copper, or at best silver, to the civilized reader of my translations.

There is a characteristic feature of this story superior to anything in Undine. It is the growth in the hero, when he knows the worst to come, of that will, or stoicism, or complete indifference to fate, which the Indians regard as equivalent to attaining *m'teoulin*, or magic power. When a man has in him such courage that nothing earthly can do more than increase it, he has attained to what is in one sense at least *Nirvana*. From an Algonquin point of view the plot is perfect.

I have given this story accurately as it was told to me by Tomah Josephs, a Passamaquoddy Indian.

How one of the Partridge's Wives became a Sheldrake Duck, and why her Feet and Feathers are Red.

N'*karnayoo*, of the old time, there was a hunter who lived in the woods. He had a brother, [Footnote: The word brother is so generally applied in adoption or friendship that it cannot here be taken in a literal sense. The brother in this case seems to have been a goblin or spirit.] who was so small that he kept him in a box, and when he went forth he closed this very carefully, for fear lest an evil spirit (Mitche-hant) should get him.

One day this hunter, returning, saw a very beautiful girl sitting on a rock by a river, making a moccasin. And being in a canoe he paddled up softly and silently to capture her; but she, seeing him coming, jumped into the water and disappeared. On returning to her mother, who lived at the bottom of the river, she was told to go back to the hunter and be his wife; "for now," said the mother, "you belong to that man."

The hunter's name was Mitchihess, the Partridge. When she came to his lodge he was absent. So she arranged everything for his return, making a bed of boughs. At night he came back with one beaver. This he divided; cooked one half for supper and laid by the other half. In the morning when she awoke he was gone, and the other half of the beaver had also disappeared. That night he returned with another beaver, and the same thing took place again. Then she resolved to spy and find out what all this meant.

So she laid down and went to sleep, wide awake, with one eye open. Then he quietly rose and cooked the half of the beaver, and taking a key (*Apkwosgehegan*, P.) unlocked a box, and took out a little red dwarf and fed him. Replacing the elf, he locked him up again, and lay down to sleep. And the small creature had eaten the whole half beaver. But ere he put him in his box he washed him and combed his hair, which seemed to delight him.

The next morning, when her husband had gone for the day, the wife sought for the key, and having found it opened the box and called to the little fellow to come out. This he refused to do for a long time, though she promised to wash and comb him. Being at length persuaded, he peeped out, when she pulled him forth. But whenever she touched him her hands became red, though of this she took no heed, thinking she could wash it off at will. But lo! while combing him, there entered a hideous being, an awful devil, who caught the small elf from her and ran away.

Then she was terribly frightened. And trying to wash her hands, the red stain remained. When her husband returned that night he had no game; when he saw the red stain he knew all that had happened; when he knew what had happened he seized his bow to beat her; when she saw him seize his bow to beat her she ran down to the river, and jumped in to escape death at his hands, though it should be by drowning. But as she fell into the water she became a sheldrake duck. And to this day the marks of the red stain are to be seen on her feet and feathers. [Footnote: Related to me by Noel Josephs, a Passamaquoddy. Notwithstanding its resemblance to Blue Beard, it is probably in every detail a very old Indian tradition. It bears a slight resemblance to several far western legends, which refer to peculiarities in the duck. It is partly repeated in a Lox legend.]

THE INVISIBLE ONE.

(Micmac.)

There was once a large Indian village situated on the border of a lake,—*Nameskeek' oodun Kuspemku* (M.). At the end of the place was a lodge, in which dwelt a being who was always invisible. [Footnote: In this Micmac tale, which is manifestly corrupted in many ways, the hero is said to be "a youth whose *teeomul* (or tutelary animal) was the moose," whence he took his name. In the Passamaquoddy version nothing is said about a moose. A detailed account of the difficulty attending the proper analysis of this tradition will be found at the end of this chapter.] He had a sister who attended to his wants, and it was known that any girl who could see him might marry him. Therefore there were indeed few who did not make the trial, but it was long ere one succeeded:

And it passed in this wise. Towards evening, when the Invisible One was supposed to be returning home, his sister would walk with any girls who came down to the shore of the lake. She indeed could see her brother, since to her he was always visible, and beholding him she would say to her companions, "Do you see my brother?" And then they would mostly answer, "Yes," though some said, "Nay,"—*alt telovejich, aa alttelooejik*. And then the sister would say, "*Cogoowa' wiskobooksich?*" "Of what is his shoulder-strap made?" But as some tell the tale, she would, inquire other things, such as, "What is his moose-runner's haul?" or, "With what does he draw his sled?" And they would reply, "A strip of rawhide," or "A green withe," or something of the kind. And then she, knowing they had not told the truth, would reply quietly, "Very well, let us return to the wigwam!"

And when they entered the place she would bid them not to take a certain seat, for it was his. And after they had helped to cook the supper they would wait with great curiosity to see Him eat. Truly he gave proof that he was a real person, for as he took off his moccasins they became visible, and his sister hung them up; but beyond this they beheld nothing not even when they remained all night, as many did.

There dwelt in the village an old man, a widower, with three daughters. The youngest of these was very small, weak, and often ill, which did not prevent her sisters, especially the eldest, treating her with great cruelty. The second daughter was kinder, and sometimes took the part of the poor abused little girl, but the other would burn her lands and face with hot coals; yes, her whole body was scarred with the marks made by torture, so that people called her *Oochigeaskw* (the rough-faced girl). And when her father, coming home, asked what it meant that the child was so disfigured, her sister would promptly say that it was the fault of the girl, herself, for that, having been forbidden to go near the fire, she had disobeyed and fallen in.

Now it came to pass that it entered the heads of the two elder sisters of this poor girl that they would go and try their fortune at seeing the Invisible One. So they clad themselves in their finest and strove to look their fairest; and finding his sister at home went with her to take the wonted walk down to the water. Then when He came, being asked if they saw him, they said, "Certainly," and also replied to the question of the shoulder-strap or sled cord, "A piece of rawhide." In saying which, they lied, like the rest, for they had seen nothing, and got nothing for their pains.

When their father returned home the next evening he brought with him many of the pretty little shells from which *weiopeskool* (M.), or wampum, was made, [Footnote: In Passamaquoddy wampum is called *waw-bap*. It is said that a single bead required a full day's work to make and finish it. It is not many years since it was made much more expeditiously in certain New York villages.] and they were soon engaged *napawejik* (in stringing them). That day poor little Oochigeaskw', the burnt-faced girl, who had always run barefoot, got a pair of her father's old moccasins, and put them into water that they might become flexible to wear. And begging her sisters for a few wampum shells, the eldest did but call her "a lying little pest," but the other gave her a few. And having no clothes beyond a few paltry rags, the poor creature went forth and got herself from the woods a few sheets of birch bark, of which she made a dress, putting some figures on the bark. [Footnote: Probably by scraping. Birch bark (*moskwe*) peeled in winter can have the thin dark brown coat scraped away, leaving a very light yellowish-brown ground. Tornah Josephs and his niece Susan, of Princeton, Maine, are experts at this work.] And this dress she shaped like those worn of old. [Footnote: This remark indicates the lateness of the Micmac version of this very old myth.] So she made a petticoat and a loose gown, a cap, leggins, and handkerchief, and, having put on her father's great old moccasins,— which came nearly up to her knees,—she went forth to try her luck. For even this little thing would see the Invisible One in the great wigwam at the end of the village.

Truly her luck had a most inauspicious beginning, for there was one long storm of ridicule and hisses, yells and hoots, from her own door to that which she went to seek. Her sisters tried to shame her, and bade her stay at home, but she would not obey; and all the idlers, seeing this strange little creature in her odd array, cried "Shame!" But she went on, for she was greatly resolved; it may be that some spirit had inspired her.

Now this poor small wretch in her mad attire, with her hair singed off and her little face as full of burns and scars as there are holes in a sieve, was, for all this, most kindly received by the sister of the Invisible One; for this noble girl knew more than the mere outside of things as the world knows them. And as the brown of the evening sky became black, she took her down to the lake. And erelong the girls knew that He had come. Then the sister said, "Do you see him?" And the other replied with awe, "Truly I do,—and He is wonderful." "And what is his sled-string?" "It is," she replied, "the Rainbow." And great fear was on her. "But, my sister," said the other, "what is his bow-string?" "His bowstring is *Ketaksoowowcht*" (the Spirits' Road, the Milky Way). [Footnote: The Spirits' or Ghosts' Road, so called because it is believed to be the highway by which spirits pass to and from the earth. The Micmac version, belittled and reduced in every way, limits this reply to "a *piece* of a rainbow." There is a grandeur of conception in the Passamaquoddy myth which recalls the most stupendous similes in Scripture.]

"Thou hast seen him," said the sister. And, taking the girl home, she bathed her, and as she washed all the scars disappeared from face and body. Her hair grew again; it was very long, and like a blackbird's wing. Her eyes were like stars. In all the world was no such beauty. Then from her treasures she gave her a wedding garment, and adorned her. Under the comb, as she combed her, her hair grew. It was a great marvel to behold.

Then, having done this, she bade her take the *wife's seat* in the wigwam,—that by which her brother sat, the seat next the door. And when He entered, terrible and beautiful, he smiled and said, "*Wajoolkoos*!" "So we are found out!" "*Alajulaa*." "Yes," was her reply. So she became his wife. [Footnote: This is the true end of this Indian Cupid and Psyche legend. But the Micmacs having, for no apparent reason, made the Stupendous Deity of the Heavens a moose (Team), have added to it another for the sake of the name, and which I give in due succession simply as an illustration of the manner in which tales are tacked together. I have very little doubt that the story as here given is an old solar myth, worked up, perhaps, with the story of Cinderella, derived from a Canadian-French source. There are enough of these French-Indian stories in my possession alone to form what would make one of the most interesting volumes of the series of the *Contes Populaires*. The Passamaquoddy version is to this effect: "There was a great being, a mighty hunter, who had a wife, of wonderful magic gifts, and a boy; and the child became blind. After a long time his sight returned, and he said so; but his mother was suspicious, and did not believe him." It is evident that she suspected that he saw by *clairvoyance*, not by literal vision. "So one day she bade her husband put on certain things which no one could behold who did not see them in truth. Then she asked the boy, 'What has your father for a sled-string?' (literally for a moose-runner haul). And he replied, 'The rainbow to haul by.' Then she asked him yet again, 'What has he for a bow-string?' And he answered, '*Ke'taksoo wowcht*;' 'The Spirits' or Ghosts' Road.' And once more she inquired, 'What has he on his sled?' To which he said, 'A beaver.' Then she knew that he could indeed see." (T. Josephs.)

We can perceive by shreds and patches such as these the *all but* loss of an early and grand mythology which has undergone the usual transmutation into romantic and nursery legends. By great exertion we might recover it, but the old Indians who retain its fragments are passing away rapidly, and no subject attracts so little interest among our *literati*. A few hundred dollars expended annually in each State would result in the collection of all that is extant of this folk-lore; and a hundred years hence some few will, perhaps, regret that it was not done.

It may be observed that in the Edda the rainbow is the heavenly road over which the gods pass. The rainbow is not the Milky Way, but it may be observed that in this tale the two are curiously compared, or almost identified. But according to Charles Francis Keary (*Mythology of the Eddas*, London, 1882), "there is small hint in the Edda of the use of the *rainbow* as a path for souls, save where Helgi says to his wife,—

"'Tis time for me to ride the ruddy road,
And on my horse to tread the path of flight,'"

which is more applicable to the Milky Way than the rainbow. "We owe," he says, "to the learned Adalbert Kohn some researches which have traced the path of the Milky Way as a bridge of souls from its first appearance in Eastern creeds to its later appearance in mediaeval German tradition." (*Zeitschrift f. v. Sp.l.c.*) In the Vedas the Milky Way is called the Gods' Path. The American Indians firmly believe that the Spirits' Road is one of their very earliest traditions, and I believe with them that they had it long before Columbus discovered this country.

Since the foregoing remarks were written, Mrs. W. Wallace Brown has obtained the following fragment, which was given as a song, and declared to be very ancient:—

"Then was woman, long, long ago:
She came out of a hole.
In it dead people were buried.
She made her house in a tree;
She was dressed in leaves,
All long ago.
When she walked among the dry leaves
Her feet were so covered
The feet were invisible.
She walked through the woods,
Singing all the time,

'I want company; I'm lonesome!'
A wild man heard her:
From afar over the lakes and mountains
He came to her.
She saw him; she was afraid;
She tried to flee away,
For he was covered with the rainbow;
Color and light were his garments.
She ran, and he pursued rapidly;
He chased her to the foot of a mountain.
He spoke in a strange language,
She could not understand him at first.
He would make her tell where she dwelt.
They married, they had two children.
One of them was a boy,
He was blind from his birth,
But he frightened his mother by his sight.
He could tell her what was coming,
What was coming from afar
What was near he could not see.
He could see the bear and the moose
Far away beyond the mountains,
He could see through everything."

The old Indian woman ended this story by saying abruptly, "Don't know any more. Guess they all eat up by *mooin*" (the bear). She said that it was only a fragment. "If you could have heard her repeat this," adds Mrs. Brown, "in pieces, stopping to explain what the characters said, and describing how they looked, and anon singing it again, you would have got the *inner sense* of a wonderfully weird tale. The woman's feet covering and the man's dress *like* a rainbow, yet not one, which made their bodies invisible, seemed to exercise her imagination strangely; and these were to her the most important part of the story." The fragment is part of a very old myth; I regret to say a very obscure one.]

STORY OF THE THREE STRONG MEN.

(Micmac.)

There was a chieftain in the days of yore. He had a great desire for a poor girl who was a servant, and who worked for him. To win this girl he first I most lose his wife. He took his wife afar into the woods to gather spruce-gum, and then left her there.

She soon found out that she had lost her way, and, wandering, she lost it more and more for many days, until she came at last to a bear's den, where, going in, she found the Chief of all the bears, who welcomed her, provided for her wants, and furnished her with pleasant food; but as the meat was raw he went into a neighboring town for fire. And as she lived with him she was to him in all things as he wished, and as a wife.

So that it came to pass, as time went on, that a new-comer was expected, and she bade the Bear provide the baby's clothes. And when the long-expected infant came it was a boy, large, beautiful, and strong; he was in everything beyond all other boys.

And as the child was born in a strange way, he very soon displayed a magic power. No baby ever grew so rapidly: when four months old he wrestled with the Bear and threw him easily upon the floor. And so the mother saw that he would be a warrior, and the chief of other men.

She loathed the life she led, and wished to leave, and live as she had done in days of old. To this the Bear would in nowise consent, and as her son was human, like herself, he loved his mother best, and thought with her.

One day he said, "Now I can wrestle well and throw the Bear as often as I choose. When I next time cast him upon the ground, catch up a club; the rest remains for you!"

They waited yet a while till he had grown so strong that the Bear was nothing in his grasp. One day they wrestled as they ever did, and then the woman, with a vigorous blow, strengthened by hate and famishing desire of freedom and a better human life, laid him in death upon the mossy floor.

They went their way back to the chieftain's town, and found him married to the servant-girl. The mother only spoke, and the wild boy tore down the wigwam of the Indian chief just with a blow, and then he called aloud unto the Lightning in the sky above, "Come down to me and help me in my need! Build a grand wigwam such as man ne'er saw! Build it, I say, and for my mother here!"

The Lightning came, and with a single flash built such a home as man had never seen.

And then he said, "Mother, I mean to go and travel everywhere, until I find another man who is as strong as I. When he is found I will return to thee."

So on he went afar until he saw a man who lifted up a vast canoe with many people in it. This he did, raising it in the water; but the boy bore it ashore, and lifted it on land.

And so the two agreed that they would go on together until they found a third equal to them in strength, if such a man were living anywhere in all the world.

So traveling by hill and lake, they went, until one day, far in a lonely land, they saw a man rolling a mighty rock, large as the largest wigwam, up a hill. But the Bear's son, lifting the stone with ease, threw it afar over the mountain-top,—threw it afar beyond the rocky range; they heard it thunder down the depths below.

Then the three strong men went to hunt the moose. He who had tossed the ship remained in camp to do the cooking, while the others went with bow and spear afar to find their game.

Now when the sun was at the edge of noon, just balancing to fall, there came a boy, a little wretched, elfish-looking child, as sad and sickly as a boy could be, who asked the man for food. He answered him, "Poor little fellow! there, the pot is full of venison, so go and eat your fill."

He ate, indeed, the dinner for the three. When he had done he did not leave a scrap; then walked into the stony mountain-side, as any man might walk into the fog, and in a second he was seen no more.

Now when the two returned and heard the tale they were right angry, being hungry men. The man; who rolled the stone stayed next in turn, but when the I little fellow came to him he seemed so famished and he shed such tears that this one also gave him leave to eat. Then, in a single swallow, as it seemed, he bolted all the food, and yelled aloud with an insulting laugh. The man, enraged, grappled him by the throat, but the strange boy flung him away as one would throw a not, and vanished in the mountain as before.

On the third day the mighty man himself remained at home, and soon the starveling child came and began to beg, with tears, for food. "Eat," said the chief, "as other people eat, and no more tricks, or I will deal with you." But as it was with him the day before, so it went now; he swallowed all the meat with the same jeering yell Then the strong man closed with the boy. It was an awful strife; they fought together from the early morn until the sun went down, and then the Elf—for elf he was—cried out, "I now give in!" So both his arms were tightly bound behind, and with a long, tough cord of plaited hide the strong man kept his prey, the lariat fast noosed about his neck. The child went on, the strong man ever following behind, holding the cord well twisted round his hand.

And so they went into the mountain-side, and ever on, a long and winding way, down a deep cavern, on for many a mile,—the light of sorcery shining from the elf made it all clear,—until at last the guide stopped in ins course, and said:—

"Now list to me. I am the servant of a frightful fiend, a seven-beaded devil, whom I deemed no man could ever conquer, he and I being of equal strength; but I believe that thou mayst conquer him, since I have found, by bitter proof, that thou canst conquer me. Here is a staff, the only thing on earth that man may smite him with and give him pain. Now, do your best; it is all one to me which of you gains, so one of you be slain, for well I wot 't will be a roaring fight."

In came the evil being with a scream, and clutched the Indian with teeth and claws. There, in the magic cavern, many a mile from the sun's rays, they fought for seven days, the stubborn devil and the stubborn man, whose savage temper gave him fresher strength with every fresh wound; the more his blood ran from his body all the more his heart grew harder with the love of fight, until he beat away the monster's seven heads. And so he slew him, and the watching elf burst into laughter at the victory.

"Now," said the Elf, "I have a gift for thee. I have three sisters: all are beautiful, and all shall be thine own if thou wilt but unbind my hands." The strong man set him free. And so he led the man to another cave, and there he saw three girls so strangely fair they seemed to be a dream. The first, indeed, was very beautiful, and yet as plump as she was lovely; then the second maid was tall, superb, and most magnificent, in rarest furs, with richest wampum bands, the very picture of a perfect bride; bet fairer than them both, as much more fair as swans outrival ducks, the youngest smiled. And the young chieftain chose her for his own.

With the three girls he went into the day. Far on the rocks above him he could see his two companions, and a sudden thought came to his mind, for he was quick to think, and so he called, "I say, let down a rope; I have three girls here, and they cannot climb." And so the two strong men let down a cord: then the first fairy-maid went up by it, and then the second. Now the chief cried out, "It is my turn; now you must pull on me!" And saying this, he tied a heavy stone, just his own weight, unto the long rope's end, then bid them haul. It rose, but as it came just to the top the traitors let it fall, as he supposed they would, to murder him.

And then the chieftain said unto the elf, "You know the mountain and its winding ways: bear me upon thy back, and that in haste, to where those fellows are!" The goblin flew, and in an instant he was by their side.

He found the villains in a deadly fight, quarrelling for the maids; but seeing him they ceased to wrestle, upon which he said, "I risked my life to bring away these girls; I would have given each of you a wife: for doing this you would have murdered me. Now I could kill you, and you both deserve death at the stake, vile serpents that you are; but take your lives,—you are too low for me,—and with them take these women, if they wish to wed with such incarnate brutes as you!"

They went their way; the women followed them along the forest paths, and ever on. Into this story they return no more.

And then the strong man said to his young bride, "I must return unto my village; then I'll come again to you; await me here." But she, as one to elfin magic born, replied, "I warn you of a single thing. When you again are at your wigwam door a small black dog will leap to lick your hand. Beware, I say; if he succeed in it, you surely will forget me utterly." As she predicted so it came to pass.

And so she waited in the lonely wood beside the mountain till a month was gone, and then arose and went to seek her love. All in the early dawn she reached the town, and found the wigwam of the sagamore. She sought a neighboring hiding-place, where she might watch unseen, and found a tree, a broad old ash, which spread its stooping boughs over the surface of a silent pool.

An old black Indian had a hut hard by. His daughter, coming, looked into the spring, and saw a lovely face. The simple girl thought it was hers, her own grown beautiful by sorcery which hung about the place. She flung away her pail, and said, "Aha! I'll work no more; some chief shall marry me!" and so she went to smile among the men.

Then came the mother, who beheld the same sweet, smiling, also girlish face. She said, "Now I am young and beautiful again; I'll seek another husband, and at once." She threw her pail afar and went away, losing no time to smile among the men.

And then in turn the old black Indian came, and looking in the spring beheld the face. He knew right well that it was not his own, for in his youth he never had been fair. So looking up above he saw the bride, and bade her come to him; and then he said, "My wife has gone away; my daughter, too. You were the cause of it; it is but right that you should take the place my wife has left. Therefore remain with me and be my own."

He fares but ill who weds unwilling witch. When night came on they laid them down to sleep, and then the bride murmured a magic prayer, begging the awful Spirit of the Wind, the giant Eagle of the wilderness, to do his worst. A fearful tempest blew, and all night long the old black Indian was out-of-doors, working with all his power to keep the lodge from being blown away. As soon as he had pinned one sheet of bark into its place another blew away, and then a tent pole rattling in the rain bounded afar. It was a weary work, but all night long the young bride slept in peace, until the morning came, and then he slept.

Then she arose, and, walking to the wood, sat down beside a stream and sang a song:—

> "There are many men in the world,
> But only one is dear to me.
> He is good and brave and strong.
> He swore to love none but me;
> He has forgotten me.
> It was a bad spirit that changed him,
> But I will love none but him."

And as she sat and sang, the sagamore her husband, paddling by in his canoe, heard the sweet song intoned in magic style, [Footnote: Not only the words, but the peculiar intonations of them, were essential to produce the proper effect of a magic song. An intelligent white man has left it on record that it required two years to learn one of these incantations of only a few lines.] and all at once recalled what had been lost,—the two strong giants, the cavern and the elf, the seven-headed monster and the fight, the sisters and the evil-minded men, and the black dog who leaped to lick his hand: it flashed upon him like some early dream brought out by sorcery. He saw her sit beside the stream, and still he heard her song, soft as a magic flute. He went to her, and in a minute he was won again.

And then she said, "This world is ever false. I know another, let us go to it." So then again she sang a magic spell, and as she sang they saw the great Culloo, the giant bird, broad as a thunder cloud, winging his way towards them. Then he came; they stepped upon him, and he soared away. But to this earth they never came again.

This very singular legend was obtained for me by Mrs. W. Wallace Brown. It is from the Micmac, and is in the original from beginning to end a song, or poem. For this reason I have given it a plain metrical form, neither prose nor poetry, such being quite the character of the original. But I, have not introduced anything not in the original.

This story consists of a very old Indian legend mingled with a European fairy tale drawn through a French-Canadian source. The incident of the Elf who eats the food of three men is to be found in another tale. In one version, the bride, finding that her husband, though utterly deprived by magic of his memory, has married again, sails away on the great bird, leaving him forever. I have naturally rejected this senseless termination in favor of one found in another form.

The calling on the Lightning to build a wigwam is probably a mistake. It is more likely that it was summoned to destroy the chiefs wigwam, but the narrator, confused with the subject of the hero's strength, changed the original. The invocations of Lightning, and subsequently of the Storm Bird are probably entirely Indian, though there are Norse invocations to Hroesvelgar, or the Eagle of the Northwest, as we read in Scott's Pirate.

The black whelp or small black dog is in this tale ominous of evil. It causes oblivion. In the Edda to dream of the same thing is the most evil of all Atli's bad dreams (vide the second lay of Gudrun, 41):—

"Seemed to me from my hand
Whelps I let slip.
Lacking cause of joy;"

and in the very same song (24) be takes a potion which causes oblivion. But there is even a third point in the Atlamal in Groenlenzku, which resembles one in the Indian tale. It is where the half enchantress Kostbera warns Hogni against leaving her:

"From home thou art going:
Give ear to counsel;
Few are fully prudent;
Go another time."

In the Norse lay we are told that to dream of a white bear indicates a storm, but here it means a strange and terrible event. Long before I met with this, I observed that the introduction, or mention, of a white bear-skin in these Indian stories invariably intimates some strange magical change.

But it is most remarkable of all, that, while the poems of the Edda have nothing but a very few incidents in common with the traditions of the western tribes, they are inspired throughout with a strange and mysterious sentiment or *manner* wonderfully like that of the Wabanaki. As regards literal resemblance the following coincidences may here be noted.

In a widely spread Norse tale a very small goblin sustains a long and obstinate contest with an immense white bear.

The Norsemen invoked the Eagle Giant of the Winds, as Scott has shown in his song of the Reimkennar. The same being is invoked in this legend.

The whelp, as an omen of evil, is mentioned in the Edda. In this tale he causes forgetfulness. A potion of oblivion is also mentioned in the Norse poem in close connection with the omen of the dog.

If we accept the termination of this tale as given in the Micmac poem it amounts to this: A certain woman causes the whelp to lick the hero's hand. This causes forgetfulness. The hero marries her, and thereby loses his first wife. In the Edda, Brynhild, who has morally the first claim to Sigurd, says of Crymhild, "She presented to Sigurd the pernicious drink, so that he no more remembers me." In the saga of Thorstein, Viking's son the hero, is made by the witch Dis to utterly forget his bride Hunoor.

The Kalmuk tale of How the Schimm-Khan was Slain contains striking analogies to this of the Three Strong Men. [Footnote: *Sagas from He Far East*, London, 1873.] In it the hero associates with three men, who take turns to cook. Their food is devoured, as in this tale, every day by a little old witch who is very strong. He overcomes her by craft. His companions, instead of drawing him up by the rope, as agreed on, leave him to perish, in order to possess themselves of a treasure. There can be no doubt as to the Hindoo origin of this and many more plots found among the red Indians. But a careful study of the Norse story convinces me that the tale did not come to the Wabanaki through any other than a Norse source.

Since writing out the foregoing poem, with the comment, I have received from Louis Mitchell the Penobscot version of it. It is about twice as long as the Micmac story, and differs from it very materially. In it the hero conquers the goblin by getting possession of his red cap. In the Norse tales the same incident occurs in different forms. He then fights with a copper demon; also with one of silver and another of gold. Each devil, while he is sharpening his sword, exclaims, "Hurry! hurry! I am hungry!" The last of the three, the *Kche mitche-hant*, or great devil, has three heads, which replace themselves when cut off; but the hero summons a lion (*pee'tahlo*) and an eagle, who devour each a head, when the demon, to save the last, surrenders. There are old "aboriginal" incidents in this Passamaquoddy tale, but the European elements predominate to such an extent as to call for the following remark from the Indian writer:—

"This story is ended. When Indians in it, as they do in many others, speak of kings and queens or ships and ivory, I think they got it all from Europe. But perhaps when the Indians came here from Asia they brought these stories with them. Thus they very often mention ivory, calling it white bone. They also mention cities. But these things are not new, for they were handed down from one generation to another."

I have to add that, while the story agrees with an universally spread Aryan fairy tale, it is very remarkable that it should add to these, several strictly Eddaic details, such as the white bear.

THE WEEWILLMEKQ'.

I. How a Woman Lost a Gun for Fear of the Weewillmekq'.

There was a man and his wife who had got together all they had for the fall hunt. They went up the St. John's River; they left the village of Foxerbica; they went twenty-five miles beyond it. They passed the falls on the upper side to get some game. They cooked and ate. They got ready to start again; they launched the canoe. [Footnote: This story and the preceding are taken *word for word* from the Indian narration. The singular precision of minute details is very characteristic of many of these legends.] They shoved the canoe twenty-five feet from the shore. The woman turned, and upset it. It went like lightning down the rapids. They had hard work to get ashore, and lost their gun, traps, kettle, and everything. They escaped with great trouble; they had trouble to save their canoe.

The man was in great grief at the loss of his gun. He sat down and sang:—

"Nici sigi psach ke-yin,
Dich m'djel mieol wagh nuch'."

I am sorry,
I am in great trouble.

There came two Indians down to the portage where the man and his wife sat. They asked him why he was so sad. He told them all. One of them was a *m'teoulin*. He asked of them, "Could you tell your gun if you saw it?" The woman cried quickly, "I could!" He was not pleased at her forwardness, but put the question again; when she as pertly answered, "Yes," for her husband. He looked sternly at her, and said, "Are you sure?" To which she cried, "Yes, yes!" Then he said, "If you are very bold, and not afraid of anything, you may get it again." And this, too, she took on herself, saying, "Oh, yes, *I'm* not afraid; *I'll* get it," making no account of her husband.

Then, by the order of the man, she went to a ledge just below the falls, where they are seventy-five feet high. There was a little projecting rock on which she could just sit,—a horrible place. Below it was a dreadful eddy, in which nothing could live. He helped her down to it, and she was in mortal terror, as such glib-tongued women generally are when there is the least danger. Then the man went away.

And as she sat there, trembling and half dead with fright, she saw Something come up out of the eddy,—even out of the worst of it. It rose; it was an awful sight,—a kind of monstrous head, with great forked horns and terrible eyes. She was stiff as a stone with fear. The lost gun lay crosswise on the prongs of the horns. It moved slowly on through the eddy, glaring at her. It came nearer and nearer; the gun was within her reach, but she was too frightened to touch it. Then the monster passed by and sank into the water, and was seen no more, nor was the gun.

They got her back with trouble from the place where she sat. The *m'teoulin* was furious with rage at her, that he had taken such pains for nothing. He said, "This serves you right for your impudence and forwardness. Learn your proper place, and never undertake to do what is none of your business." He then condoled with the husband, but said, "If you could give me all you could think of, I could never get your gun again."

By this women may learn not to speak too quickly, or propose to do men's duties, "*Hu 'sami n'zama wiuch wee lel n'aga samee n'gamma wiool petin'l.*" (P. "Too quick with the tongue, slow with the hands.") [Footnote: Though the Weewillmekq' is a worm inhabiting the forest and found in dry wood, it is certainly identified, or confused, by the Passamaquoddy Indians with the alligator, or some kind of a horrible water-goblin, which appears to have many points in common with the *Chepitchcalm,* or dragon of the Micmacs. This story was related to me by Tomah Josephs, now Indian governor at Princeton, Maine.

Among various notes I find the following:—

"The weewillmekq' becomes human at times, even now."

"Six years ago," said T. J., "I was in the woods collecting boughs, and I saw a *weewillmekq'* on a tree. The thunder kept approaching the tree on which it was, and finally struck it. It seemed to me as if the worm had attracted the lightning." (August 26, 1883.)

"The Weewillmekq' is a small worm, sometimes two or three inches long. It is seen sometimes in the water as large as a horse. Then it has horns. It is a very horrible-looking little worm."]

II. *Muggahmaht'adem, the Dance of Old Age, or the Magic of the Weewillmekq'.* [Footnote: This mysterious being is called *Wee-wil-li-ah-mek* in Penobscot The correct pronounciation is very nearly *Wee-wil-'l-mekqu'* for both Penobscot and Passamaquoddy, but this would be a difficult utterence for any one who has never listened to the Algonquin soft gutturals.

Mrs. W. Wallace Brown informs me that "the *Weewillmekqu'* is a snail." This would account for its being thought to inhabit both land and water.]

(Passamaquoddy.)

Of old times. There lived in a village many Indians. Among them was a handsome young man, very brave, a great hunter. And there was a beautiful girl. What was her name? Mahli-hahn-sqwess, or Kaliwahdazi,— I don't remember which. But she was proud and high-tempered, and, what was worse, a great witch, but nobody knew it. She wanted the young man to marry her, but he was very busy getting ready for the fall and winter hunt, and had no time to attend to such a thing; and told her so very plainly.

Yes, he must have been very plain with her, for she was very angry, and said to him, "You may go; but you will never return as you went." She meant that, he would be ill or changed. He gave no heed to her words; he did not care for her nor fear her. But far away in the woods, far in the north, in midwinter, he went raging mad. The witch had struck him, when far away, with her magic.

He had with him an elder brother, a great brave, a very fierce man. He, not being able to do aught else, did the most desperate thing a Wabanaki Indian can do. He went down to the river, and sang the song which calls the *Weewillmekq'*.

"We que moh wee will l'mick,
We que moh m'cha micso,
Som'awo wee will l'mick!
Cardup ke su m'so wo Sawo!"

I call on the Wee-will-l'mick!
I call on the Terrible One!
On the One with the Horns!
I dare him to appear!

It came to him in all its terrors. Its eyes were like fire; its horns rose. It asked him what he wanted. He said that he wished his brother to be in his right mind again.

"I will give you what you want," said the Weewillmekq', "if you are not afraid."

"I am not afraid of anything," said the Indian.

"Not of me?"

"Not of you nor of Mitche-hant, the devil himself."

"If you dare take me by my horns and scrape somewhat from one of them with your knife," said the monster, "you may have your wish."

Now this Indian was indeed as savage and brave as the devil; and he had need to be so to do this, for the Weewillmekq' looked his very worst. But the man drew his knife and scraped from the horn till he was told that he had enough.

"Go to your camp," said the Worm. "Put half the scrapings into a cup of water. Make your brother drink it."

"And the other half?" asked the Indian.

"Give it to the girl who made all this trouble. She needs medicine, too."

He returned to camp, and gave the drink to his brother, who recovered. When the hunt was at an end they went home.

They arrived at night. There was an immense lodge in the town, and a dance was going on. The younger brother had prepared a cool drink,— sweet with maple-sugar, fragrant with herbs,—and in it was the powder of the horn of the Weewillmekq'. The witch, warm and very thirsty from dancing, came to the door. He offered her the cup. Without heeding who gave it, she drank it dry, and, turning to her partner, went on in the dance.

And then a strange thing happened. For at every turn of the dance she grew a year older. She began as a young girl; when at the end of the room she was fifty years of age; and when she got back to the door whence she started she fell dead on the floor, at the feet of him who gave her the drink, a little, wrinkled, wizened-up old squaw of a hundred years.

Aha, yes? wood enit atokhahyen, muggoh mah't adem. This is the story of the Dance of Old Age. But you may call it *Sektegah*, the Dance of Death, if you like it better. [Footnote: This extraordinary story was related to me by Noel Joseph, at Campobello, August 26, 1883. I am indebted to Mrs. W. Wallace Brown for the incantation song. The Weewillmekq' has, as it appears in several tales, an extraordinary resemblance to the Norse dragon. It cures mental diseases. It seems to be the same with the *Chepitchcalm*.]

III. Another Version of the Dance of Old Age.

(Passamaquoddy.)

It was in the autumn, the time when Indians go up the rivers to their hunting-grounds, that two young men left home. They ascended the stream; they came to a branch, where they parted: one going alone, another with his married brother. This latter, with the brother, had left in the village a female friend, a witch, who had forbidden him to go hunting, but he had not obeyed her.

And she had cause to keep him at home, for, when he was afar in the woods, and alone, he met one day with a very beautiful girl, who fascinated him, and gave herself to him. And when he said that he did not know how to conceal her from his friends she told him that she was a fairy, and could make herself as small as a newly born squirrel, and that all he need do was to wrap her up in a handkerchief and carry her in his pocket. When alone, he could take her out, enjoy her company, and then reduce and fold her up and put her away again.

He did so, but from that hour, while he carried the fairy near his heart, he began to be wicked and strange. This was not caused by her, but by the girl at home. He was entirely changed; he grew devilish; he refused to eat, and never spoke. His sister-in-law began to fear him. When she offered him food he cried out, "Unless I can devour one of your children I will have nothing!"

When his brother returned and heard all this, he, too, offered him meat, but met with a refusal and the reply, "Give me one of your little children." To which he answered, "The child is so small that it will not satisfy you. Let me go and get a larger one." Then he ran to the village and informed his friends of what had come over the brother. And as they knew that he was about to become a *kewahqu'* (*chenoo*) they resolved to kill him.

But there was a young man there, a friend of the sufferer, who said that he could save him. So all who were assembled bade him try.

And when night came he went apart, and began to sing his *m'teoulin*, or magic song. When it ended there was a loud sound as of some heavy body falling and striking the earth, which fairly shook. The next morning he called all his friends and the married brother, and showed them a human corpse. "Now leave me," he said. "Go to my friend and tell him that I have food for him." The Indians did so, and in horror left the two cannibals to devour their disgusting meal. When the insane youth was satisfied, his friend asked, "Have you had enough?" He replied that he had. [Footnote: The human body which supplied the meal was probably in reality a deer, or some such animal.] Then the magician said, "You are bewitched by the girl who forbade you to go hunting; she knew you would find a maid better than she is. Now come with me."

They went to a small lake; they sat down by its side; the sorcerer began his magic song. And as he sang the waters opened; from the disturbed waves rose a huge Weewillmekq', a creature like an alligator, with horns. And, as the terrible being came ashore, the magician said, "Go and scrape somewhat from his horn and bring it here!" The young man had become fearless; he went and did as he was bid: he scraped the horn, and brought the scraping.

"Now, my friend," said the magician, "let us try this on a tree." There was a large green beech growing by them. It was simply touched with the fragment from the horn when another color spread all over the bark as rapidly as the eye could follow it: in an instant it was dead, and in a few minutes more it fell to the ground, utterly rotten, as if it were a century old.

"Now," said the sorcerer, "we will experiment with this on the witch who wishes to destroy you." So as it was night they went to the village. A dance was being held, and the beautiful tall witch having paused to rest, the two men approached her. The young man placed his hand on her head; he held in it a scraping of the horn of the *weewillmekq'*. As he did so she grew older in an instant,—she became very old; a pale color rippled all over her; she fell, looking a hundred years, dead on the floor, shriveled, dried, and dropped to powder.

"She will not trouble you any more," said the sorcerer. "Her dance is over."

This is the same story as the preceding; but I give it to show now differently a tale may be told by neighbors. In one it is the *spretae injuria formae*, the wrath of rejected love, which inspires the witch to revenge; in the other it is jealousy. In one she inflicts madness; in the other she turns him into a cannibal demon, as Loki, when only half bad, was made utterly so by getting the "thought-stone" or heart of a witch. This legend was sent to me by Louis Mitchell. It is written not by him, but by some other Passamaquoddy, in Indian-English.

TALES OF MAGIC.

M'teoulin, or Indian Magic.

The study of magic as it is believed in or understood by the Indians of America is extremely interesting, for it involves that of all supernaturalism or of all religion whatever. But if we, declining all question as to the origin of monotheism, limit ourselves definitely to what is known of Shamanism alone, we shall still have before us an immense field for investigation. Shamanism is the belief that *all* the events and accidents of life are caused or influenced by spirits, and as fear of suffering is in all men, but particularly the savage, the strongest moral emotion, the natural consequence is a greater fear of *evil* invisible beings. The result of it is a faith that everything which is obscure or invisible is supposed to be the work of mysterious agents, generally evil. Thus all disease whatever, all suffering, pain, loss, or disaster, or bad weather, is at once attributed either to a spirit or to some enemy who practices witchcraft. The Shaman is the priest or doctor, who professes to be able, by his counter-charms, to counteract or neutralize this devil's work.

It will be long ere the scholar definitely determines whether Shamanism as it now exists originated spontaneously in different countries where the same causes were to be found, or whether it is *historical*; that is, derived from a single source. I believe that while darkness, hunger, fear, and similar causes could not fail to create a rude religion anywhere, as Moncure Conway has shown, yet that the derivation from one beginning, or at least later modifications from it, has been very great indeed. Investigation indicates that it was in Assyria, at a very remote age, that Shamanism had, if not its origin, at least its fullest development. The reader who will consult Lenormant's work on Chaldean magic will learn from it that the fear of devils and the art of neutralizing their power were never carried to such an extent elsewhere as in the Land of Bel. Now as Shamanism has at the present day its stronghold among the Turanian races of Central Asia, it may greatly strengthen the theory, somewhat doubted of late, of the early Accadian predecessors of the Chaldeans and their Turanian origin, if we can only prove that their magical religion was the same as that of the Tartars. So far as my reading has aided me, I am inclined to believe that they are identical. "Magic" went so far among the former that, while they discovered natural remedies for natural ills, they never doubted that one was as much the result of sorcery as the other. This theory spread everywhere.

Shamanism, or a vague fear of invisible evils and the sorcerer, may indeed have sprung up independently in Tartary, Central Africa, Finland, and North America. But it is almost incredible that the use of a drum inscribed with magical figures, the spirit flight of the angakok or Shaman, and twenty other characteristics of the art should have become, without transmission, common to all these countries. Shamanism has probably been at the root of all religions; there was a great deal of it in all those of the Semitic races, and, admitting this, it is not difficult to see how from Chaldea and Babylon it may have found its way into Africa, where black savages, who would have rejected a higher religion, would grasp greedily at what they sympathized with. The only real difference between the Voodoo and Pow-wow practices is that the former is, so to speak, the *blacker* and more revolting. This is because a low state of culture has induced the believers in it to retain more of the coarse witchcraft on which Shamanism was based, or out of which it grew.

For wherever Shamanism exists, there is to be found, in company with it, an older sorcery, or witchcraft, which it professes to despise, and against which it does battle. As the Catholic priest, by Bible incantations or scriptural magic, exorcises devils and charms cattle or sore throats, disowning the darker magic of older days, so the Shaman acts against the real *wizard*. Rink tells us that among the heathen Eskimo the Shaman is sacred, and witchcraft a deadly crime, but that the latter is the secret survival of a more ancient religion. *Voodoo*, whether practiced, as it is to-day, in Philadelphia, New York, Havana, or Senegambia, deals with alleged devils, poisons, chicken bones, the ivory root, unnatural orgies,—all, in short, that can startle and astonish ignorant natures; it is the combination of the oldest faith with its successor. Far higher forms are those of the magic of the black *Takowri* whom one meets divining about the streets of Cairo, or of the Arab proper, which brings us fairly to the Cabala and the Jew, Cornelius Agrippa and Eliphas Levi.

It is not difficult to understand how Shamanism with its drums and darkened rooms, its conjuring of evil-doers and extraction of diseases in tangible forms, should have spread from Central Asia to the Laplanders and Eskimo, and thence to the red Indians. Very little attention has been paid to the intercourse actually existing at the present day between these races. I have met with a Passamaquoddy Indian who spoke French well, who had been educated at a mission school, and who had been among the Eskimo. As regards legends and folk-lore, no one can read the Eskimo tales and those of this volume and not feel that the Algonquin is to the man of the icy north what the gypsy is to the Hindoo. As regards the early religion of both races, it is simply *identical*, and it is far too peculiar in its many similar details to have simply sprung up, as many might assume, from the common likeness in customs of all savages. For there is in both a great deal of "literary" culture, especially in the Algonquin, and it would be little less than miraculous that this too should have assimilated by chance. It does not help the "opposition" to point out that Algonquin legends, declare that their ancestors came from the west. Even so, they came from the Pacific coast, where Eskimo Shamanism exists in its most decided forms. But in any case it cannot be denied that in the red Indian mythology of New England, and of Canada and New Brunswick, we have a collection of vigorous, icy, powerful legends, like those of a strong northern race, while those of the middle continent, or Chippewa, are far feebler and gentler. Hiawatha-Manobozho is to Glooskap as a flute to a war trumpet.

It is absurd to laugh at or pity the Indian for believing in his magic. Living as he does in the woods, becoming familiar with animals, and learning how much more intelligent and allied to man they are than civilized man supposes, he believes they have souls, and were perhaps originally human. Balaam's ass spoke once for every Christian; every animal spoke once for the Indian. If a child can be put to sleep by singing to it, why cannot insensibility to pain or a cure be caused by the same process? He is told that the wafer becomes the body of Christ; this may confirm his belief that the Indian god Manobozho turned bits of his own flesh or his wife's into raccoons, for food. If it is difficult for any educated or cultivated man to conceive how, if any condition or phase of supernaturalism be admitted, any other can be denied, how can the Indian be logically blamed for believing anything? But the greatest cause of all for a faith in magic is one which the white man talks about without feeling, and which the Indian feels without talking about it. I mean the poetry of nature, with all its quaint and beautiful superstitions. To every Algonquin a rotten log by the road, covered with moss, suggests the wild legend of the log-demon; the Indian corn and sweet flag in the swamp are the descendants of beautiful spirits who still live in them; Meeko, the squirrel, has the power of becoming a giant monster; flowers, beasts, trees, have all loved and talked and sung, and can even now do so, should the magician only come to speak the spell. And there are such magicians. Why should he doubt it? If the squirrel once yielded to such a power in man, it follows that some man may still have the power, or that he himself may acquire it. And how much of this feeling of the real poetry of nature does the white man or woman possess, who pities the poor ignorant Indian? A few second-hand scraps of Byron and Tupper, Tennyson and Longfellow, the jingle of a few rhymes and a few similes, and a little second-hand supernaturalism, more "accepted" than felt, and that derived from far foreign sources, does not give the white man what the Indian *feels*. Joe, or Noel, or Sabattis may seem to the American Philistine to be a ragged, miserable, ignorant Indian; but to the *scholar* he is by far the Philistine's superior in that which life is *best* worth living for.

The magic of the Passamaquoddy and Penobscot, like the magician himself, is called *meteowlin*, *m'deoolin* or *m'teoulin*. It is the same effectively as *meda*, which is from the same root. It is a power, but opinions differ as to how it is acquired. It is certain, as I was told by an old Passamaquoddy Indian, of Sebayk, near Campobello, that some children are born *m'teoulin*. They manifest it, even while babes, by being capricious, eccentric, and malicious.

Others acquire the art as they grow older. From all that I have heard I infer that *m'teoulin* takes two forms,—one of witchcraft, the other of magic. The former is innate, or may be acquired; the latter, for aught I know, may be sometimes inborn, but is generally acquired by fasting, abstinence of other kinds, and ceremonies. The two are distinctly different. Rink found in Greenland and Labrador that the Eskimo, as I have said, made this difference.

I will now give, word for word, the remarks of certain Indians on this subject, beginning with those of an intelligent and prosperous old man, who is certainly enlightened and Christianized very much beyond the average, of his race. I had asked him if there were any *m'teoulin*, or magicians, living. He replied:—

"There are. Many at St. John and Sebayk are still *m'teoulin*. I saw this myself thirty-five years ago at St. John's. There was a deaf Indian there. The white men were abusing him. They spat on him. By and by a *m'teoulin* from St. John's came, a man of thirty-five or forty. I saw this. The *m'teoulin* asked them not to abuse the deaf and dumb Indian. They turned on the *m'teoulin*. Then he screamed so horribly, so awfully, and looked so like a devil that the men were frightened. They fell on their knees, and could not move. They let the man go."

This is precisely what is narrated by many writers of the Shaman screaming and distorting of the features. Very few people know of what the human voice is capable. It can not only be trained to divine song, but to such demoniacal howling as to deafen and appall even the guardians of a lunatic asylum. In Lapland, Central Asia, or on Nootka Sound the initiated are trained in remote solitudes to these utterances, to which no one can listen without terror. My informant continued:—

"Two or three weeks after I was in another place. We spoke of the *m'teoulin*. The white folks ridiculed them. I said there was one in Fredericton, and I said I would bet ten dollars that he would get the better of them. And they bet that no Indian could do more than they could. So the *m'teoulin* came. And first of all he screamed so that no one could move. It was dreadful. Then he took seven steps through the ground up to his ankles, *just as if it had been light snow*. When I asked for the ten dollars, the white men paid. I gave it to the *m'teoulin*."

Among the Greenland Eskimo the sorcerer, writes Rink, "after meeting with *tomassuk*, or guardian spirits, sometimes manifests it by his feet sinking into the rocky ground *just as if in snow*." He uses the very words of the Indian who described the same thing to me. And very recently in Philadelphia, in fact while I was writing the preceding remarks, a spiritualist named Gordon performed the very same trick. Having been detected, a full account of the manner of action appeared in the Press of that city. It was done by a peculiar method of stooping, and of concealing the stoop behind a skirt. It was a very odd coincidence that the explanation should thus present itself while I was seeking it.

This Shaman Eskimo trick was known to the Norsemen. In the Saga of Thorstein it is said that Ogantun, a noted sorcerer, when stabbed at, "thrust himself down into the ground, so that only the soles of his feet could be seen;" and of Kol it was said that "he could pass through the earth as well as walk upon it."

"Women are sometimes *m'teoulin*. There is one at Psesuk (Bar Harbor) now, this summer. You have met her. She is ——'s wife. [Footnote: I am acquainted with all the parties, but for obvious reasons suppress their names.] If you offend her she can hurt you in strange ways.

"She is a good doctor. Once she cured a man. When he got well he could not pay her for the medicine. His name is Louis ——. She asked for her money; she asked many times; she could not get it. He was going to the woods, far away, to trap; he said he would pay her when he returned, but she wanted it then. She said, 'I will never forget this; I will be revenged.' He went far up the St. John River with his traps; he set them in the stream for beaver. All that he caught that winter was sticks, and sometimes an eel. Then at the end of the day he would say to his man, 'It is of no use.' And then they could hear the witch laughing behind the bushes, and tittering when he came home. So it went on long. Then he was sorry, and said, 'I wish I had paid that woman what I owed her.' And at once they heard a voice from the bushes, or rocks, say, 'Louis, that will do. It is enough.' And the next day they caught two beaver, and every day two, and so on, till the season was over.

"This happened in 1872, in Miramichi Waters."

There does not appear to be any single approved method of acquiring *m'teoulin*. Some, as I have said, are born to it, but they appear to be wizards or witches. Others are formally trained from boyhood by the experienced magicians. Others acquire certain gifts by certain ceremonies or penances. Of this kind was the power obtained in the manner narrated in the following story, which I heard from an old Passamaquoddy:—

"There was once a young man who wished to become a very wise and brave warrior, like his father. And his father said to him, 'I get all my luck of every kind from my dreams. You can have such dreams; any man can, if he will do a certain thing; but that thing is not easy for a young man like you. You must sleep seven nights with a virgin, and never touch her.'

"The young man thought this over for a few days, and then asked his father how it could be arranged or managed.

"'I will tell you,' replied the old man. 'Find a girl; the more beautiful she is and the more you want her, the stronger the magic will be. Go to the parents for their daughter as a wife. Cheat them so. Before you marry get seven bear-skins, and let no man except one know anything about it. Make him clean them. One skin should be cleaned every twenty-four hours. Seven days must pass so.'

"The young man was accepted by the parents; he sent the seven bear-skins to the young woman; they were married; they went to their wigwam. He lay on the bear-skins; he directed his wife to make another bed and sleep on it. They lay apart. The bride thought this was strange; she told her mother of it. The mother said, 'Never mind. By and by it will be all right.' The wife thought it was all wrong. When seven nights had passed the bridegroom disappeared. He was not seen in his village for twenty-five or thirty years. Then he returned to his father. He could divine all things by dreams. He had but to take the magic bear-skin and sleep on it, and dream. He could tell where to find good hunting or fishing. He *foredreamed* war with the Mohawks. Can any man do this? They say so, and I have known many who tried it in vain. They could not pass the trial successfully."

"There are stones in the forest with names on them. They give great power to dream. I have seen in my dreams the *m'teoulin* of ancient times,—the magicians, my father told me, of long ago. I have seen them diving under the waters from one island to another. I have seen them dive ten miles.

"When I was, young, J. N., who was a great *m'teoulin*, offered to teach me the art. I could have become one, but I would not. I did not think it was right.

"Once old J. N. and my grandfather hunted in the woods. It was near Katahdin, the Great Mountain. [Footnote: Katahdin, like the Intervale near North Conway, is haunted and enchanted ground, abounding in fairies and other marvelous beings. But there is not a mile square of New England which has not its legends.] And they wanted everything. They had got out of everything. One night old N. said, 'I can bear this no longer. Would you like a nice pipe of tobacco? We have had nothing but meat for four weeks.' So he went away for a short time; perhaps it was an hour. He returned with a box. There was in it three pounds of tobacco; there was cheese, rice, and sugar; there was fifty pounds of provision in all."

This famous *m'teoulin* was long a popular governor of the Passamaquoddies. I have a curious old brass candlestick, said to be one hundred and fifty years old, which he owned all his life. The following remarkable reminiscences of this very clever old sagamore were given to me by Marie Sakis, a Penobscot:

"The old governor was a great *m'teoulin*. He had got it among the Chippewas. He said that it would come to pass that he would die before the next snowstorm. No, he did not care himself, but my husband's mother did, when she heard this, and she cried. Then he said, 'Well, I will try to live, or else die in a month; but it will be a hard fight.' So he made him a bow, and strung it with his wife's hair; [Footnote: In a Chippewa legend a boy confers magic power on a bow by stringing it with his sister's hair.] and having done this, he shot an arrow through the smoke-hole of his wigwam. [Footnote: This is also mentioned in a legend where it is said that every arrow killed a supernatural enemy.]

All this was at Nessaik, near Eastport. Then he said to his wife, 'Take one of your leggins and put it on my head.' She did so. Then he took medicine. A rainbow appeared in the sky, and a great horse-fly came out of his mouth, and then a large grasshopper. He cried to his wife, 'Do not kill it!' And then came a stone spear-head. [Footnote: This is all in detail perfectly Shamanic. The smell of the fresh fish after such a fight is the same in an Eskimo legend. The horse-fly (*gan*) is Lapp.]

'Now,' said the governor, 'this is all right so far, but the great struggle is yet to come. It is a *wee-wilmekq'* who has done this.' (You know what that is: the Passamaquoddies call it *weewilmekq'*. It is a worm an inch long, which can make itself into a horrid monster as large as a deer; yes, and much larger. It is *m'teoulin*; yes, it is a great magician.) 'I am going to fight it. You must come with a small stick to hit it once, and only a mere tap.' [Footnote: In the legend of Partridge, a mere tap stuns the water-fairy.] But she would not go. So he went and fought with the Weewillmekq'. He killed it. It was a frightful battle. When he returned he smelt like fresh fish. His wife bade him go and wash himself; but let him bathe as much as he could, the smell remained for days. The pond where he fought has been muddy, and foul ever since.

The governor could with a gimlet bore a hole in any tree in the woods, and draw from it as he pleased; any kind of wine or other liquor. Once he was far in the forest with some white gentlemen; he wished to entertain them. He did this, to their astonishment. He produced tobacco in a miraculous manner when it was wanted. Then, returning to Eastport, he went to Mr. Pearce, who kept a store, and showed him that a certain amount of wine had disappeared from his barrels, and paid him for it. He never drank wine or spirits himself.

He once went hunting. He took his wife with him; she was *enceinte*. It was in midwinter. She had a great yearning for green corn. He put a dish on the ground, and there fell from above ears of fresh-boiled green corn into it. 'There,' said he, 'as I promised, you have it.'

She had a silver cross and beads. One day she lost it, and grieved very much. He said, 'Put that wooden dish upside down, near the fire.' It was done, and when she turned it up the cross was under the dish. And he said the Ketawks, or Spirits, had brought it."

The following legend, told me by Tomah Josephs, sets forth another manner by which *m'teoulin* may be acquired.

"There were two Indian families camped away at some distance from the main village. In one lived a young man, and every night he would go to the other wigwams to see some girls. His mother warned him that he would come to harm, for there was danger abroad, but he never minded her.

Now, one night at the end of winter, when the ground was bare of snow, as he was walking along he heard something come after. It had a very heavy, steady tramp. He stopped, and saw a long figure, white, but without arms or legs. It looked like a corpse rolled up. He was horribly frightened, but when it attacked him he grew angry. The object, though it had no arms, fought madly. It twined round him; it struck itself against him, and thrashed itself, bending like a fish all about. And he, too, fought as if he was crazy. He was one of those whose blood and courage go up, but never down; he could die, but never give in till dead. Before daylight the Ghost suggested a rest, or peace; the Indian would not hear of it, but fought on. The Ghost began to implore mercy, but the youth just then saw in the north *Kival lo kesso*, the break of day. Then he knew that if he could but endure the battle a little longer he should indeed get a great victory.

Then the Ghost implored him, saying, 'Let me go, and whatever you may want you shall get, and good luck all your life.' Yet for all this he would not yield, for he knew that by conquering he would win all the Spirit had to give. And as the first sun-ray shone on him he became insensible, and when he awoke it was as from a sleep. But by his side lay a large, old, decayed log, covered with moss. He remembered that during the fight he had seemed once to plunge his fist, by a violent blow, completely into the enemy up to his elbow, and there was a hole in it corresponding to this wound. He had torn away the other's scalp-lock, stripping the skin down to the waist; he found a long, hairy-looking piece of moss ripped from the end of the log to the middle. And all about lay pieces of moss and locks of his own hair, testifying to the fury of the fight.

He was terribly bruised and torn, but that he did not heed, for now he was another man, and a terrible one. His mother said, 'I warned you of danger:' but he had conquered the danger. He had all the strength of five strong men, and all the might and magic of the Spirit; yes, the Spirit itself was now in him. After this he could do anything, and find game where no one else could. To conquer a ghost gives power."

To conquer the dead, or to fight terrible spirits, to thereby absorb their power, and finally to keep them in a struggle until the day shines on them, is both Norse and Celtic, if not, indeed, world-wide. But the grim spirit of this narrative is Norse; it is that of the hero wresting from a corpse's hold the sword of victory.

> "Farewell, daughter!
> Fleet give I thee,
> Five men's bane,
> If thou it believe."

But the great element or chief cause of magic power among, the Indians is that of Will. It manifests itself in many forms, mere courage being one. Thus the *Weewillmekq'* confers supernatural ability or other favors only on those who are not afraid of it. The demon Log, as we have just seen, gives strength and prosperity to a man for simply fighting like a bull-dog. Beyond courage, pluck or bottom is with these Indians as nearly allied to magic as poetry was among the Greeks, or with an Eschenwaya. When the true magician "gets mad," and continues to get madder till the end, he is invincible. Allied to this is perseverance. The Rabbit is rewarded with skill as an enchanter merely for continuing to try. His very failures have this in them, that he keeps on resolutely, though in a wrong road. No one can fail to be struck, in these legends of the Northeast Algonquins, how often a boy, or adult, when asked if he can do a difficult thing, replies, "I can try." All of this apotheosis of pluck, perseverance, and patience is *far* more developed among these legends than in those of the Chippewas or other western and southern tribes, at least so far as I am familiar with them. It exists wherever there are red Indians, but the Eastern Algonquin seems to have thought it out more and made more of it than others have done. Therefore his cycle of myths, or his Edda, occupies a higher place. It is less chaotic; it is more consistent; it is a chorus in which every voice is trained to respond to or correspond with the leader. In this respect it has a remarkable resemblance to the Scandinavian myths and poems. In its theory that magic power may be obtained by "penitence,"—I do not mean here "repentance,"—that is by self-inflicted pain, it agrees with the Hindoo, and in fact more or less with all religions. But it is only, I believe, in the red Indian and Hindoo creeds that it is distinctly admitted that man can attain the power to do both good and evil, or whatever he pleases, if he will only pay for it by suffering. The doctrine of power through penance is so simple and obvious in its origin that it would long precede monotheism. A man exercises himself with great exertion in lifting stones, as in an Eskimo tale, till he is strong; he practices shooting arrows and running after them, as in the story of the Chief's Son, till he can outrun them. Then the secret of such marvelous deeds is supposed to exist in the bow, and it becomes a fetich.

A very important part of *m'teoulin* is the materials employed. In Old World magic these are exclusively objects which startle or disgust, parts of the human body, dead reptiles, or things singular and rare. Among the Indians, very commonplace articles are employed indifferently with those of the former kind. The magic consists not in them, but in the magician and his methods. He has had, let us say, his dreams, or received, while alone in the forest, his inspirations, which have told him what to do. He takes the objects suggested, and with them performs his wonder works. Sometimes he tells others to do the same with the same things, but in this case he is still the motive force; it is *his* enchantment. In illustration of this I give the following legend:—

Far in the woods was an Indian town; near it lived two old people, who had two beautiful daughters, and no son. The girls were very shy. They seldom let themselves be seen. They would not listen to the young men.

The chief of the tribe had a fine son, a great hunter, and skilled in mysteries. [Footnote: In Passamaquoddy, *N'paowlin*: a man learned in mysteries, a scholar. This is my own Indian name. It is apparently the same with: *boo-oin*; that is, pow-wow man.] The young man wanted one of the girls. His father went to their parents and obtained their consent, but the girls refused to be married.

There lived in the village a young man who was neither strong, handsome, nor clever at any kind of work. Hearing that the chief's son had failed to get one of the shy or proud girls, he said—but all in jest, for he had but a poor opinion of himself—that he was the right kind of a man to get them. "If they had, for example, only seen *me*, now," he exclaimed, "they would have wished to be married at once!" Then they all laughed, and proposed that they should go that night and try to see the girls, and how they would receive the plain looking youth.

So they went quietly, about supper-time, and entered so suddenly that the girls had not time to hide behind the curtain, and so were obliged to receive the visitors. After supper they engaged in playing *Mingwadokadjik*. In this game a ring is hidden in the ashes or sand, and each player, with a pointed stick, makes a plunge until the ring is hit, and brought out. (This is Indian *poker*.—T. B.)

So the evening passed, and nothing was said of marriage; and at last the guests went away, and for some time the young man made a jest of his having gone courting. One day he was far and alone in the woods, when he met an old woman of very strange appearance. She was wrinkled and bent with extreme age, and her head was braided up with a very great number of *sakalobeek*, or hair-strings, which hung down to her heels. After greeting him civilly, she asked him if he was really anxious to marry one of the beauties whom he had visited. "O *Nugumee*" (grandmother), he replied, "I do not care about it." "Only if you did," she replied, "I can give you the one you want, if you will only say so."

Now the young man saw that the old woman was in earnest, and he replied that in fact he would be very glad to get one of the girls, but that no girl worth having would look at him. Then the old dame, taking one of her hair-strings, said, "Roll this up, and carry it in your pouch for a while; [Footnote: One of the infallible ancient methods to make anything into a fetich, or amulet, is to carry it a long time about the person. Familiarity, as Heine observes (*Reisebilder*), gives a silent life, or apparent sympathy, to even old clothes. Thus domestic well-known objects become fairies, and thus they talk to children.] and then go, and, catching an opportunity, toss the cord upon her back. But take care that she does not know that you have done this, and let it be indeed a secret to all."

So he took the *sakalobe*, and, visiting the girls once again, threw it on one of them, more hopeful of success this time. And the cast succeeded, though she said nothing then. But the next day, alone in the woods, he met her, for she had followed him. And she said, "*Tamealeen?*" "Where are you going?" "I am going hunting," he replied. "But, if you have not lost your way, what are you doing here?" "I am not lost in the woods," she replied, but said no more. Then he, seeing how it was, said, "It would be better, though, if I returned with you to your parents, and told them that I found you lost, and showed you the way home." And having done this, the girl's father, noting that she liked the young man, asked him if he wished to marry her; and as both were willing, and something more, the wedding feast was soon ready, the friends invited, and the couple settled down.

Some days after, the husband, seeing his wife wearing the magic hair-string, asked her, "Where did you get that pretty *sakalobe*?" "I found it," she replied, "in my *'ntuboonk*" (usual sitting place in the wigwam). This caused the young man to reflect how kindly he had been treated by the old fairy or witch, and how easily he, without any merit, had won his wife, and then to think of the deserving young chiefs son who had failed. So, taking him into the woods, they found the old woman, who, kind as ever, did for the chief's son what she had already done for his friend, and gave him also a magic hair-string. And using it in the same way he in like manner won the other sister; and it was indeed well, for she was the one whom he wanted most. And the two men whose wives were sisters (*wechoosjik*), were on the best of terms and much together.

Now the young chief reflected that his brother-in-law had been very kind to him, for little cause, and thought how he could repay him. So he asked him one day if he would like to be a swift runner. "Truly I would," replied the other. "Then go and gather some feathers, and let them blow when the wind is high, and chase them. You will soon be able to outstrip the wind, and when the art comes it will never depart from you." Then he did this, and became so swift that no man or beast could escape him.

Yet again the chiefs son said, "Would you like to become strong and very active?" And as he of course said "Yes," the friend replied, "Dress yourself in the worst and raggedest garments, and attack the first man you find. He will catch you by the clothes; but do you slip out of them and run." This he did; the first man whom he met was a lunatic, who gladly grappled for a fight. So he slipped out of the clothes and ran; but the madman thought the apparel made the man, and beat it a long time, and left it for dead. But after he had done this with many men he indeed became strong and active.

Then the chief's son said, "I will teach you quickness of sight, so that you may perceive animals while hunting, though other men may not. Take a handful of moose's hairs; hold them firmly in a roll between your thumb and finger; hold them up in a high wind and let them go. So you will be able to perceive, in time, all the moose. And to see deer, or any other animal, you must take their hair and treat it in the same way." So he did; and by means of this magic became so keen of sight that he beheld every beast.

Yet again the chief's son said, "Would you see birds where no other men can?" And he, assenting, was told to strip the feathery part from a bird's quills (*chekakadega*), and, blowing it into the air, look carefully in the direction in which it flew. And having practiced this also, he became very perfect in the art. [Footnote: The secret of these spells is very apparent. But the teacher would make the pupil believe that the successful result would greatly depend on the color and kind of the fur or feathers employed. It is curious to observe how, in the over-refinement of "sport" among gentlemen, the idea that this or that is "good form" and "the correct thing," which *must* be done, has had the effect of establishing much which is mere fetich. A fox in England and a bear in Canada must be killed in a certain way by men of caste.]

Now, having learned all these things, he asked the chief's son how he could learn to see the fishes of the sea. And being told that he must collect all kinds of fishes' bones, and burn them and pound them to dust, he did so; and, having blown them up into the wind, he could see all manner of fish and call them to him.

This young man went afar in his thoughts; for reflecting that the whales were giant-like in power, he wondered what might be done by magic with them. And his friend said that it was true that the whales could give to man unearthly power and exceeding long life. "For," said he, "they never die till they are killed, and by their aid one may live on till life borders on immortality." So burning a piece of whale-bone (*pootup-awigun*), he pounded it to powder, and, standing on a rock that jutted out into the sea, the sorcerer blew the dust seawards. And erelong he saw dark spots far away, and as they grew to be more numerous they became larger, and yet more numerous anon, and for every grain of dust which he blew there came a whale; and yet he blew again seven times. Then the whole school of immense creatures came towards him; and he that was largest, or the sagamore of the whales, swimming close to the man on the rock, said, "Why hast thou called me?" And he replied, "Make me strong."

And the Whale answered, "It is well. Put thy hand in my mouth!" And, doing this, he found and took out a golden key. [Footnote: This is a manifestly modern addition. There is every indication that the story itself is ancient, probably Eskimo.] "Keep that," said the Whale. "While you have it you will be safe against man, beast, or illness. The foe shall not harm you; the spirits which haunt the wilderness shall pass you by; hunger and pain shall not know you; death shall not be in your road."

So the young man thanked the great magician, and went home; and as it had been promised it came to pass. All was ever well with him; trouble and trial were with him no more. Those who were, in his village never knew hunger; the wild game abounded, and came to them when called; no enemy attacked them; the sun and moon smiled on them; they sang the songs of the olden time, and played the flute in peace.

In time the old chief drew near the end of his life, and his son asked the friend if his father's days could not be prolonged. But the magician thought it best to let him pass in peace; and he did so. Then the young chief offered his place and power to his brother-in-law (*wechoosul*); but he refused it, and passed his, life in aiding his friend in every way by his power and wisdom. *Kespeahdvoksit* (here the story ends).

This legend is little more than an enumeration of the recipes popularly employed to obtain certain powers. It may be observed that it is limited to all that a real Indian requires. It is very different from what a white man or an Asiatic savage would have wanted; and there is just enough truth and common sense in the methods recommended to make the whole plausible. The reader will observe that the magic hair-string and locks of hair play the same important part in *m'teoulin* that they did in Old World magic. This is hardly one of the coincidences which can be attributed to spontaneous development from similar causes. It may be such, but there may be also an Eskimo sidegate through which it entered from the other side.

Another magic means was the influencing high and mysterious powers. Of this the following is an admirable illustration:—

Tumilkoontaoo, or the Broken Wing.

(Micmac.)

An Indian family lived on the sea-shore. They had two sons; the eldest of these was married, and had many small children. They lived by fishing; they chiefly caught eels.

It came to pass that the weather was so stormy that they could not fish. The wind blew terribly night and day; the waves were like dancing hills. Hunger made them fierce. One day the father told his boys to walk along the shore and see if no fish had been cast on the beach.

A young man went; he went far along; and as he went the wind was ever worse; it blew so fiercely that he could hardly stand. It seemed to come from a point of land. He resolved to pass it, and when there he saw the cause of the tempest. Upon a *kwesopskeak'*—a high and rocky ledge, a bold cliff, but surrounded by the water—sat the Wind-Bird, or storm-sagamore himself, flapping his wings, and thereby raising all the wind.

Then the young man, who was brave and wise, resolved to outwit the wind-god. And approaching him and addressing him as *Nikskamich*, "My grandfather," he inquired, "are you cold!" And he answered, "Nay;" but the young man insisted that he must be suffering, and offered to carry him on his back to the main-land. [Footnote: It would appear that while the bird flapped his wings he did not fly. I believe this was the same with the Norse Hrosvelgar.] And the offer being accepted, he carried the mighty bird from one weedy, slippery rock to another, up and down, jumping anon, and wading through the pools. But at the last rock he, with full intention, stumbled and fell as if by accident, yet managed it so well as to break one of the wings of the eagle, as he indeed meant to do. Yet he made great show of being very sorry, and, having set the wing, bade the bird keep quiet, and not move his wings for many days; not till the wound was healed should he stir them. "Sit still, *Nikskamich*," he said, "and I will bring you food; I will be attentive; you shall want nothing." And the god sat still: there was a calm on the water; no leaves moved in the forest; there was no wind in all the world.

The young man went home; there was not a breeze, the canoe went smoothly over the sea, the eels could be seen in the depths, the Indians caught fish by thousands; never before had they caught so many. And the sagamore of the birds sat still; the Wind-Bird waited to get well; the young man fed him every day.

There can be too much of what is good; good turns to evil, sweet to sour. After many days of quiet calm the sea was covered with *Ogokpegeak*, a scum which is caused by sickness among the fish, and which is thrown off by them, for they suffer in still water. Then the fisherman can no longer look down into the sea; then he cannot use the spear.

Then the young man, examining the wing of the storm-bird, said, "Grandfather, it is much better; move it but a little now, that I may see!" So he moved it; he gave a flap, and lo! a slight ripple passed over the surface of the sleeping sea. And striking lightly with his wings, again there came a breeze, and the *Ogokpegeak*, or the scum, was blown away, and the Indians fished again, and all was well.

So they had the Wind-Bird for a friend, and the sea was smooth or stormy as they willed. But these Indians wished for more than they could manage. They grew tired of catching small fish; they wanted whales. "Let us go and catch the Bootup!" said the elder brother. "How will you take him?" asked the younger. "I will entice him with the *peepoogwokan*," said the elder, "with my pipe." So he sat by the sea; he played on the pipe; he played, but no whale came. So they went back to their small fishery.

This is manifestly the beginning and end of a very ancient Indian mythical tale. The Micmacs have tacked on to it a ridiculous fragment of an indifferent French nursery tale, without an end and without any connection with the Indian beginning. The tradition is probably entirely Eskimo. Among the Greenlanders there is a caste of whale-fishers, separate and apart, and this story, in its second stage, was applied to teach, *Ne sutor ultra crepidam*,—that all should stick to their trades, and that though a sorcerer might rule the winds it did not follow that he could win the whales.

I have spoken before of the curious identity of the Indian storm-king, or Wind-Bird, with that of the Norse Hrosvelgar. When among the Chippewas, west of Lake Superior, I met with a white man who had received the name of Thunder-Bird from the Indians still further west.

The magicians of all countries, be they of Africa, Asia, or North America, are invariably represented by travelers as holding their flock in subjection, and never being doubted as to power or skill. But there are skeptics or Agnostics among the men of the woods as well as among those of civilized cities. There are shrewd fellows who cannot only detect impostors, but turn their tricks to their own advantage. An amusing illustration of this is given in the following story:

Fish-Hawk and Scapegrace. [Footnote: Wiskumagwasoo and Mahgwis. The Mahgwis, or "Scapegrace," is a kind of sea-gull.]

(Micmac.)

Two men met and talked: one was Fish-Hawk, the other was Scapegrace. Now the Fish-Hawk can fly higher than any other ocean bird, and he is proud and particular as to his food; he is only beaten by the eagle. When he dives and takes a fish the eagle pursues him; he lets it drop; the great sagamore of the birds catches it; but to less than the chief he yields nothing. But the Scapegrace will eat anything he is heavy in flying; he is slow and of low degree.

So when the Scapegrace proposed to the Fish-Hawk that they should become partners the proud bird was angry in his heart, but said nothing, as he was crafty, and as it occurred to him that he could punish the other; and this he was the more willing to do because the Scapegrace actually proposed to fly a race with him! So he said, "Let us go together to a certain Indian village." And they went off together.

The Fish-Hawk arrived there far before the other. And on arriving he said, "Beware of him who will come after me. You will know him by these signs: he is ugly and heavy; he will bring with him his own food. It is coarse and common; in fact it is poison. He wishes to kill you; he will offer it. Do not eat of it, or you will die."

Then having been very well entertained himself, he took his departure. Scapegrace soon appeared, but was treated with great reserve. He offered his food, and the people pretended to eat it, but took good care to quietly throw it away. Then he told the chief that he was seeking a wife, and asked if there were girls to marry in the town. To which the chief replied, "Yes, there is a mother with several daughters, of the *Amalchoogwech'* or Raccoon tribe."

He went to see the girls. A bad name had gone before him. One of them stood before the lodge. She saw him, and cried, "*Mahgwis wechooveet*!" "Scapegrace is coming!" They received him as if he had been Sickness. He was welcomed like filth on fine clothes. They cried out, "*Ulummeye*!" "Go home!" He asked the mother if she had daughters. She answered, "Yes." He asked her if she would give him one. She replied, "I will not." So he went his way.

Now when he had gone Fish-Hawk came again, and asked if Scapegrace had been there. He inquired if all had passed as he predicted. They said it had. Then it occurred to him to pass himself off for a great prophet, a wise magician, well knowing that he could make much of it. So he said, "It is well. Remember that you would have all died but for my foresight. That wizard would have poisoned you all. But have no fear. In future I will watch over you."

Then, he said to a man of the people that if at any time he should see a large bird flying over the village it would be an omen of great coming danger. "Then," he said, "think of me; call on me, and I will come." So he departed.

The man thought it all over for a long time. He was shrewd and wise. "He foretold the coming of Scapegrace," he reflected. "Now he pretends to be a very great sorcerer. We shall see!"

Sure enough, in a few days he saw a bird flying on high. "That," said he, "must be the *Wis-kuma-gwasoo*." He called him, and he came. "You spoke," he said, "of danger to our town. What is it?"

"There is great danger. In a few days your town will be attacked by a Kookwes. [Footnote: In Passamaquoddy *Kewahqu'*, a cannibal giant, who is also a sorcerer.] Unless you save yourselves you will all be devoured."

"What shall we do to be saved?" asked the man. "When will he come?"

"In seven days," replied the Fish-Hawk. "Before that time you must take to your canoes and flee afar. You may get beyond his reach, but you cannot before that time get beyond the horrible roar of his voice. And all who hear it will drop dead."

"How can we escape this second danger?" asked the man.

"You must all close your ears, so that you can hear nothing. When the time is over you may return."

The man's name was Oscoon. [Footnote: Oscoon (M.): the Liver.] He led the people away. He closed their ears; he did not close his own. Once he heard a far-away whoop. It was not very terrible. But he said nothing. After a time, the scouts who were sent out returned. They reported that the Kookwes had departed. They had not even seen him. It was a great escape.

The people thought much of Oscoon. They made him their chief. In a few days the Fish-Hawk returned. He spoke to Oscoon: "Did the giant come?" "He did." "You escaped?" "By following your advice, we did." "And in which direction did he go?" [Footnote: Here the Fish-Hawk inadvertently betrays himself. In the Edda, Loki changes himself into a falcon and flies to Jotunheim to make mischief, as usual. Odin also changes himself to a hawk or eagle when he is chased by the giant Suttung. There is a strong Norse color to all this tale. The Fish-Hawk is very Loki-like and tricky.] "Surely you, who know so much about him, must know that better than we do." Then the Fish-Hawk saw that he was found out. He flew away, and never returned to the town to play the prophet.

He who would cheat must watch his words well.

As in the preceding tradition, there has been tacked to this a fragment of a very poor French tale about a king, a great city, a royal carriage, and the forest of wild beasts, borrowed from so many old European romances. But what is here given is apparently really Indian, and it shows with spirit and humor how men tricked one another and rose in life by trickery, in the days of old.

There are naturally contradictory opinions on such a subject as to what constitutes the morality of magic. The old Shaman or Manitou regarded witchcraft as wicked. The Roman Catholic has taught the Indian that all sorceries and spells except his own are of the devil. Hence it came that I got from two Passamaquoddy Indians, next-door neighbors, the following opinions:—

Tomah.—"There was once a man who hated another. So he prayed until he became a snake," etc.

Another Indian.—"If a man wanted to be *m'teoulin* he must go without food, or sleep, or saying his prayers, for seven days. Yes, that certainly. He must go far into the woods. He must go again when his power was used up."

The faith in and fondness for magic were so great among the Algonquins that there is not one even of their most serious histories into which it has not been introduced. The Passamaquoddies will narrate an incident of their wars with the Mohawks. The first time it will all be probable enough; but hear it again, when the story-teller has become more trustful, and some of the actors in it or the scene will be sure to end like a Christmas pantomime in fairy-land. With them *m'teoulin* covered everything; it entered into every detail of life. I do not think that it was so deeply felt even by the ancient Babylonians or the modern Arabs and Hindoos as by our red men. It is no wonder they prefer the Catholic religion to the Protestant.

There is a Micmac legend which is so magical and mystical, so inspired with Eskimo Shamanism, that it would not be remarkable if it had been originally a sacred song. This is

The Giant Magicians.

There was once a man and his wife who lived by the sea, far away from other people. They had many children, and they were very poor. One day this couple were in their canoe, far from land. There came up a dense fog; they were quite lost.

They heard a noise as of paddles and voices. It drew nearer. They saw dimly a monstrous canoe filled with giants, who greeted the little folk like friends. "*Uch keen, tahmee wejeaok?*" "My little brother," said the leader, "where are you going?" "I am lost in the fog," said the poor Indian, very sadly. "Ah, come with us to our camp," said the giant, who seemed to be a good fellow, if there ever was one. "Truly, ye will be well treated, my small friends, for my father is the chief; so be of good cheer!" And they, being much amazed at this gentleness, sat still in awe, while two of the giants, each putting a tip of his paddle under their bark, lifted it up and put it into their own, as if it had been a chip. And truly the giants seemed to be as much pleased with the little folk as a boy would be who had found a flying squirrel. [Footnote: A story like this of giants in a canoe would very naturally originate about the Bay of Fundy, where, in the dense and frequent fogs, all objects assume greatly exaggerated apparent dimensions. One often beholds there, on the shore, "men as trees walking."]

And as they drew near the beach, lo! they beheld three wigwams, high as mountains, in size according to that of the giants. And coming to meet them was the chief, who was taller than the rest.

"Ha!" he cried. "Son, what have you there? Where did you pick up that little brother?" "*Noo*, my father, I found him lost in the fog." "Well, bring him home to the lodge, my son!" So the giant took the small canoe in the palm of his hand, the man and his wife sitting therein, and carried them home. Then they were taken into the wigwam, and the canoe was laid carefully in the eaves, but within easy reach, about a hundred and fifty yards from the ground.

Then an abundant meal was set before them, but the benevolent host, mindful of their small size, did not give them more to eat than they would have needed for about ten years to come, and informed them in a subdued whisper, which could hardly have been heard a hundred miles off, that his name was Oscoon. [Footnote: Mr. Rand suggests that this may indicate the dark color of his tribe. Eskimo legends speak of people among them who were black.]

Now it came to pass, a few days after, that a company of these well-grown people went hunting, and when they returned the guests must needs pity them that they had no game in their land which answered to their size; for they came in with strings of such small affairs as two or three dozen caribou hanging in their belts, as a Micmac would carry a string of squirrels, and swinging one or two moose in their hands like rabbits. Yet, what with these and many deer, bears, and beavers, they made up in the weight of their game what it lacked in size, and of what they had they were generous.

Now the giants became very fond of the small folk, and would not for the world that they should in any way come to harm. And it came to pass that one morning the chief told them that they were to have a grand battle, since they expected in three days to be attacked by a Chenoo. Therefore the Micmac saw that in all things it was even with the giants as with his own people at home, they having their troubles with the wicked, and the chiefs their share in being obliged to keep up their magic and know all that was going on in the world. Yea, for he would be a poor *powwow* and a necromancer worth nothing who could not foretell such a trifle as the day and hour when an enemy would be on them!

But this time the Sakumow (M.), or sagamore, was forewarned, and bade his little guests stop their ears and bind up their heads, and roll themselves in many folds of dressed skins, lest they should hear the deadly war-scream of the Chenoo. And with all their care they hardly survived it; but the second scream hurt them less; and after the third the chief came to them with a cheerful countenance, and bade them arise and unpack themselves, for the monster was slain, and though his four sons, with two other giants, had been sorely tried, yet they had conquered.

But the sorrows of the good are never at an end, and so it was with these honest giants, who were always being pestered with some kind of scurvy knaves or others who would not leave them in peace. For anon the chief announced that this time a Kookwes—a burly, beastly villain, not two points better than his cousin the Chenoo—was coming to play at rough murder with them. And, verily, by this time the Micmac began to believe, without bating an ace on it, that all of these tall people were like the wolves, who, meeting with nobody else, bite one another. So they were bound and bundled up as before, and put to bed like dolls. And again they heard the horrible shout, the moderate shout, and the smaller shout, until *sooel moonoodooahdigool*, which, being interpreted, meaneth that they hardly heard him at all.

Then the warriors, returning, gave proof that they had indeed done something more than kick the wind, for they were covered with blood, and their legs were stuck full of large pines, with here and there an oak or hemlock, for the fight had been in a forest; so that they had been as much troubled as men would be with thistles, nettles, and pine splinters, which is truly often a great trouble. But this was their least trial, for, as they told their chief, the enemy had well-nigh made Jack Drum's entertainment for them, and led them the devil's dance, had not one of them, by good luck, opened his eye for him with a rock which drove it into his brain. And as it was, the chiefs youngest son had been so mauled that, coming home, he fell dead just before his father's door. Truly this might have been deemed almost an accident in some families; but lo! what a good thing it is to have an enchanter in the house, especially one who knows his business, as did the old chief, who, going out, asked the young man why he was lying there. To which he replying that it was because he was dead, his father bade him rise and walk, which he did straight to the supper table, and ate none the less for it.

Now the old chief, thinking that perhaps, his dear little people found life dull and devoid of incident with him, asked them if they were aweary of him. They, with golden truth indeed, answered that they had never been so merry, but that they were anxious as to their children at home. He answered that they were indeed right, and that the next morning they might depart. So their canoe was reached down for them, and packed full of the finest furs and best meat, when they were told to *tebah'-dikw'*, or get in. Then a small dog was put in, and this dog was solemnly charged that he should take the people home, while the people were told to paddle in the direction in which the dog should point. [Footnote: Strange as it may seem, there is not the least exaggeration in this. Lieutenant-Colonel Barclay Kennan told me that when surveying in the far North Pacific he had an Eskimo dog which, in the thickest fog, would scent the land at a great distance, and continually point to it.] And to the Micmac he said, "Seven years hence you will be reminded of me." And then *tokooboosijik* (off they went). The man sat in the stern, his wife in the prow, and the dog in the middle of the canoe. The dog pointed, the Indian paddled, the water was smooth. They soon reached home; the children with joy ran to meet them; the dog as joyfully ran to see the children, wagging his tail with great glee, just as if he had been like any other dog, and not a fairy. For, having made acquaintance, he without delay turned tail and trotted off for home again, running over the ocean surface as if it had been hard ice; which might, indeed, have once astonished the good man and his wife, but they had of late days seen so many wonders that they were past marveling.

Now this Indian, who had in the past been always poor, seemed to have quite recovered from that complaint. When he let down his lines the biggest fish bit; all his sprats were salmon; he prayed for goslings, and got geese; moose were as mice to him now; yea, he had the best in the land, with all the fatness thereof. So seven years passed away, and then, as he slept, there came unto him divers dreams, and in them he went back to the Land of the Giants, and saw all those who had been so kind to him. And yet again he dreamed one night that he was standing by his wigwam near the sea, and that a great whale swam up to him and began to sing, and that the singing was the sweetest he had ever heard.

Then he remembered that the giant had told him he would think of him in seven years; and it came clearly before him what it all meant, and that he was erelong to have magical power given to him, and that he should become a *Megumoowessoo*. This he told his wife, who, not being learned in darksome lore, would fain know more nearly what kind of a being he expected to be, and whether a spirit or a man, good or bad; which was, indeed, not easy to explain, nor is it clearly set down in the chronicles beyond this,—that, whatever it might be, it was all for the best, and that there was a great deal of magic in it.

That day they saw a great shark cruising about in their bay, chasing fish, and this they held for an evil omen. But, soon after, there came trotting towards them over the sea the same small dog who had been their pilot from the Land of the Giants. So he, full of joy, as before, at seeing them and the children, wagged his tail and danced for glee, and then looked earnestly at the man as if for some message. And to him the man said, "It is well. In three years' time I will make you a visit. I will look to the southwest." Then the dog licked the hands and the ears and the eyes of the man, and went home as before over the sea, running on the water.

And when the three years had passed the Indian entered his canoe, and, paddling without fear, found his way to the Land of the Giants. He saw the wigwams standing on the beach; the immense canoes were drawn up on the water's edge; from afar he beheld the old giant coming down to welcome him. But he was alone. And when he had been welcomed, and was in the wigwam, he learned that all the sons were dead. They had died three years before, when the shark, the great sorcerer, had been seen.

They had gone, and the old man had but lingered a little longer. They had made the magic change, they had departed, and he would soon join them *in his own kingdom*. But ere he went he would leave their great inheritance, their magic, to the man.

Therewith the giant brought out his son's clothes, and bade the Indian put them on. Truly this was as if he had been asked to clothe himself with a great house, since the smallest fold in them would have been to him as a cavern. But he stepped in, and as he did this he rose to great size; he filled out the garments till they fitted; he was a giant, of Giant-Land. With the clothes came the wisdom, the *m'teoulin*, the *manitou* power of the greatest and wisest of the olden time. He was indeed *Megumoowessoo*, and had attained to the Mystery.

This very remarkable and evidently ancient tale is one of that kind which the keepers of tribe chronicles among the pagan Indians do not tell to the world, and which they conceal from white men. It is not a fragment, nor is it unfinished, as some readers may suppose. Its plot is of a much higher nature than a novel, which ends in a marriage. To an Indian, whose ideas of earthly happiness were not in money, houses, and lands, personal power was the one thing to be most desired. As a Passamaquoddy said once to me, "To be rich in those days meant to be a great hunter and always have plenty of meat for everybody." Hence the desire to be great and strong, to be able to entice wild animals, to run like the wind, to be crafty in all things, especially in making war; hence to have prophetic dreams. All of this was to be attained by *m'teoulin*, or magic. The highest ambition of an Indian was to become a *Megumoowessoo*, a mystical being, which is explained differently as fairy, faun, sylvan deity, but which means one who enjoys all the highest privileges of humanity allied to the supernatural. This is what the hero of this story gets by favor of the giant.

It may be observed that in this tale the Indian cannot explain to his wife what he nevertheless perfectly understands; that is, the exact nature of a *Megumoowessoo*. The giant, by speaking of his own kingdom, gives the true key of the whole mystery. He has attained magic power so far as one can exercise it in this life. Like Glooskap he can be, or unlike him prefers, to be habitually, a giant. He has battled with the Chenoo and Kookwess; he has, like Hercules, fulfilled his mission; and now he departs for his own realm, that of the

Megumoowessoo, as Arthur went to Fairy-Land, as Buddha to the unknown Nirvana,—that is, to something beyond the conception of poet or theosophist.

I suspect that the period of seven years, and again of three years, had been employed by the Indian in preparing himself by penance for *m'teoulin*. The respect of the Indians for the number *seven* is so remarkable, that if it be true that *Deus imparibus numeris gaudet*, they are in that respect, at least, like deities. Whenever *seven* or a white bear's skin occurs in these tales, there always lies hidden a magical mystery.

It is not the least remarkable feature of this tale that it abounds in that quiet small humor which recalls the adventures of Captain Lemuel Gulliver. The Indian, like, the Norseman, was such an *implicit* believer in his own myths, and he had evolved them so entirely from himself without borrowing,—since we may regard him as one in this respect with the Eskimo,—that no human characteristic detracted from the dignity of the Manitou.

There is a strong suggestion in this story that the giants were whales. This and the incident of their inhabiting a mysterious country beyond the sea and the fog would identify them with the enchanted land of the Eskimo, visited by the Angakok in their trances, and by others in *kayaks*. This country was named *Akilinek*, "a fabulous land beyond the sea." The whole story of Malaise, the man who traveled to Akilinek, is in every detail extremely like an Indian tale. (Rink, page 169.) It has also a Norse affinity. The land of the giants was supposed by both Icelanders and Indians to be in the North Atlantic. There is a Norse tale of a man changed to a whale which indicates a common origin with the one here given.

It is believed that the *m'teoulin* can, when speaking, make themselves heard to whom they will, at any distance. They, can confer with one another secretly when miles away, or make themselves known to many. I was informed by an Indian in all faith that an old witch who died in 1876, twelve miles from Pleasant Point, was heard to speak in the latter place when at her last. A very intelligent Passamaquoddy told me that when Osalik (Sarah) Hequin died he himself heard all she said, though sixty-five miles distant. I am certain that he firmly believed this. This woman died a strange death, for she was found standing up, dead, in the snow, with her arms extended and "hands sticking out." It is generally believed that she was killed by other *m'teoulin*.

There are really very few ideas in modern mesmerism not known to Eskimo or Indian Shamans. Clairvoyance is called by the Passamaquoddies *Meelah bi give he*.

GLINT-WAH-GNOUR PES SAUSMOK.

N'loan pes-sans, mok glint ont-aven
Glint ont-aven, nosh mor-gun
N'loan sep-scess syne-duc
Mach-ak wah le-de-born harlo kirk
Pes-sauk-wa morgun pa-zazeu.
Dout-tu eowall, yu' eke ne-mess comall
Dow-dar bowsee des ge-che-ne-wes skump,
Na-havak dunko to-awk w'che-mon wh'oak
No-saw yu-well *Mooen* nill
Mask da-ah gawank la me la-tak-a-dea-on
Di-wa godamr Kudunk-ah dea-on
Glor-ba dea-on glom-de-nec
Glint-wah-gnour pes sausmok.

THE SONG OF THE STARS.

We are the stars which sing,
We sing with our light;
We are the birds of fire,
We fly over the sky.
Our light is a voice;
We make a road for spirits,
For the spirits to pass over.
Among us are three hunters
Who chase a bear;
There never was a time
When they were not hunting.
We look down on the mountains.
This is the Song of the Stars.

"Ahboohe b'lo maryna Piel to-marcess"
We poual gee yuaa
Mar-yuon *cordect* delo son
Ne morn-en nute magk med-agon
On-e-est Molly duse-al *ca-soo-son nen.*

Tumbling end over end, goes Piel to *mercess*,
With feathers on his eyes.
To the maple-sap ridge *we are going*,
Our lunch a cod-fish skin;
One est Molly's daughter goes with us.